Regional
Economic Policy
and
its Analysis

Regional Economic Policy and its Analysis

HARVEY ARMSTRONG and **JIM TAYLOR**
University of Lancaster

Philip Allan

First published 1978 by

PHILIP ALLAN PUBLISHERS LIMITED
MARKET PLACE
DEDDINGTON
OXFORD OX5 4SE

0 86003 015 6 (hardback)
0 86003 116 0 (paperback)

Set by Outline 77
Printed in Great Britain by The Camelot Press Limited,
Southampton

To our wives, Susan and Lynnette

Contents

Preface

Textbooks are usually written either to replace existing textbooks or to fill a gap in the existing literature. This book falls squarely into the second category. Existing texts on regional economics divide into two main types: those concerned mainly with economic theory and the techniques of regional analysis, and those concerned mainly with regional problems and policies in specific countries. The intention of this book is to provide a link between the theory and practice of regional economics. Other texts should therefore be regarded as complementary, and not alternatives, to this one.

The book has been written for students pursuing courses in regional economics, regional policy and regional planning. We have assumed that our readers will have had a sound training in the basic principles of economics. Our intention has not been to provide hard-and-fast answers to urgent regional problems — indeed, we believe that easy solutions do not exist. We seek only to stimulate a greater awareness of regional problems and the problems facing regional policymakers, and to present the student with a theoretical framework which can be used to analyse these problems. The increasing interest in regional policy in many different parts of the world indicates a growing need for specialist regional economists and we hope that this book will encourage more young economists to consider this field more seriously. We should also point out that although the material is presented in what we consider to be a logical order, each of the three sections can be read independently. In other words, the student is not required to have read the earlier chapters in order to understand those that follow.

Three themes run through this book. They can be summarised by asking three questions. Why do regional problems arise? What policies can be devised to tackle these problems? How should these regional policies be evaluated? The questions are simple; the answers, unfortunately, are not — which is the reason we decided to write this book. In our attempt to answer these questions, we have relied heavily upon examples drawn from United Kingdom and European experience of regional policy. This geographical concentration simply reflects our greater familiarity with European material. We hope, however, that this book will have a wider appeal since our primary objective has been to present a *general* analytical framework within which regional problems and policies can be studied and evaluated.

When we first planned this book we had intended to divide the work such that each of the authors was responsible for specified chapters. As things turned out, however, every single chapter bears the marks of both authors, with the result that we must share the blame equally for each and every part of this book.

Our debt of gratitude knows no boundaries — regional or otherwise. In particular, we would like to thank Tony Thirlwall in prosperous Kent, and Brian Ashcroft and Gavin McCrone in not-so-prosperous Scotland for kindly reading the draft chapters of this book. All three contributed extensive comments which not only saved us from making several blunders, but also led to significant changes in both content and exposition. Our debt of gratitude to John Rhodes and Barry Moore, who have pioneered the evaluation of regional policy in the United Kingdom, should also be made clear. Without their help and generous provision of papers in advance of publication, parts of this book, and in particular the final chapter, simply could not have been written. Nearer to home, many of our colleagues and students at Lancaster deserve thanks for their encouragement and help, particularly, V. Balasubramanyam, Rod Whitaker and Ron Akehurst. The errors which persist have defied our attempts to relocate them. They remain entirely our own responsibility.

Finally, we wish to thank our diligent and understanding typist, Margaret Gudgin, whose ability to meet deadlines and translate illegible script never ceases to amaze us. She has done a marvellous job. We are also grateful to Linda Mogford for typing some of the earlier drafts of various chapters. Finally, to our wives and children we say a mammoth 'thank you' for their understanding and support. They deserved considerably more of our time then they got on too many occasions during the writing of this book.

November 1977

1
The Origins and Objectives of Regional Economic Policy

In spite of its relatively recent arrival, regional economic policy is now firmly established as a major branch of economic policymaking in many nations of the world. This is particularly true in the nations of Western Europe, such as Britain and France, though the developing nations — particularly those in the more advanced stages of development such as Brazil and Malaysia — have also moved in the same direction.

There can be no doubt that the emergence of regional policy was primarily an offshoot of the Keynesian revolution. The disastrous experience of the worldwide depression during the 1930s, coupled with the subsequent high degree of control over economic activity during the Second World War, convinced many governments that they had both the power and indeed the responsibility to prevent such a disaster happening again. Moreover, the commitment to full employment at the *national* level inevitably forced governments to seek methods of achieving full employment in each major *region* of the economy. The existence of regional unemployment disparities had, of course, been a serious political issue in the UK during the 1920s and 1930s, but little could be done to reduce these disparities until the Keynesian revolution had provided governments with the power to deal effectively with high levels of *national* unemployment. This point is vividly illustrated in table 1.1 and figure 1.1. At the height of the 1930s depression in the UK, the unemployment rate in Wales and Scotland exceeded 30%, and it exceeded 20% in all other regions except southern England. There was little that regional policy could hope to achieve in the face of unemployment rates of over 14% even in the 'most prosperous' regions.

1

Table 1.1 *Unemployment rates in the UK regions, January 1933*

Region	Unemployment rate (%)
London	14.2
South East	17.0
South West	19.6
Midlands	20.2
North East	29.8
North West	25.7
Wales	37.8
Scotland	30.2
Northern Ireland	28.9
UK	23.4

Source: Historical Abstract of British Labour Statistics, tables 110 and 162.

Note: % unemployed = [number of persons (insured and uninsured) registered as unemployed x 100] ÷ (number of insured employees aged 16 to 64 at mid-year)

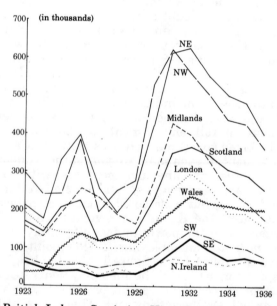

Source: British Labour Statistics: Historical Abstract, table 162.

Figure 1.1 *Number of persons registered as unemployed, June each year 1923-36*

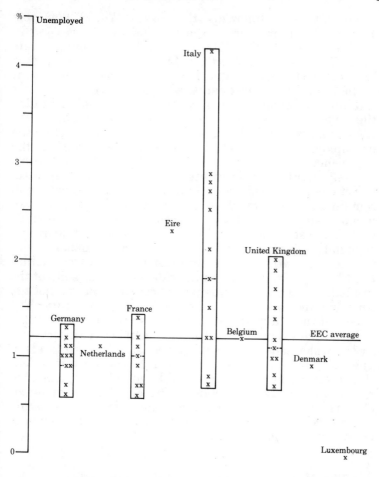

Source: Eurostat, *Population and Employment in the Countries of the Community 1970-1974,* Commission of the European Communities, 1975.
Eurostat, *Regional Statistics: Population, Employment and Living Standards 1973-1974,* Commission of the European Communities, 1975.

Notes:
1. Each cross represents a separate region.
2. National average values are shown as a broken line.

Figure 1.2 *Regional unemployment disparities in the European Economic Community, 1974* (registered unemployment as a percentage of the civilian population.)

The situation following the Second World War was entirely different. During the first post-war recession in 1949, for example, the highest regional unemployment rate in the UK was 6.5% in Northern Ireland, followed by 4.0% in Wales and 3.0% in Scotland. The vast pool of unemployment of the 1930s had almost vanished, thanks largely to greater international cooperation in economic policymaking and to the extension of macroeconomic policy following the Keynesian revolution. This does not mean, however, that the unemployment problem has been solved — far from it, as the experience of the 1970s has made all too clear. But it seems unlikely that the tragic events of the 1930s will be repeated.

Yet even if recessions could be avoided, there would still remain the problem of serious regional discrepancies in unemployment. Successive recessions since the war have revealed in stark detail the deep-rooted nature of underlying regional problems. Regional unemployment disparities in the member nations of the European Economic Community (EEC), for example, remain as wide as ever, in spite of the gradual emergence of regional policies in almost all of the nine member nations of the enlarged Community. The extent of these disparities in 1974 is shown in figure 1.2.

If the achievement of full employment is to be interpreted in the wider sense of removing persistently high levels of unemployment in certain regions of the economy, it is clear that macroeconomic policies will have to be supplemented by an active regional policy. The elimination of major slumps is certainly a necessary condition for removing serious regional unemployment disparities, but equally certainly, it is not a sufficient condition.

1.1 The Nature of Regional Policy Objectives

In stressing the importance of reducing regional differences in unemployment rates, we have taken a traditional view of the purpose of regional policy. The reduction of regional unemployment disparities has been, and still is, the dominant goal of regional policy in the UK: 'the primary objective of United Kingdom regional policy is to bring the supply and demand for labour in the Assisted Areas more closely into balance by safeguarding existing employment and creating new jobs in those areas' (Regional Development Programme 1977).

The dominance of the unemployment objective in the UK

clearly highlights a unique feature of regional policy objectives: there are very few purely 'regional' objectives. Almost all the objectives of regional policy are *national* objectives, and regional policy exists so that national goals can be attained. In this case, the national goal of full employment cannot be attained without a regional policy designed to eliminate regional pockets of unemployment that persist even during periods of boom.

The concentration on the unemployment objective in UK regional policy is easily understood. Regional problems have arisen largely due to the decline of the older industrial areas and 'the regional problem has always been viewed as a continuing one, in the sense that traditional industries have shed labour over a long period and it is probable that they will continue to do so' (Regional Development Programme 1977). Gradually, however, other objectives have been added to that of reducing unemployment in depressed areas. Indeed, as long ago as 1940 the far-sighted Barlow Report on the Distribution of the Industrial Population (White Paper 1940) argued that one of the prime goals of regional policy should be to attain a better balance in the geographical distribution of population and industry in the different regions of the country for both social and strategic reasons. Regional and urban problems were seen as being essentially different sides of the same coin. A better regional balance of industry and population would ease the congestion and other problems of the large cities, especially those in Greater London.

When the various statements of policymakers concerning regional policy are assembled, six broad objectives can be identified (Diamond 1974):

(i)   to reduce unemployment in areas where it is persistently high;
(ii) to reduce the pressure of population in already congested areas;
(iii) to increase the average rate of utilisation of national resources;
(iv) to reduce interregional differences in the pressure of demand in order to relieve inflationary pressures;
(v)   to preserve and strengthen regional cultures and regional identities;
(vi) to achieve a better balance between the population and the environment.

This list of objectives shows that the problems which are

believed to be associated with regional imbalance are extremely wide in scope. They include social and environmental objectives as well as economic objectives. To this list we can also add the political objectives of regional policy. In many countries, Canada being a prime example, regional disparities pose a perpetual threat to political unity. The rapid rise of the *Parti Quebecois* and its commitment to separatism demonstrates the growing problems of holding the Canadian Federation together. If Quebec does decide to take over many of the functions that are currently the responsibility of the Canadian central government, this would have serious implications for the rest of Canada since there are also forces in the Canadian West demanding greater powers, particularly with respect to fiscal affairs, than they currently possess. The political and economic consequences of such devolution, however, are still extremely difficult to forecast. This is no less true of the UK, where calls for greater devolution of political and economic powers by Scottish and Welsh nationalists have resulted in part from the relatively poor economic performance of Scotland and Wales during recent decades. In addition, further integration within the EEC will depend to a significant extent on the ability of the Community to prevent regional disparities within Europe from widening even further.

The threat to the political unity of nation states may also lie behind the emergence of regional policies in countries where regional disparities in living standards coincide with regional racial disparities, as is the case in Malaysia. The regions of Malaysia with the lowest per capita income levels are seen to have a predominantly Malay population, whereas the regions with high concentrations of Chinese tend to have relatively high per capita incomes (see figure 1.3). The development of a regional policy in Malaysia has therefore been heavily influenced by the need to reduce regional, and consequently racial, disparities in per capita income.

We would indeed expect a regional policy to be founded upon more than simply economic objectives, and this should be borne in mind throughout the remainder of this book, which is primarily concerned with the *economic* analysis of regional policy. It may be the case, of course, that economic and non-economic objectives are closely interrelated. A popular deterministic view is that many non-economic problems result from the economic imbalance between

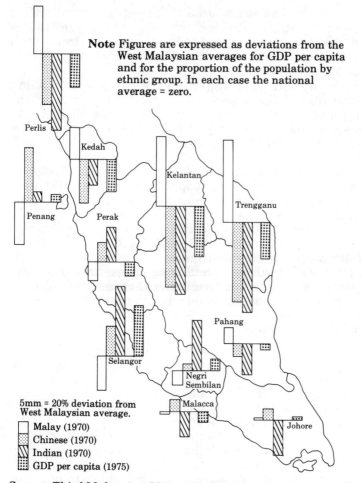

Note Figures are expressed as deviations from the West Malaysian averages for GDP per capita and for the proportion of the population by ethnic group. In each case the national average = zero.

5mm = 20% deviation from West Malaysian average.

☐ Malay (1970)
▦ Chinese (1970)
▨ Indian (1970)
▥ GDP per capita (1975)

Source: Third Malaysian Plan, 1976-1980, Kuala Lumpur, 1976.

Figure 1.3 *Ethnic population distribution and regional per capita income in West Malaysia*

regions. Whether there is a causal link, however, between economic and non-economic problems, and if so in which direction it operates, is debatable. Blackaby (1976) points to the evidence of a link between crime and unemployment. Indeed, he goes further by arguing that '.... one may legitimately expect in Northern Ireland that the recruitment of young men into the Provisional IRA was helped by the fact that there were large numbers who had nothing else to do but to stand on street corners'. A related view is that it is possible to justify regional policy on economic grounds alone and treat any associated reduction of social, environmental or political problems as a bonus. This view, to put it mildly, is also controversial.

Unfortunately, the vague and sometimes conflicting statements of the objectives of regional policy by the policymakers themselves are nowhere near sufficient. The economic analysis of regional policy requires a much more precise statement of objectives than we have yet obtained. An alternative, and more rigorous, approach to the specification of the economic objectives of regional policy is to begin from macroeconomic policy objectives rather than from the statements and comments of policymakers. Traditionally, macroeconomic policy has been concerned with two broad economic objectives for society: the objective of maximising economic efficiency, and the objective of attaining an equitable distribution of income. It is possible to go a step further than this by specifying these two objectives in more detail. In addition to the general objective of achieving a more equitable distribution of income, we have five other objectives (Stilwell 1972) — namely, the efficiency objectives:

(i)   to prevent the under-utilisation of resources (which implies the existence of an optimum rate of utilisation);

(ii)   to secure a better allocation of resources between various uses (which implies the existence of an optimum allocation of resources);

(iii) to achieve a satisfactory rate of growth of productive capacity (which implies the existence of an optimum rate of growth);

(iv)   to prevent excessive inflation (which implies the existence of an optimum rate of inflation);

(v)   to avoid chronic and persistent disequilibria in the balance of payments.

All five efficiency objectives are concerned, in one way or another, with raising national output. An increase in output can be achieved directly by raising the utilisation rate of resources, or by raising the marginal product of resources through an improved allocation. The reduction of regional imbalance assists in the attainment of both these objectives. It contributes directly to the improved utilisation of resources by reducing unemployment in regions where it is high. Similarly, regional policy can be used to control the growth of the major conurbations, which are seen to be suffering increasingly from congestion and other related urban problems.

The influence of inflation and balance of payments problems on the objective of raising national output is less obvious at first sight. The existence of both inflation and a fundamental disequilibrium in the balance of payments, however, means that the objective of increasing national output has often been sacrificed in order to reduce inflation and attain a balance of payments equilibrium. There is no doubt that the objectives of price stability and balance of payments equilibrium have severely constrained the policymakers' attempts to raise national output by utilising the unused resources of depressed regions. It will be argued in a later chapter that a reduction in regional differences in the pressure of labour demand may help to reduce inflationary pressures in the economy as a whole, thus helping the policymaker to achieve the objectives of price stability and a faster growth of output at the same time.

The proposition that the purpose of regional policy is to help the policymaker to achieve *national,* rather than purely regional, goals is controversial in so far as it appears to deny the existence of regional objectives. Specific regional policy goals — such as the preservation of rural communities in the Scottish Highlands and Islands — do, however, exist and have resulted in active policies. But they have been overshadowed in practice by the heavy emphasis placed on national objectives in the construction of regional policies.

1.2 The Conflict between Objectives

Policy objectives can, and often do, conflict. We are all familiar with the problems of conflicting objectives in the operation of macroeconomic policy: rapid growth, stable prices, and balance of payments equilibrium appear to be extremely difficult objectives to achieve simultaneously. The problem of conflicting objectives is no less severe in the development and execution of regional policy.

Some examples will help. Consider the policy of stimulating growth in a depressed region. There is a widely held view that rapid regional growth tends to be an unbalanced process, with increases in productive capacity tending to be drawn towards specific growth poles. If this is a realistic model of regional growth, and if there are significant advantages to firms resulting from geographical concentration, it may be necessary for policymakers to encourage development in specific growth poles with the result that the welfare gap *within* regions may actually have to be widened if the welfare gap *between* regions is to be narrowed.

A second example is that it may be necessary to sacrifice a number of regional policy objectives in the medium term if these conflict with other policy objectives, such as increasing the rate of growth of the national economy or reducing pressure on the balance of payments by stimulating the expansion of export industries. Developing countries, for example, may find that the most efficient method of expanding the economy is to concentrate scarce investment resources in specific regions, and these may be the regions which already have a relatively high per capita income level. The objective of reducing regional differences in per capita income may therefore have to be sacrificed until the economy is sufficiently prosperous to be able to spread its new capital equipment more widely (see Lefeber 1964).

Finally, it becomes far more difficult to implement a regional policy during periods of prolonged depression, especially if this is accompanied by a chronic deficit in the balance of payments and a high rate of inflation, as occurred in Britain during 1975 to 1977. With high unemployment even in the so-called prosperous regions, it becomes increasingly difficult to argue the case for diverting industry to the depressed regions. Furthermore, the need to expand exports during a time of severe balance of payments deficit leads to a relaxation of controls on the location of new factory buildings which are to be used for the production of exports.

1.3 The Problems of Specifying and Quantifying Policy Objectives

The objectives of regional policy, whether derived from the broad objectives of macroeconomic policy or from the statements of policymakers, are either too general or too vague to be of much practical value. They are not sufficiently precise for the efficient construction and evaluation of regional policy. As a result, the analysis of regional policy has been riddled with ambiguity and misunderstanding.

The equity objective is an excellent example of the need for precision in the specification of policy objectives. It is not clear from the equity objective as it stands just what regional policy is supposed to achieve. It is quite possible, for example, that a regional policy which successfully led to an equalisation of regional per capita incomes might well have *regressive* effects on the *distribution* of income. This would happen if a region experienced a rise in its per capita income relative to the nation as a whole, but where most of the income gain accrued to high income households resident in the depressed region. In other words, it is important to distinguish between 'place prosperity' and 'people prosperity' (West 1973). The first does not necessarily imply the second. British assisted areas consist of localities of widely divergent affluence. Regional policies benefit both affluent and depressed localities alike. Even in the poorest of localities, not all those who benefit from regional policies will be low on the welfare scale. A further twist to the divergence between 'place prosperity' and 'people prosperity' is added by the fact that owners of capital (and other resources) may not be resident in the same region as the resources they own. Industrial subsidies may simply increase the earnings of capital owners who are themselves resident in other regions.

A further example of the need for greater precision in the specification of objectives is that equity inovlves more than just the reduction of differences in per capita income levels. The stability of income is also important. Two regions may have exactly the same per capita income *level,* taking the average over a number of years, but its variation over time may be considerably greater in one region than another. Since income-earners are likely to prefer a stable to an unstable income, such additional dimensions of equity must be taken explicitly into account. Hence, in spite of the difficulties involved, there is a clear and pressing need to introduce greater precision into the specification of policy objectives. The absence of clear objectives has greatly retarded the economic analysis of regional policy.

Precise specification of objectives is essential for three distinct reasons:

(i)   for the purpose of delimiting an appropriate set of regional policy areas;

(ii) for the purpose of devising a policy (which involves the selection of an efficient set of policy instruments)

capable of achieving the specified objectives;
(iii) for the purpose of evaluating regional policy.

The importance of precise objectives for the selection of policy instruments is obvious. The tools selected depend upon the job to be done; different goals require different types of policies for their achievement. The selection of a coherent set of policy instruments forms the subject matter of the second part of this book.

Similarly, it is impossible to estimate how effective regional policies have been, or will be, unless we are clear what they are designed to achieve. Without clarifying the objectives of regional policy, evaluation degenerates into measuring the *effects* of regional policy rather than measuring the *effectiveness* — and there is a world of difference between the two. We discuss this distinction in detail in the final section of the book.

Less obvious is the role that regional policy objectives play in delimiting assisted areas. Without a clear set of objectives, the delimitation of areas for policy purposes becomes a purely arbitrary procedure. Consider, for example, the method by which assisted areas have been designated and redesignated in the United Kingdom. Under the Local Employment Act of 1972 (as amended by the Industry Act of 1972), the Secretary of State designates assisted areas according to 'all the circumstances, actual and expected, including the state of employment and unemployment, population changes, migration, and the objectives of regional policy' *(Trade and Industry, 1977)*. With such a vague set of criteria for delimiting assisted areas, almost any part of the UK is a candidate for designation, and it is not perhaps surprising that the assisted areas have tended to multiply until they threaten to swallow up the whole nation (see figure 1.4). Since it is not clear what regional policy is trying to achieve, it is also not clear which areas should be made eligible for regional assistance.

The danger of delimiting assisted areas without first formulating precise policy objectives is vividly illustrated by earlier methods of delimitation used in Britain. Between 1960 and 1966, every local employment exchange area jwith an unemployment rate exceeding 4½% was delineated as a development district, and therefore an area eligible for assistance. This method had the advantage of using a precise indicator — the unemployment rate. Unfortunately,

Special Development Areas

Development Areas

Intermediate Areas

Northern Ireland

* New Towns also eligible for
Special Development Area
incentives.

*Glenrothes
*Livingston

Skelmersdale

Source: Department of Industry, *Incentives for Industry.*

Figure 1.4 *The Assisted Areas of the United Kingdom (at June 1977)*

it was *too* precise. The apparent implication to be drawn
from this method of delimiting assisted areas is that the sole
aim of regional policy at that time was to reduce
unemployment below 4½% in all local areas. But even
though unemployment was regarded as the essence of the
regional problem, few would set the objectives of regional
policy so narrowly. In other words, a failure to specify *all* the
objectives of regional policy resulted in the division of the
UK into two sets of areas (viz. assisted and non-assisted) on
the basis of a single simplistic indicator.

If detailed regional policies are to be constructed and their
effectiveness assessed, it is desirable for the objectives to be
expressed in quantitative terms. First, numerical targets
should be set for each objective. Second, the time period
within which the targets are to be achieved should be stated.
Third, weights should be attached to each objective so that
priorities can be set. What this means is that some objectives

may be more important than others and this fact should be recognised. Using regional policy to tackle unemployment may, for example, be more important than using it to reduce inflation. If a particular policy simultaneously assists in the attainment of one objective while hindering the attainment of another, the setting of priorities is essential even though it is an extremely difficult task.

In practice, of course, it is difficult to get policymakers to specify objectives too precisely and even more difficult to get them to set numerical targets. Policymakers are reluctant to quantify their policy objectives because they are acutely aware of the danger to their own political position of setting targets and failing to achieve them. This is particularly true where policymakers feel that circumstances are beyond their control, as in the United Kingdom where 'specific objectives for regional policy in terms of jobs or of unemployment rates are not established in advance, as these variables depend heavily on national and world economic conditions' (Regional Development Programme 1977). It is sad but not surprising that policymakers have taken the easier option of specifying their policy objectives in vague and general terms.

One hopeful sign for the future has been the movement away from the traditional emphasis on unemployment. In the past, there has been an excessive tendency to rely upon regional unemployment rates as a proxy indicator for the economic malaise of regions. Assisted areas have been designated on the basis of unemployment rates, policies selected on the basis of their ability to reduce unemployment irrespective of their other implications, and the effectiveness of regional policies has been judged against their ability (or inability) to reduce regional unemployment. It is now widely realised that regional problems are too complex, and the objectives of regional policy too diverse, for one indicator to take on such a herculean task. Indeed, the unemployment rate is not even an efficient measure of unemployment since it provides information only about those who *register* as unemployed. Those who fail to register as unemployed — and this applies to a large number of unemployed married women — are ignored.

As a result of these limitations, a whole battery of regional indicators is now in use. Most popular are output and income measures, such as GDP per capita, which avoid many of the weaknesses of regional unemployment rates. Figure 1.5 shows the regional dispersion of GDP per head within the

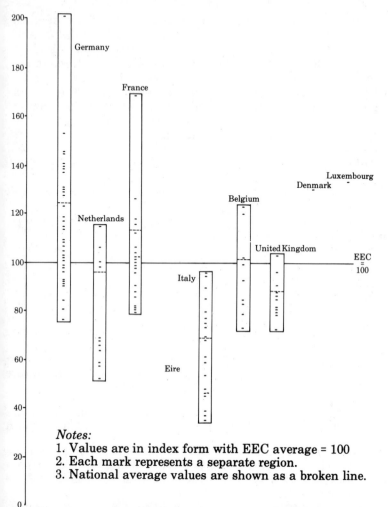

Notes:
1. Values are in index form with EEC average = 100
2. Each mark represents a separate region.
3. National average values are shown as a broken line.

Source: Eurostat, *Regional Accounts: Economic Aggregates, 1970,*
        Commission of the European Communities, 1976

Figure 1.5 *Regional gross value added (at market prices) per head*
        in the European Economic Community, 1970

EEC in 1970. This trend towards the use of multiple
indicators was greatly strengthened in Britain by the Hunt
Report (White Paper 1969), which identified a number of
intermediate or 'grey' areas of Britain on the basis of a range
of economic indicators. These included, alongside
unemployment rates and per capita incomes, measures of

employment growth, activity rates, the structure of local employment, the range of job opportunities available, and migration rates. Table 1.2 shows the relative positions of the UK regions on the basis of several principal economic indicators. Table 1.3 shows a similar set of indicators for the Canadian Provinces. It can be seen that the broad geographical patterns of regional 'prosperity' correspond fairly closely no matter which indicator is used. The coincidence, however, is by no means perfect.

Table 1.2 *Some indicators of economic prosperity in the standard regions of the United Kingdom*

Region	GDP per head 1974		Male Activity rate[a] 1971		Female activity rate[a] 1971		Unemployment rate 1974		Net migration rate 1973-76	
	UK=100	Rank	GB=100	Rank	GB=100	Rank	UK=100	Rank	Rate	Rank
South East	117	(1)	101	(2)	105	(2)	59	(1)	-0.33	(10)
East Anglia	93	(5)	98	(8)	91	(8)	74	(2)	+1.08	(1)
South West	93	(5)	96	(9)	88	(9)	100	(5)	+0.73	(2)
West Midlands	99	(2)	103	(1)	106	(1)	81	(3)	-0.22	(8)
East Midlands	96	(3)	101	(2)	101	(4)	81	(3)	+0.18	(4)
Yorks/ Humberside	93	(5)	100	(4)	98	(6)	104	(6)	-0.03	(5)
North West	95	(4)	100	(4)	104	(3)	130	(7)	-0.28	(9)
North	90	(9)	99	(7)	94	(7)	174	(10)	-0.11	(6)
Wales	84	(10)	97	(9)	84	(10)	141	(8)	+0.24	(3)
Scotland	93	(5)	100	(4)	99	(5)	152	(9)	-0.13	(7)
N Ireland	74	(11)	—	—	—	—	226	(11)	-0.78	(11)
United Kingdom	UK=100	—	GB=100	—	GB=100	—	UK=100	—	—	—

An activity rate is the percentage of those of working age who are registered as either employed or unemployed.

Notes:
1. With the exception of net migration rates, indicators are expressed in index form with United Kingdom (or Great Britain as appropriate) = 100.
2. Each net migration rate refers to the annual average for the period 1973 to 1976, and is the net migration of the region expressed as a percentage of the mid-1971 population of the region.

Sources: Regional Statistics, 1975 and 1976; *Census of Population,* 1971; Office of Population Censuses and Surveys of England and Wales; General Register Offices of Scotland and Northern Ireland.

The trend towards multiple indicators is to be welcomed. It represents the first inevitable step along the path towards constructing a more precise set of regional policy objectives. Clearly, progress is being made in providing a more adequate data-base from which suitable indicators can be constructed. But there is no room for complacency. The gap between the existing data-base and that required for the

Table 1.3 *Some indicators of economic prosperity in the Canadian Provinces, June 1974*

Province	Average weekly earnings and salaries		Unemployment		Participation rate (males and females combined)[a]		Employment change index	
	Canada =100	(Rank)	Canada =100	(Rank)	Canada =100	(Rank)	1961 =100	(Rank)
Newfoundland	95	(5)					139	(5)
Prince Edward Is	70	(10)	210	(5)	88	(5)	156	(3)
Nova Scotia	86	(9)					130	(8)
New Brunswick	87	(8)					134	(6)
Quebec	97	(4)	131	(3)	97	(4)	131	(7)
Ontario	103	(2)	73	(2)	104	(1)	148	(4)
Manitoba	91	(6)					128	(10)
Saskatchewan	90	(7)	55	(1)	103	(2)	129	(9)
Alberta	101	(3)					162	(2)
British Columbia	110	(1)	108	(4)	101	(3)	163	(1)
Canada	100	—	100	—	100	—	143	—

[a] The participation rate is the recorded labour force expressed as a percentage of the population 14 years of age and over.
Source: Statistics Canada, January 1975.

delimitation of assisted areas, for policy formulation and for policy evaluation, remains wide. As yet, there has been little attempt to tie specific indicators to the objectives that they are meant to represent and quantify. There has also been no determined attempt to fix targets and priorities to individual objectives.

Conclusion

Despite the many problems that policymakers face in trying adequately to specify and quantify their policy objectives, we have nevertheless seen — in Britain and elsewhere — the emergence of quite a complex set of regional policy instruments. Furthermore, policymakers have created a system of policy areas so that distinct policy packages can be applied to different regions depending upon the extent of each region's problems. Thus, although the objectives of regional policy remain vague and imprecise, the policy instruments are numerous and in some cases quite powerful.

It is somewhat surprising that a complex set of regional policy instruments should have been constructed before the aims of regional policy have been clearly spelled out. Only if the objectives are spelled out in greater detail will it become possible to analyse and evaluate regional policy more efficiently.

Selected references

Cameron (1974); Diamond (1974); Lefeber (1964); Leven (1964);
McCrone (1969), Introduction and Chapter 1; Regional Development Programme (1977); Stilwell (1972), Chapters 1 and 2.

PART 1

The Emergence, Persistence and Costs of Regional Imbalance

Why do regions grow at different rates? Are there any self-regulating mechanisms within the economic system which help to redress regional economic imbalance? What are the problems that emanate from regional economic imbalance? These are the questions we discuss in the first part of this book.

Our aim is not to provide clear-cut answers to these questions, but rather to provide a suitable framework which can be used to attack these and related questions from various angles.Thus, we begin (in Chapter 2) by examining some of the more widely discussed explanations of why regions grow at different rates. Since one of the main conclusions reached in the regional growth chapter is that interregional linkages play a major part in determining the economic performance of individual regions, the discussion of why regions grow at different rates is followed (in Chapters 3 and 4) by an examination of interregional movements of capital, labour and commodities.

After investigating the causes of regional imbalance, we proceed to discuss why regional imbalance poses problems for policymakers. The most obvious undesirable outcome of regional disparities is the problem of persistent and severe regional differences in unemployment. The regional unemployment problem is therefore examined in Chapter 5. We then turn in Chapter 6 to three further (and rather less obvious) arguments in support of the case for regional policy. Firstly, we examine the argument that regional policy may help to defuse some of the inflationary pressures that build up in the 'more prosperous' regions. Secondly, the view that a regional policy can help to solve some of the problems caused by urban growth is critically examined. Finally, we turn to a more recent argument — namely, that the economic integration of different countries, as in the European Economic Community, may lead to a worsening of regional problems.

2
The Emergence of Regional Economic Disparities

The fact that regions grow at different rates is well known. In spite of a good deal of research by economists, economic historians and economic geographers, however, there is still no generally accepted explanation of why these regional growth differences occur.

Explanations of why regions grow at different rates have been developing along two main routes. Economists have turned to the standard macroeconomic models of growth and converted them into regional growth models. The emphasis, however, has been heavily weighted towards abstract theoretical models, the usefulness of which is limited by their restrictive assumptions. In addition, lack of adequate regional data has presented problems in devising suitable empirical tests. Economic historians and economic geographers have taken a more practical route and investigated in detail the actual development of specific regions in order to discover the primary factors responsible for the changing geographical pattern of economic activity over time. These studies have tended to stress the disequilibrating forces at work in regional growth processes.

A number of different, though not entirely unrelated, explanations of regional growth differences are discussed in this chapter. The reason for considering a range of different explanations is that each separate theory may have something to contribute to a more general theory of regional growth disparities.

2.1 The Meaning of Regional Growth Disparities

As a preliminary to investigating why regions grow at different rates, we must begin by defining the term 'regional

21

growth disparities'. Different definitions exist depending upon the meaning attached to the word 'growth'. The simplest definition is the rate of increase of *real output*, which is useful if we are interested in examining the policy implications of regional differences in the growth of productive capacity. Greater concentration of productive capacity in a small number of regions, for example, may yield economies of large scale production whilst at the same time having a detrimental effect on the regions suffering from absolute decline. The investigation of regional differences in the growth of productive capacity draws attention to these types of problems. More often, however, it is the growth of output *per capita* that is of greatest interest to the policymaker. For this reason, it is important to see what the various growth theories have to say about regional differences in the growth of output per capita. In the present chapter, we therefore confine ourselves to examining two aspects of regional growth: the growth of real output and the growth of output per capita.

The various definitions of growth do not necessarily say the same thing. Two regions with the same rate of growth of output, for example, will have quite different rates of growth of output per capita if their populations are not growing at the same rate. Furthermore, it is quite possible for regional differences in per capita output to be narrowing at the same time as productive capacity is becoming more and more concentrated in a small number of regions. Indeed, this has been a feature of many nations during the present century and is a phenomenon of regional growth that requires more attention.

2.2 The Neoclassical Approach to Explaining Regional Differences in Growth

The theory
The basis of neoclassical models of growth is the aggregate production function. The output of an economy is asserted to depend upon its productive capacity, the latter being determined by the supply of factor inputs. Two special features of neoclassical models are that factors of production are assumed to be substitutable and that factor prices are perfectly flexible. The consequence is that no factor of production can remain unemployed, at least not for long, since the unemployment of a factor results in a fall in that

factor's price and hence an increase in the amount of the factor demanded.

The importance of these two special features of the neoclassical model is best brought out by briefly considering the aggregate production function used in the modelling of the Harrod-Domar theory of growth:

$$Q = \min\ (aK,\ bL)$$

which asserts that $Q = aK$ *or* $Q = bL$, whichever is the smaller of the two, and where Q is output, K is available capital inputs and L is available labour inputs. In other words, capital and labour must be used in a fixed ratio to produce any given level of output. It follows that since the capital/labour ratio is fixed by the state of technical knowledge, the maximum level of output that can be produced is set by either the stock of capital ($Q = aK$) or the stock of labour ($Q = bL$) depending upon the technically required capital/labour ratio. For example, if there are 100 identical machines each requiring two workers for their operation, then a labour force of 220 would result in only 200 finding work, whereas a labour force of 180 would result in only 90 machines being operated. No automatic mechanism exists in this world of 'fixed coefficients' for bringing about full employment. The neoclassical system is quite different. If there exists unemployed labour, wages fall and so make it profitable for firms to employ more labour, and similarly with all other factor inputs.

The simplest version of the neoclassical model asserts that output is a function only of capital and labour inputs, the economy being assumed to experience zero technical progress:

$$Q = F(K, L) \tag{1}$$

Since output in any one year depends on the supplies of capital and labour, it is intuitively obvious that the rate of output growth over time can be expressed as a function of the rates of growth of capital and labour. By assuming constant returns to scale (i.e. doubling the input of both capital and labour will double output), we can obtain a more precise representation of this simple growth model:

$$\dot{Q} = \alpha \dot{K} + (1 - \alpha)\dot{L} \tag{2}$$

where $\dot{Q}$, $\dot{K}$ and $\dot{L}$ refer to rates of change of Q, K and L respectively, and where α and $1-\alpha$ can be interpreted as the respective contribution of capital and labour to aggregate output (see Appendix A). Hence, a 4 % annual growth of the capital stock and a 2 % annual growth of the labour supply would result in an annual output growth of 2.6 %, given $\alpha = 0.3$ and $1-\alpha = 0.7$. To obtain the rate of growth of output per worker ($\dot{Q} - \dot{L}$), $\dot{L}$ can be subtracted from both sides of equation 2:

$$\dot{Q} - \dot{L} = \alpha(\dot{K} - \dot{L}) \tag{3}$$

which shows that output per man can only increase if capital growth exceeds the growth of the labour supply. In other words, the capital/labour ratio (i.e. capital per worker) must increase for output per man to increase. This positive relationship between capital per worker and output per worker is shown in figure 2.1.

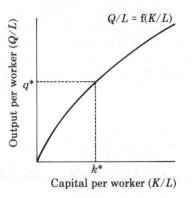

Note
$Q = F(K, L)$ implies $Q/L = f(K/L)$ assuming a linear homogeneous production function e.g. a Cobb-Douglas production function with constant returns to scale. See Appendix A.

Figure 2.1 *The aggregate production function.*

This brings us to an important feature of the neoclassical model. Output per worker will, as we have seen, increase as each worker is provided with more capital equipment — a process known as 'capital deepening'. But this cannot continue indefinitely. Capital, like labour, suffers from decreasing marginal returns. The increase in output per worker will therefore be at a diminishing rate as shown in figure 2.1. Eventually, a position such as k^* will be reached beyond which the level of investment per period will not be sufficient to equip an expanding labour force with the machines needed to maintain the capital/labour ratio at that level. The capital stock will have to expand at the same rate as the expansion of the labour force if the capital/labour ratio is not to fall. But as the capital/labour ratio expands, more and more investment will be required per period to maintain the K/L ratio at this higher level. It can be shown, in fact, that there exists an equilibrium level of the capital/labour ratio, such as k^* in figure 2.1 (see Appendix A). In turn, the equilibrium level of the capital/labour ratio implies an equilibrium level of output per worker (q^*). Above k^*, the labour force would grow more rapidly than the capital stock, resulting in a falling capital/labour ratio. Below k^*, the capital stock would grow more rapidly than the labour force, resulting in a rising capital/labour ratio. Only at k^* do capital and labour grow at the same rate, thus guaranteeing the stability of the capital/labour ratio. Furthermore, the constant returns to scale assumption guarantees that output will grow at the same rate as capital and labour. In these circumstances, the economy is in long-run equilibrium.

What conclusions can we draw from our brief discussion of the simplest neoclassical growth model? First, we have seen that output grows without limit as the supply of capital and labour increases. Second, output *per worker* can increase only through an increase in capital per worker. Third, over the long run, output per worker will be constant since an equilibrium capital/labour ratio will be established. An increase in output per man is therefore possible only in the medium term; that is, until the long-run capital/labour ratio has been reached.

More realism can be built into the neoclassical model by allowing for technical progress — a potentially important source of growth. The most convenient way of allowing for the effect of technical progress on output growth is to regard it as an additional and separate element in the production function. Each unit of capital and labour is assumed to benefit equally from technical progress which descends on to an unsuspecting economy 'like manna from heaven'. A typical model which includes this type of technical progress (A) is as follows:

$$Q = A(t)\,F(K, L) \tag{4}$$

As technical knowledge progresses over time (t), it is assumed to improve the productivity of capital and labour equally. Clearly, this depiction of technical progress is oversimplified. Alternative models exist in which technical progress augments the efficiency of either only capital or only labour, but they are not considered here. Nor are the more realistic models which assume that technical progress does not apply to all existing factor supplies but is 'embodied' only in new capital or new labour (see Branson 1972 for an excellent introductory treatment). Nevertheless, even the *neutral, disembodied* version of technical progress shown in equation 4 represents an improvement on the previous version.

Again assuming constant returns to scale, we can rewrite equation 4 in terms of rates of change (see Appendix A):

$$\dot{Q} = \dot{A} + \alpha\dot{K} + (1-\alpha)\dot{L} \tag{5}$$

where $\dot{A}$ is the rate of technical progress. For example, with zero growth of the capital stock and the supply of labour, a 3 % rate of technical progress would cause output to grow at the same rate. This extended version of the neoclassical model does at least allow for the possibility of a steady growth in output per worker over the long run. This is easily seen by rewriting equation 5 to obtain the rate of growth of output per worker ($\dot{Q} - \dot{L}$):

$$\dot{Q} - \dot{L} = \dot{A} + \alpha(\dot{K} - \dot{L}) \tag{6}$$

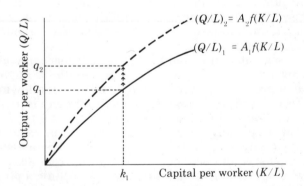

Figure 2.2 *The aggregate production function with technological progress*

from which we can see that even if the capital stock and the labour force grow at the same rate, output per man will increase provided there is technical progress (i.e. $\dot{A} > 0$). The same result is depicted in figure 2.2. The upward shift in the production function caused by technical progress results in an increase in output per worker from q_1 to q_2 at any given capital/labour ratio such as k_1.

Moreover, as we have shown, output and capital grow at the same rate in the long run (i.e. $\dot{Q} = \dot{K}$), which allows us to rewrite equation 6 as follows:

$$\dot{Q} - \dot{L} = \frac{\dot{A}}{1 - \alpha} \tag{7}$$

This is the long-run equilibrium version of equation 6. Hence, equation 6 is the growth model we would use to explain why one economy may grow at a different rate from another economy over the medium term.

Although this discussion of the neoclassical theory of growth has been superficial, it has nevertheless covered sufficient ground to demonstrate the potential usefulness of the neoclassical approach to explaining regional growth differences. Using the neutral, disembodied technical progress version of neoclassical growth theory there is a choice between the medium-term model and the long-run equilibrium model. Since we are interested here in explaining why regions grow at different rates over relatively short time periods (e.g. a decade), the medium-term model is the appropriate one to use. If we were interested in determining the long-run equilibrium growth rate of a regional economy, the long-run model would be appropriate.

By converting equation 5 into a *regional* growth model, it becomes immediately apparent that the neoclassical approach provides three reasons for regional differences in output growth: technical progress, the growth of capital stock and the growth of the labour force. We assume that regional differences in factor shares, α and $1 - \alpha$, are negligible and can be ignored. The regional growth equation can be written as follows:

$$\dot{Q}_r = \dot{A}_r + \alpha \dot{K}_r + (1 - \alpha) \dot{L}_r \tag{8}$$

where the subscripts refer to region r.

Similarly, if this model is to be used to explain *regional differences* in the growth of output per worker, we must 'regionalise' equation 6:

$$\dot{Q}_r - \dot{L}_r = \dot{A}_r + \alpha\,(\dot{K}_r - \dot{L}_r) \tag{9}$$

which asserts that output per worker can increase, in the medium term, for one of two reasons: either through technical progress or through capital deepening. Regional differences in the growth of output per worker are explained entirely by regional differences in the rate of technical progress and by regional differences in the rate of increase of capital per worker. In the context of an economy in which investment opportunities vary significantly between regions, differential rates of capital accumulation can be expected to have a marked impact on regional differences in the growth of output per worker.

In a regional context, the growth of capital and labour depends not only upon indigenous changes in regional factor supplies, but also upon interregional movements of capital and labour. Indeed, these geographical movements of mobile factor inputs are an essential feature of regional growth. Factor inputs are considerably more mobile between regions than between nations, and regional growth differences are likely to be strongly influenced by factor movements, which are assumed to respond to regional differences in factor returns.

Capital and labour do not, however, respond perfectly and instantaneously to regional differences in factor returns. A more reasonable assumption is that capital is more mobile than labour, but that significant frictions to mobility exist for both factors. The greater mobility of capital implies that it is those regions with the fastest indigenous growth of labour that will grow the most rapidly, since the lower wages being paid in such regions will induce capital to move into them from regions where wages are higher. Given that capital is more mobile than labour, the neoclassical theory of migration predicts that capital will flow into low-wage regions faster than labour will flow out of such regions and into higher wage regions (Smith D.M. 1975).

Whether or not differences in technical progress are likely to be an important influence on regional growth rates is difficult to assess. Little is yet known about the geographical diffusion of technical progress. *A priori*, we would expect technical knowledge to be highly mobile; this would imply that the rate of technical progress should be similar in all regions — a viewpoint supported by the recent empirical work of Dixon and Thirlwall (1976). On the other hand, detailed empirical analysis by geographers of the spatial diffusion of technology (see for example Berry 1974 and Morrill 1968) suggests that the diffusion of technical progress between regions is by no means instantaneous and seems to follow well-defined channels.

A serious disadvantage with the neoclassical approach to explaining why regions grow at different rates is that the model is far too aggregative as it stands. As a result, it conceals a potentially important source of regional growth. If the regional economy has two sectors, one being a declining sector with low labour productivity and the other being an expanding sector with high labour productivity, output growth will occur as a direct consequence of the movement of labour from the low productivity sector to the high productivity sector. Resource shifts between industries *within a region* may therefore be an important source of regional output growth, a factor which may in some circumstances be important in explaining why regions grow at different rates.

A further criticism of the neoclassical approach to explaining regional growth differences is the excessive concentration on the influence of supply factors. Though this may be acceptable in national models, the openness of regional economies and the different resource endowments and production conditions in different regions make it more likely that the demand for a region's export commodities will have a marked effect on its growth. Later in this chapter, an export demand model of regional growth will be considered.

A weakness of the neoclassical approach as presented above is the assumption of constant returns to scale. This is a major point of difference between neoclassical growth theory and the growth pole theories which are considered below. Neoclassical models that assume constant returns to scale assume away what may be an important source of regional growth differences — namely, internal and external economies of scale. Internal economies arise within the firm as a direct consequence of the growth in its size, whereas external economies accrue to firms located in a specific area as a consequence of the spatial concentration of firms. We shall be returning to these scale economies below. It is possible, however, to relax this assumption in neoclassical models.

A number of other criticisms can be levelled against the neoclassical approach to explaining the growth process, such as the assumption of only two factors of production both of which are homogeneous, but at least it provides a useful starting point for understanding some of the possible sources of regional growth differences.

Two applications of the neoclassical model
The lack of adequate regional data makes it difficult to test hypotheses produced by even the simplest of neoclassical models. Nevertheless, attempts have been made to test the neoclassical model in a regional setting and two of them are considered here, one for the USA, the other for the UK.

The best known attempt to test and evaluate the neoclassical regional growth model empirically is undoubtedly that by Borts and Stein (1964). They begin with the simplest neoclassical growth model in which only one commodity is produced, and in which capital and labour are assumed to migrate towards the region offering the highest rate of return. Capital will migrate from high to low wage regions (i.e. towards the regions where the marginal product of capital is highest), whilst labour will migrate in the opposite direction. Such a model offers two testable hypotheses:

(i)   Capital growth will be highest in low wage regions. As a result of capital inflows and labour outflows from these regions, the capital/labour ratio should also increase most rapidly in low wage regions.

(ii) Low wage regions should also exhibit the most rapid growth of wages as a result of a rising capital/labour ratio.

Some of the results obtained by Borts and Stein are given in table 2.1. The simple one-commodity neoclassical model is not supported. Only during 1929-1948 did the low wage regions exhibit a more rapid growth of capital, wages, and the capital/labour ratio than the high wage regions. Introducing more realistic assumptions concerning labour and capital migration does not alter this conclusion. If, as earlier, we assume that capital suffers from fewer frictions to its geographical mobility than labour, then it is the low wage regions which we would expect to experience the most rapid growth of output. But we would still expect these low wage regions to experience the most rapid capital accumulation

Table 2.1 *The relationship between the level of wages and the percentage growth of capital, labour and wages in the USA, 1919-57*

Period		Percentage growth of capital[1,2]	Percentage growth of labour	Growth of capital/ labour ratio	Percentage growth of wages
1919-1929	High wage areas[3]	60	22	38	43
	Low wage areas	53	23	30	36
1929-1948	High wage areas	86	31	55	168
	Low wage areas	139	29	110	220
1948-1953	High wage areas	37	13	24	29
	Low wage areas	32	13	18	28
1948-1957	High wage areas	69	20	49	55
	Low wage areas	67	23	44	58

Notes:
1. Figures in all cases refer to the non-agricultural sector.
2. Capital growth is measured in terms of the growth of factor income payments to owners of non-agricultural capital.
3. The 48 continental states of the USA are divided into high and low wage areas on the basis of average wages and salaries per employee.
Source: Borts and Stein (1962), table 1; Borts and Stein (1964), table 3.1.

(hypothesis (i)) even though the retention of population may prevent either the capital/labour ratio or wages from growing rapidly (hypothesis (ii)).

Borts and Stein argue that the single commodity assumption of the neoclassical model is its most critical weakness. Using a more realistic version of the neoclassical model, in which regions produce not one commodity but many commodities, output growth can be achieved through intersectoral shifts of productive factors as well as through interregional shifts. This suggests that regions possessing both a high productivity growth sector and a low productivity declining sector will grow rapidly because of the shift of factors from the low to the high productivity sector. This modification to the neoclassical model improves the match between fact and theory considerably. The significant exceptions to this modified explanation of regional growth differences are those regions which lack a high productivity growth sector. Borts and Stein conclude by suggesting that whilst neoclassical theory (suitably modified) may provide a reasonable explanation of regional growth differences in the USA in the past, the model is unlikely to be as useful in the future, mainly because the major structural changes in the US economy have now been

completed (i.e. the movement of labour out of agriculture).
Explanations of future growth differences in the USA will
have to incorporate the increasing influence of migration
flows and the influence of changes in the demand for
regional exports. The crucial influence of regional export
demand was in fact already visible in the USA during the
period studied by Borts and Stein. The superior growth
performance of high wage areas during 1948-1953 seems to
have been the result of regional export demand stimulated
by the Korean War. Moreover, in some of the regions which
had exhausted their potential for transferring labour
internally, such as New England, their continued decline
could be attributed to a decline in the demand for their
principal export commodities. Finally, the role of export
demand may go some way towards explaining the
apparently perverse growth of capital and capital/labour
ratios in high wage regions. Following Borts (1960), we can
define the marginal efficiency of investment in a region as:

$$\text{MEI} = \text{MPK} \ (P_x \ / \ P_k)$$

which emphasizes the fact that the profitability of
investment is not simply a function of the price of capital
(P_k) and the physical productivity of the investment (MPK),
but is also a function of the price of the region's exports (P_x).
Hence, a high wage region with a low marginal product of
capital may still exhibit rapid capital growth provided the
demand for its exports is high.

In an analysis of regional growth differences in the UK,
Dixon and Thirlwall (1976) use the disembodied technical
progress version of the neoclassical model to estimate the
relative significance of technical progress ($\dot{A}$) and capital
deepening ($\dot{K} - \dot{L}$) on regional growth rates in the UK.
Unfortunately, paucity of data severely limits the usefulness
of their findings but their application is nevertheless
interesting and suggestive of further research. They begin
with the medium-term model, which attributes the growth of
output per worker ($\dot{Q} - \dot{L}$) to technical progress and to
increases in capital per worker (i.e. capital deepening). The
basic model can be written as follows (equation 9 above):

$$\dot{Q}_r - \dot{L}_r = \dot{A}_r + \alpha(\dot{K}_r - \dot{L}_r)$$

$\dot{Q}_r - \dot{L}_r$ is available from published data, but since regional
capital stock data are not available, the rate of change in real

wages ($\dot{w}$) is used as a proxy for $\dot{K} - \dot{L}$ (see Appendix A). Finally, the coefficient α is approximated by assuming that it will be equal to capital's share of total output.

Unfortunately, this basic model as it stands is of little value. In addition to the dubious accuracy of using $\dot{w}$ as a proxy for $\dot{K} - \dot{L}$, it suffers all the usual weaknesses of neoclassical models. Capital deepening and technical progress, for example, are likely to be related since new techniques of production will be embodied in new capital stock. The model, of course, assumes disembodied technical progress. Similarly, the model assumes constant returns to scale, and the existence of economies of scale may exert an upward bias on the estimated effect of technical progress. Finally, as in the Borts and Stein analysis, the model as it stands ignores the effect that resource shifts into high productivity sectors within regions may have on a region's productivity growth.

In view of such problems, Dixon and Thirlwall extend their analysis by using a more complex model to estimate the relative contribution of the following factors to regional growth differences in the UK over the period 1958-68:

1. technical progress
2. capital deepening
3. increasing returns to scale
4. resource shifts (from low to high productivity industries).

Table 2.2 *Components of productivity growth in the manufacturing sector of the United Kingdom regions, 1958-68*

Region	Rate of growth of labour productivity[1,2] (A)	Capital deepening (B)	Increasing returns to scale (C)	Intraregional resource shifts (D)	Technical progress (E)
SE	4.9	2.20	0.08	0.20	2.42
E Anglia	5.8	1.54	0.44	1.40	2.42
SW	4.6	2.12	0.18	− 0.10	2.42
W Midlands	4.6	1.97	0.11	0.10	2.42
E Midlands	7.2	4.11	0.17	0.50	2.42
Yorks/Humberside	3.9	1.60	− 0.02	− 0.10	2.42
NW	5.3	2.52	− 0.12	0.40	2.42
N	3.8	2.00	− 0.02	− 0.60	2.42
Wales	3.7	0.97	0.21	0.10	2.42
Scotland	4.8	1.80	− 0.02	0.60	2.42
N Ireland	7.2	4.30	− 0.02	0.50	2.42
United Kingdom	4.9	2.35	0.03	0.10	2.42

Notes:
1. A = B + C + D + E
2. The rate of growth of labour productivity is expressed as a percentage per annum.
Source: Dixon and Thirlwall (1976), table 6.8.

The main results are reproduced in table 2.2. Notice the importance of *both* technical progress and capital deepening in determining the rate at which labour productivity grows *within* each region. Since technical progress was assumed to be idential in all regions due to the high degree of mobility of technical knowledge, it plays no role in explaining regional *differences* in productivity growth. Regional differences, in fact, emerge as the result of regional differences in capital deepening and, to a lesser but still significant extent, as a result of regional differences in intraregional resource movements from low to high productivity sectors.

They point out, however, that the results must be treated cautiously: the study period (1958-1968) is far too short to be confident about the 'numbers' obtained.

2.3 The Export - Base Approach

Neoclassical theories of regional growth are unsatisfactory in an open, trading system of regions. Their failure to handle the effects of aggregate demand causes them to miss entirely a factor leading to differential regional growth which many regard as of major importance — namely, the demand for regional exports by the 'rest of the world'. It is inevitable that neoclassical models cannot handle this effect. Not only are they supply-based rather than demand-based models, the simplest variants also assume a single commodity and therefore ignore the possibility of different regions specialising in commodities with different rates of growth. This, as we saw earlier, was one of the main conclusions of the Borts and Stein study.

The export-base model of regional growth emerged from several historical studies of the growth and development of resource-based regions (Innis 1920, North 1955). The early work on the model stressed that many regions, particularly in north-western North America, were developed from 'without' rather than from 'within'. Capital and labour flowed into these regions in order to exploit their rich natural resource base. As world demand for the natural resources expanded, the necessary transport links were forged with the outside world, leading to the integration of these regions with world markets. Shipping lines and railroads were therefore brought into these regions for the purpose of exploiting their natural resources.

Hence, the central proposition of the export base model is that in several cases the initial stimulus to a region's economic development can be traced to the exploitation of its endowment of natural resources. The geographical distribution of natural resources may therefore help to explain why regions grow at different rates. But the analysis cannot stop here. We must proceed further if the export-base model is to explain the continuing and sustained expansion of a region — or indeed its decline (Stabler 1968, Scott 1966).

If the export-base model is to prove useful, it must do two things. It must first explain why regional specialisation occurs. The regions of north-western North America, which can be regarded as classic examples of regions where demand influences have dominated regional growth, have continuously specialised in the production and export of primary products, either in their raw state or with some initial processing. More generally, the export-base model must be expanded to cover regional specialisation in any type of commodity, whether it be based on raw materials, manufacturing or service industries. Second, export-base theory must concern itself with the circumstances under which a region will continue to grow and under what circumstances it will decline.

The regional trading system is undoubtedly open and free of restrictions within national boundaries. In such a situation, it is possible to draw upon the theory of comparative advantage as an explanation of regional patterns of production and export specialisation. The best known explanation of the origins of comparative advantage, and hence export specialisation, is the Heckscher-Ohlin theorem, which argues that regions will specialise in the production and export of commodities that use their relatively abundant factor intensively. Regions with abundant supplies of raw materials will therefore specialise in raw material-intensive commodities, labour-abundant regions in labour-intensive commodities and capital-abundant regions in capital-intensive commodities.

Obviously, the Hekscher-Ohlin theorem must assume interregional immobility of factors of production, for otherwise 'regional factor abundance' has no meaning. This assumption of immobility is reasonable for raw materials, but less reasonable for labour and entirely unreasonable for capital, which is likely to be quite mobile between regions. In such a situation it is therefore probable that regions favourably endowed with raw materials will specialise in the production of raw materials for export as this is their relatively cheap factor. In a neoclassical framework, capital will tend to flow into such regions in response to the high returns available to it. Hence, not only do we find the regions with the fastest rate of growth of immobile factor inputs growing faster than other regions, as the single commodity neoclassical model predicts, we also find regional specialisation occurring as well. Not surprisingly then, the regions of north-western North America have specialised in the production of raw materials and their related byproducts. Capital and labour have been drawn into these regions in response to the high returns paid to them.

Once specialisation is established, the role of external demand for a region's output becomes obvious. The more open a region is, the more important are changes in export demand in the explanation of a region's growth. If we assume that a region cannot itself influence its export selling price, then rising export demand and rising export prices will give a stimulus to the region's income and output. This will tend to bid up the relative prices of the non-abundant factors which in turn will be induced to migrate into fast-growing regions. The widening of regional growth rates will continue unchecked until the external stimulus to exports ends or until factor shortages arise. There may also be another constraint. There will be a tendency for other regions to 'jump on the bandwagon'. The more mobile that factors are between industries, the more likely is this to happen. Hence, even if the influence of external demand continues to favour a particular commodity over a long period and even if regional factor immobilities do not impose serious limits on output expansion, a region may find competitors arising amongst other regions and the export price being forced down as new suppliers enter the world market. The lower is occupational, spatial and industrial factor mobility, the longer will a particular region be able to exploit any advantage that world demand confers upon it.

Notice how the growth process tends to become cumulative in these export-base models. The stimulus to export demand has both a multiplier effect on regional income and possibly an accelerator effect on investment as well (Hartman and Seckler 1967). In addition, higher factor prices relative to other regions will draw in labour and capital. The inflow of labour will raise the demand for those goods which are produced and consumed locally, such as transportation, trade, personal services and government services. Subsidiary industries supplying specialist services to the export sector will also emerge as growth proceeds. These form part of the full range of agglomeration and localisation economies which, alongside any internal economies of scale existing in the export industries, will give further stimulus to the export sector by reducing production and distribution costs. Over time, we may see subsidiary industries become less dependent on the original export sector and they may begin to export in their own right.

The original export activity does not necessarily continue to grow indefinitely. Indeed, anything is possible. Low-cost locations can, for a wide variety of reasons, become high-cost locations. The pattern of demand may change and swing away from the export commodity in question. A cumulative reversal of the growth process outlined above may rapidly set in. Provided factor prices are flexible, however, and provided factors are sufficiently mobile between industries, the law of comparative advantage will allow the region to survive through the reallocation of productive factors to more viable export commodities. During this period of reallocation, the region may also lose labour and capital to faster growing regions.

The export-base theory, in its more extended form, is a seductive one. Its advantage over the neoclassical approach is that it stresses the role of demand factors. Yet it was roundly condemned soon after its appearance mainly because, in its simplest form, it merely describes the historical development of regions dependent on raw material exports. It offered little insight into the conditions likely to have a dominant effect on growth. The role of factors internal to a region, for instance, such as local initiative and government development programmes, are entirely ignored. Whilst the more naive export-base model is guilty of such omissions, however, those which incorporate induced investment effects, factor supply influences and the effects of external economies of scale are less open to this criticism. Perhaps the greatest weakness of the theory is that beyond the occasional mention of income elasticity of demand, no systematic explanation of the determinants of the demand for a region's exports is attempted, and without this it is impossible to predict regional growth differences.

2.4 The Polarisation Hypothesis

The polarisation hypothesis differs from other models in three ways. First, it is principally concerned with the conditions leading to the reinforcement of growth differences between regions. Second, it stresses a wide range of different mechanisms which could contribute to the perpetuation of regional growth differences. Third, one hesitates to call the polarisation hypothesis either a theory or even *an* hypothesis. It is really a group of ideas, concepts and bits-and-pieces culled from numerous theories.

The polarisation process occurs at different levels of spatial aggregation. It is reflected at the national level in the polarisation of economic development in specific regions; and within regional economies it is reflected in the polarisation of economic development in urban centres. Since much has been written about the cumulative causation mechanism, and particularly about the process of polarisation of economic development, it will be useful to discuss this mechanism in some detail.

The theory of polarised growth attempts to explain why economic development tends to become increasingly concentrated in certain 'poles of development', giving rise to growth disparities between different geographical areas. The roots of polarisation theory lie in the work of Perroux (1950), Myrdal (1957) and Hirschman (1958). Perroux's notable contribution is the distinction between geographical space and economic space, the latter being defined in terms of the transactions and economic linkages between firms and consumers in an economy. Many processes are 'polarised' rather than 'homogeneous' (i.e. equally dispersed) in economic space. As such they may, or may not, manifest themselves in polarised form in geographical space. To see this, consider the example of a firm with many plants scattered around the regions of an economy. The firm may be self-sufficient in the sense of being vertically integrated, with the various plants being strongly linked to one another. These linkages define an economic space which is highly polarised — that is, nodal economic space — focussing upon the headquarters. But the manifestation of this process is certainly not, in this case, polarised in geographical space.

The theory of polarised regional growth, by definition, stresses the tendencies of economic mechanisms to become polarised *simultaneously* in both geographical and economic space. The 'why and how' of geographical polarisation is our concern here. The crux of the polarisation hypothesis is the self-reinforcing nature of regional growth — the process of cumulative causation. In polarisation models, it is the initial headstart that is all-important, for once a region embarks on the process of economic development, the workings of the economic system inexorably enable it to grow at the expense of other regions in the economy. The result is a vicious spiral of economic growth which may enable a region to continue to grow rapidly long after its initial advantages have withered away.

Many hypotheses have been advanced under the heading of polarisation theory to explain this process of cumulative causation. One of the most convincing and potent of explanations, and one stressed by both Perroux and development economists, is the presence of economies of scale, both external and internal. Such considerations are usually deliberately excluded from the neoclassical model and failure to incorporate them represents a major weakness of that approach in explaining regional growth disparities. If an industry is subject to significant internal economies of scale, the firms that grow quickly will gain a competitive advantage over rivals and growth will become cumulative. This assumes, of course, that the scale economies are of the type that emanate from the growth of a plant rather than from the growth of the enterprise.

More important in a regional setting, however, than economies internal to the plant, may be the cost reductions resulting from the spatial proximity of related activities. A number of alternative classifications of these *external economies* exist. Following Isard (1956) and Hoover (1963), we can distinguish between economies of localisation and economies of urbanisation. Economies of localisation arise from the geographical concentration of plants in the same industry. They include transfer or linkage economies that arise because of the geographical proximity of plants that have input-output ties with each other. A large number of studies of linkage economies have been carried out. These linkage economies deserve special mention because they reveal some of the reasons why nodal points of transport networks are points where distribution and assembly costs can be minimised for certain types of industry.

Economies of localisation arise for a variety of reasons. Most important are the advantages emanating from the proximity of plants at the various stages of production in the same industry which arise from the potential for specialisation in production. The effect is a reduction in long-run average costs. Increased specialisation leads to increased efficiency in production, with specialisation taking several organisational forms. Separate firms may, for example, be established as specialist plants within the complex, or groups of firms may come together to set up joint facilities, subcontracting being a typical feature of production. But specialisation in the production process is by no means the only economy of localisation. The geographical association of many plants and firms in the same industry strongly facilitates research and innovation in that industry. It also creates a pool of labour with the required skills and experience upon which all can draw. Very importantly in a world distinctly not perfect in information flows, such geographical concentration strongly reduces the risk and uncertainty of industrial activity and innovation.

All this may seem a remarkably strong case for polarised development and the reader may well wonder why many firms decentralise (although few decentralise far from the major urban areas). Not all these external economies need manifest themselves, in fact, in geographical space. Moreover not only are external economies more mobile in some cases than others, but the mobility of external economies may also be increasing as transportation networks develop and as production becomes more efficient. If external economies are mobile, then associations between plants will be insensitive, within limits, to the distance between them. If the external economies are immobile, however, the association between plants will lead to the geographical concentration of the activities. The crucial point is that not all linkages and external economies are sensitive to geographical separation.

A classic example of economic polarisation not leading to geographical polarisation is the government-induced movement of motor vehicle assembly plants to Merseyside and Scotland in the early 1960's. Vehicle assembly plants are highly linked activities, both in terms of physical product flows and the provision of services. They were expected to generate much ancillary development around the new plants. This did not happen because the linkages established by these firms at their original English mother plant locations proved remarkably insensitive to distance and were preserved after the new branch plants were created. It may also have been due to the inability of local suppliers to meet the input requirements of the new assembly plants. The development of national and multinational firms with their own nodal linkages in economic space may be weakening the goegraphical 'pull' of external economies.

Agglomeration or urbanisation economies arise from the geographical association of a large *number* of economic activities, which are not necessarily in the same industry. They arise because of the concentration of many facilities jointly serving different industries. These include urban transportation and commuting facilities; well organised labour markets and large pools of workers with different types of skill; the provision of social overheads and government services; and a vast range of legal and commercial services — lawyers, accountants, consultants, freight-forwarding agencies, financial institutions, and so on. Urban centres also offer attractions to market-oriented activities, with many service trades falling into this category. Finally, social and cultural facilities may have a strong effect on the location decisions of entrepreneurs, industrial managers and migrant households.

As well as the economies arising from the concentration of economic activities in urban centres, cities seem to be excellent breeding grounds for invention and innovation. The pace of invention and innovation appears to be positively related to the growth and size of cities (Pred 1965). This may seem a little strange. Yet the stimulus to invention relies on more than just personal genius. In part it also depends upon the demand for inventions by industrialists and on the interplay of industrialist and inventor. One invention will often call for others before it can be put into operation. Above all, urban areas offer excellent conditions for invention, innovation and the diffusion of innovation (Berry 1974).

There can be little doubt that localisation and urbanisation economies have had a considerable role to play in the geographical polarisation of economic development. Once begun, this concentration has a cumulative effect on the growth of a locality, which becomes progressively more efficient as development proceeds. The growth of the cotton textile industry in Lancashire up until the First World War provides an excellent example of this. The spinning side of the production process became concentrated in the southern districts around the import termini for raw cotton at Manchester, whilst weaving became increasingly concentrated in the northern districts of East Lancashire. Sub-areas even specialised within spinning and weaving, their locational advantages becoming reinforced through time by the development of further skills and expertise and by the development of ancillary trades and specialist suppliers of machinery, tools and spare parts. Specialist commercial, marketing and transportation facilities also developed in the two main urban foci of the region — Liverpool and Manchester. Innumerable other examples of intraregional specialisation could be quoted: in steel, vehicles, shipbuilding, timber and many other industries.

The enhanced attractiveness of existing growth centres sets up a whole series of 'backwash' effects which operate to the detriment of the less developed regions. The efficiency of growth centres as locations for investment makes them a magnet for capital movements, which has particularly severe effects in underdeveloped countries because of the general scarcity of capital. In addition, the growth centres tend to drain the less developed regions of their economically active and most efficient workers, thus reducing the capacity of these regions to 'catch up'.

Interregional trade has similarly disturbing effects on the less developed regions. The economies of underdeveloped countries frequently exhibit the well-known phenomenon of dualism whereby one part of the economy is highly capital-intensive whilst the remainder is highly labour-intensive. Growth centres are typically dominated by rapidly growing, capital-intensive and technologically advanced industries. At first, the rapidly growing regions may simply by-pass the less developed regions and trade predominantly with the rapidly growing regions of other countries. Over time, as interregional trade develops, the less developed regions will gradually be drawn into the market economy, bringing many economic benefits to these regions. There may, of course, be costs as well since the smaller, less efficient firms which had formerly survived by virtue of their isolation may simply be overwhelmed by the more efficient industries of the growth centres once interregional trade begins to take place.

Even economically advanced nations may experience regional and industrial dualism. Holland (1976b) has argued that industries in the 'heartland of the modern capitalist economy' exhibit what he terms *meso*-economic structures. Growth centres are dominated by large, efficient, oligopolistic firms, many of which belong to multinational corporations. In the less developed regions of advanced countries, traditional *micro*economic industrial structures may persist in spite of their inability to compete in international markets. They continue to survive partly because the attentions of the growth centre industries are focussed on the larger prosperous regions and on international markets. They may also survive because of anti-monopoly policies. In these circumstances, the less developed regions suffer not because of a collapse of their indigenous industries, but rather from being saddled with an inefficient industrial structure. Nor can they rely on being able to attract meso-economic firms away from the growth centres with the temptation of lower labour costs. Such firms will prefer to exploit the advantage of even lower labour costs by locating in underdeveloped countries as 'capital ... strides the world in seven-league boots, over-stepping problem regions in both developed and less developed countries' (Holland 1976b). Whether the existence of multinational corporations actually makes it more difficult to operate a regional policy in both developed and underdeveloped nations, however, has still to be demonstrated.

It would be wrong to end our brief discussion of polarisation theory without some mention of the spread or trickling-down effects that emanate from growth centres. As a nation develops, transport links between regions are likely to improve with the result that enterprising firms will begin to search for new investment opportunities in underdeveloped regions. Reinforcing this, the powerful internal and external economies reaped by growth centres may give way to diseconomies such as urban congestion, pollution and the bidding-up of factor prices, particularly land values and wages. Finally, the government may not stand idly by. It may deliberately attempt to stimulate growth in the less developed regions through regionally-discriminating expenditure on economic development. Available evidence appears to lend some support to the view that regional disparities in per capita income do indeed tend to narrow over the long run. This certainly appears to have been the case for many of the economically advanced nations of the world (Williamson 1965).

2.5 The Export-Base Model and Cumulative Causation: A Reconciliation?

In recent work on the theory of regional growth, attempts have been made to link up the influence of export demand and the process of cumulative causation (see Kaldor 1970 and Dixon and Thirlwall 1975). This approach adds a degree of sophistication to the previous rather intuitive nature of earlier formulations of the export-base model by emphasising the beneficial feedback effect of a region's growth on the competitiveness of its exports and thus on its subsequent growth.

The model consists of four functional relationships. The first component attempts to explain the rate of change of labour productivity:

$$\dot{q} = a + \lambda \dot{Q} \tag{10}$$

where:
$\dot{q}$ = the rate of change of labour productivity
a = autonomous productivity growth
$\dot{Q}$ = the growth rate of output
λ is a constant known as the Verdoorn coefficient.

This relationship, which is commonly known as Verdoorn's Law, forms the basis of the model. It asserts that the rate of growth of labour productivity is determined by the rate of growth of output. The faster the rate of growth of output, the faster will be the rate of growth of labour productivity.

In the second part of the model, the rate of domestic inflation is defined as the difference between cost inflation (wage inflation plus the rate of change of the profit mark-up on wage costs) less the rate of change of labour productivity:

$$\dot{P} = \dot{C} - \dot{q} \tag{11}$$

where:
 $\dot{P}$ = the rate of price inflation
 $\dot{C}$ = the rate of cost inflation

The third component is the export-demand part of the model and argues that the rate of growth of exports depends upon the price inflation in the economy doing the exporting, the inflation rate in other regions, and the growth of world income. The model is summarised as follows:

$$\dot{X} = \eta \dot{P} + \delta \dot{P}_f + \epsilon \dot{Z} \qquad (12)$$

where:
 $\dot{X}$ = the rate of growth of regional exports
 $\dot{P}_f$ = the rate of world price inflation
 $\dot{Z}$ = the rate of growth of world income
 η, δ and ϵ are the respective elasticities.

(Note that equation (12) is derived from the demand equation $X = P^{\eta} P_f^{\delta} Z^{\epsilon}$. Note also that η will be negative, and δ and ϵ will be positive.) Equation (12) simply argues that the faster the rate of growth of world income, and the smaller the inflation rate in the economy in question compared to the world inflation rate, the faster the rate of growth of exports. Finally, a simple export-base relationship is used to link output growth and the growth of exports:

$$\dot{Q} = \gamma \dot{X} \qquad (13)$$

Putting the four relationships together, we can now see the interrelated nature of the model. In particular, the model demonstrates how an expansion of export demand will have a cumulative effect on a region's output growth through the Verdoorn Law (equation 10):

$$\dot{q} = a + \lambda \dot{Q} \qquad (10)$$
$$\dot{P} = \dot{C} - \dot{q} \qquad (11)$$
$$\dot{X} = \eta \dot{P} + \delta \dot{P}_f + \epsilon \dot{Z} \qquad (12)$$
$$\dot{Q} = \gamma \dot{X} \qquad (13)$$

In this system of four equations, we expect $\lambda, \delta, \epsilon$ and γ to be positive and η to be negative. The reasons are obvious and do not require discussion.

To see how the model works, consider the effect of an increase in the growth of world income. This has a positive effect on export growth, which in turn leads to an increase in the region's rate of growth of output. The effect of the increase in the growth rate of output is to raise the rate of growth of labour productivity which subsequently results in an increase in the export competitiveness of the region by reducing the rate of domestic inflation. It is at this point that the second-round effects begin since the improvement in the region's competitive position induces a further increase in its exports; and so the process continues. Figure 2.3 traces

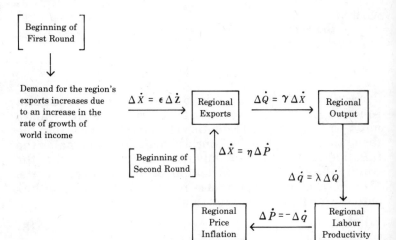

Figure 2.3 *Cumulative growth induced by an increase in the growth of world income*

out the pattern of the first-round effects of an increase in world growth. The second and subsequent rounds will be the same except for the fact that the additional increase in exports induced during each round will become smaller and smaller. (We assume that the model is stable. For conditions under which the model is unstable see Dixon and Thirlwall 1975.)

An arithmetic illustration will help. Consider two regions, A and B, which are identical in every respect other than that region B's exports have a greater income elasticity of demand than region A's exports. It can easily be shown that the equilibrium rate of growth will be higher in B than in A.

Given the following information about A and B, we can compute their respective equilibrium growth rates by solving equations (10) to (13) for $\dot{Q}$:

Region A	*Region B*
$\dot{q}_A = 2 + 0.5\,\dot{Q}_A$	$\dot{q}_B = 2 + 0.5\,\dot{Q}_A$
$\dot{P}_A = 4 - \dot{q}_A$	$\dot{P}_B = 4 - \dot{q}_B$
$\dot{X}_A = -1\dot{P}_A + 1\dot{P}_f + 1\dot{Z}$	$\dot{X}_B = -1\dot{P}_A + 1\dot{P}_f + 2\dot{Z}$
$\dot{Q}_A = 1\dot{X}_A$	$\dot{Q}_B = 1\dot{X}_B$

Let $\dot{P}_f = 1$ and $\dot{Z} = 2$ for both A and B.

Equilibrium growth rate
Solving for $\dot{Q}$ by substituting (10), (11) and (12) into (13) we obtain:

$$\dot{Q} = \frac{\gamma\,[\,\eta(\dot{C} - a) + \delta\dot{P}_f + \epsilon\dot{Z}]}{1 + \gamma\,\eta\lambda}$$

Using this formula to calculate the equilibrium growth rates in A and B we obtain:

$$\dot{Q}_A = 2\% \qquad \dot{Q}_B = 6\%$$

Hence, the difference in output growth between regions A and B is explained in this example entirely by the higher income elasticity of demand for region B's exports. According to this model, regional growth differences can also be explained by regional differences in: autonomous productivity growth (a), cost inflation $(\dot{C})$, the price elasticity of demand for the region's exports (η), the cross elasticity of demand for the region's exports (δ), the relationship between output growth and the growth of exports (γ) and the Verdoorn coefficient (λ).

We suggested earlier that this model of regional growth helps to reconcile the export base and polarisation theories, the link being provided by the Verdoorn Law. The model gives a region's export sector a crucial role, and by adding the Verdoorn Law it shows how the process of growth can 'feed upon itself'. In some circumstances this can lead to an unstable or explosive growth situation in which a region's growth rate can improve (or deteriorate) indefinitely. In other more likely circumstances, the model is stable and the growth rate climbs to some equilibrium level and settles there. This feature should not mislead us into thinking that regional disparities will necessarily stabilise. It is quite conceivable for two regions to attain stable but *different* growth rates. In such circumstances regional differences in output and output per man could continue to widen over time.

Unfortunately, the model suffers many of the problems inherent in all export-base models. It contains no explanation of just what determines regional export specialisation and how this will change over time. There is also some uncertainty concerning what the Verdoorn Law actually encompasses.

The Verdoorn coefficient (λ) supposedly reflects the influence of economies of scale — both internal and external — on the growth of labour productivity. In addition to scale economies, however, the Verdoorn coefficient may reflect the influence of less obvious factors, such as the induced effects of output growth on technical progress and capital deepening. The Verdoorn Law thus appears to be a more complicated function than it seems at first sight. Induced technical progress and induced capital deepening will vary between industries, for example, which means that different regions can be expected to have a different 'Verdoorn effect' depending upon their particular industry-mix. Regional differences in the industrial structure can consequently be expected to give rise to regional growth differences for reasons other than those already itemised in the above illustrative example.

Clearly, the model analysed in this section must be regarded as only a very partial reconciliation of the export-base and polarisation theories of regional growth. The simple Verdoorn equation, whilst adding a useful 'cumulative feedback' aspect to the export-base model, also masks and misses much that is valuable in the more intuitive and descriptive polarisation approach. Much that is valuable in the polarisation approach is masked by collapsing the effects of internal and external economies of scale, technical progress and capital deepening into the simple Verdoorn equation. In addition, the Verdoorn equation misses entirely many of the other polarisation effects identified by the theory of cumulative causation.

Conclusion

Each of the various theories of regional growth discussed in this chapter presents the policymaker with a distinct explanation of regional growth disparities. Neoclassical growth theory stresses the role of factor supplies and of capital and labour migration. Export-base models stress the need for a viable and expanding export sector if a region is to grow quickly. Polarisation models highlight the need to create conditions *within* depressed regions that are favourable to self-fuelling growth. Each approach, therefore, has something special to offer the policymaker who is seeking to influence the pattern of regional growth.

Our discussion of regional growth disparities, however, has revealed just how far economic theory has yet to progress before the regional growth process can be more fully understood. The various theories of regional growth offer widely divergent explanations for the emergence of regional imbalance: they are unanimous, however, in one respect. All the theories emphasize that the speed with which a region develops is largely dependent on its *links with other regions*.The fact that regions rely heavily on trade with other regions means that it is impossible to examine the growth of one region in isolation from other regions. The neoclassical model, which stresses the role of factor supplies in determining how fast a region grows, must allow for the interregional migration of labour and capital in addition to the growth of the indigenous supplies of factors. Similarly, theories such as the export-base model which focus on the demand for a region's commodities as the primary determinant of growth are forced to consider the trade links between regions.

In the next two chapters, we consider in greater detail the role played on the one hand by the interregional migration of labour and capital, and on the other hand by interregional trade.

Selected references

Borts and Stein (1962); Branson (1972), Chapters 19 and 22; Dixon and Thirlwall (1975); North (1955); Stabler (1968); Todd (1974).

3
Regional Imbalance and Factor Migration

In the previous chapter considerable stress was placed on the role that interregional movements of capital and labour play in the growth of regions. In this chapter we examine in greater detail the determinants of labour and capital movements and the effects they are likely to have on regional disparities. In spite of its many limitations, we begin with the simple static classical theory of factor migration. This provides us with a 'benchmark' from which we can proceed to more realistic and more useful models.

Traditional economic theory argues that regional disparities in real wages and the rate of return on capital will automatically be eliminated by the self-correcting nature of the economic system. If regional differences in factor prices emerge, we can supposedly rely upon the classical equilibrating mechanism to restore equilibrium as workers migrate from low wage to high wage regions and as capital moves in the opposite direction. According to this theory, regional differences in factor prices would disappear provided there were no further disturbances to the balance of demand and supply for factors of production in each region.

This view is far too simplistic, however, as it stands. As more realistic assumptions are introduced into our simple classical model, these predictions begin to break down. Indeed, it can be forcefully argued that factor migration may actually be de-stabilising rather than stabilising in its effects on regional disparities. Factor migration may have the perverse effect of increasing regional differences in factor prices rather then reducing them.

Moreover, we should take care not to misinterpret the classical model of factor migration, which argues only that regional differences in the price of *homogeneous* factors of production will be eliminated, not that regional differences in per capita income will be removed. Indeed, it is quite possible for factor prices to be identical in all regions (for each separate homogeneous factor of production) at the same time that per capita incomes differ substantially. This would occur if some regions relied heavily on high-skill/high-wage occupations whilst other regions relied on low-skill/low-wage occupations. The ratio of workers to non-workers may also vary between regions, which would have the effect of depressing per capita incomes in regions where the ratio was low. Finally, per capita income will vary between regions depending on the residential location of wealth holders. Per capita income levels may therefore diverge markedly between regions for reasons other than the existence of regional differences in the price paid to homogeneous factors of production.

3.1 Interregional Labour Migration

A simple classical theory of labour migration
We begin by specifying the limiting assumptions of our classical model:

(i)   Perfect competition exists in all markets.
(ii)   Production functions exhibit constant returns to scale.
(iii)   Factor migration is costless and there are no other barriers to migration.
(iv)   Factor prices are perfectly flexible.
(v)   Each factor of production is of homogeneous quality.
(vi)   Owners of factors of production (i.e. labour and capital owners) are completely informed about factor returns in all regions.

Let us begin our discussion with an elementary example. The economy is assumed to consist of two regions, East and West. For simplicity, each region is assumed to produce the same single commodity and to use the same techniques of production. Since we shall concentrate initially on labour migration, each region is assumed to have an identical capital stock which is also wholly immobile. Given that the labour market is perfectly competitive, we know that the real wage must equal the marginal product of labour since employers will be maximising profits. (Note that this condition is identical to equalising marginal costs and

(i) *The initial position.*

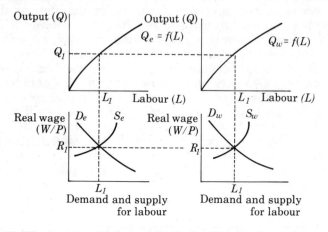

(ii) *The supply of labour falls in the East and a real wage differential emerges.*

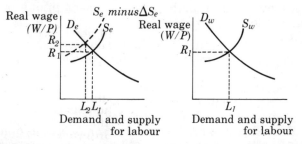

(iii) *Labour migration removes the real wage differential.*

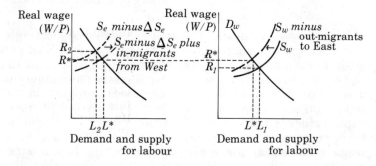

Figure 3.1 *The equilibrating effect of labour migration*

marginal revenue under perfectly competitive conditions.) Since the marginal product of labour declines as the level of employment increases — because of diminishing marginal returns — more labour will be employed only if the real wage falls. This provides us with the demand for labour, which is inevitably identical in the two regions since we have assumed that they possess identical production functions. On the supply side of the labour market, more labour will be supplied as the real wage increases. Initially, the supply functions of labour are assumed to be identical in both regions. Since both the demand for labour and the supply of labour are identical in the two regions, it follows that the wage differential will be zero.

The power of labour migration to bring about factor price convergence can now be shown. To do this, we must disturb the idyllic situation established in part (i) of figure 3.1. In a changing world, regions will experience fluctuations in both the demand and supply for labour. Consider, for example, the effect of a decrease in the supply of labour in the East. This could occur gradually as the result of natural population change, or more suddenly through, for example, the raising of the school-leaving age or the reduction of the retirement age. The labour supply function shifts from S_e to $(S_e - \Delta S_e)$ in the East. Under the assumption of wage flexibility this results in an increase in the real wage in the East from R_1 to R_2. A regional real wage differential of $(R_2 - R_1)$ has thus emerged.

Given that labour is perfectly informed and that there are no costs or other barriers to migration, there will be a movement of labour from the West to the East in response to the real wage differential. Immigration to the East leads to an increase in the labour supply in that region, whilst emigration has the opposite effect in the West. Labour migration will continue until identical wage rates are once more etablished in both regions. The new equilibrium wage will be established at R^*, at which point the motivation for further migration vanishes. In addition to eliminating the regional wage disparity, the migration also gives rise to a real allocative gain to the nation as a whole. Workers have migrated from the West, where the marginal product of labour is low, to the East, where it is higher.

Since we have deliberately begun by constructing a migration model under the most extreme assumptions, it should be no surprise to find that its predictive performance is poor. It will nonetheless be useful to examine briefly the actual behaviour of migrants. This will help us to identify the more serious flaws in the classical model and will hopefully point the way towards a more realistic analysis of labour migration.

Interregional labour migration in the UK, 1961-76

Table 3.1 sets out the *net* flows of migrants between the UK regions for selected periods between 1961 and 1976. It shows that net migration to the traditionally depressed regions of N Ireland, Scotland and, to a lesser extent, the most

Table 3.1 *Components of regional population change, 1961-76* (Figures are *average annual* changes expressed as a percentage of the regional population as at mid-1971.)

Region	1961-1971[3]			1971-1973[3]			1973-1976[3,4]		
	Population change[1]	Natural change	Net migration[2]	Population change[1]	Natural change	Net migration[2]	Population change[1]	Natural change	Net migration[2]
SE	+0.56	+0.58	-0.02	+0.08	+0.29	-0.21	-0.24	+0.09	-0.33
E Anglia	+1.22	+0.50	+0.72	+1.57	+0.36	+1.21	+1.27	+0.19	+1.08
SW	+0.99	+0.40	+0.59	+1.13	+0.14	+0.99	+0.63	-0.10	+0.73
W Mids	+0.75	+0.78	-0.03	+0.41	+0.50	-0.09	+0.01	+0.23	-0.22
E Mids	+0.87	+0.66	+0.21	+0.85	+0.41	+0.44	+0.34	+0.16	+0.18
Yorks/Humbs	+0.40	+0.55	-0.15	+0.20	+0.28	-0.08	+0.02	+0.05	-0.03
NW	+0.33	+0.50	-0.17	+0.06	+0.25	-0.19	-0.27	+0.01	-0.28
North	+0.20	+0.53	-0.33	+0.03	+0.21	-0.18	-0.10	+0.01	-0.11
Wales	+0.34	+0.36	-0.02	+0.47	+0.15	+0.32	+0.21	-0.03	+0.24
Scotland	+0.04	+0.66	-0.62	-0.06	+0.30	-0.36	+0.04	+0.09	-0.13
N Ireland[5]	+0.69	+1.13	-0.44	+0.31	+0.85	-0.54	-0.13	+0.65	-0.78
United Kingdom	+0.52	+0.58	-0.06	+0.30	+0.31	-0.01	-0.00	+0.09	-0.09

Notes:

1. Population change equals natural change plus net migration.

2. Includes 'other changes' such as movements in armed forces and in residents at educational establishments and prisons.

3. 1961-71 and 1971-73 estimates refer to standard regions as defined at 31.3.1974. The 1973-76 estimates refer to standard regions as defined at 1.4.1974.

4. 1975-76 estimates are provisional. The remainder are revised estimates.

5. 'Other changes' are not available for N Ireland for 1973-76.

Sources: Office of Population Censuses and Surveys of England and Wales; General Register Offices of Scotland and Northern Ireland.

northerly regions of England has been consistently negative. Superficially, this net outflow of people from the traditionally less prosperous regions provides support for the simple classical model of migration. Indeed, it can be argued that had it not been for the jobs created by regional policy in these regions, the net migration losses may have been even greater.

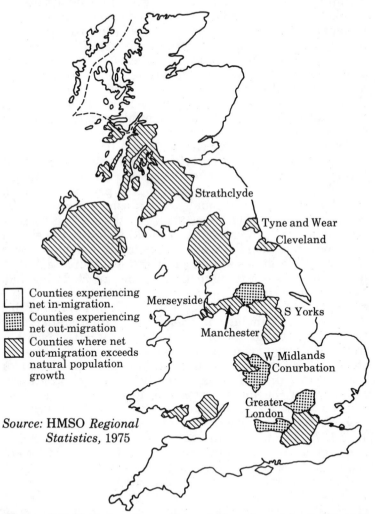

Figure 3.2 *Net migration and population change in the United Kingdom 1973-74*

On the other hand, table 3.1 shows that the traditionally more prosperous SE and W Midlands regions have also been net exporters of people, and to an increasing extent during the 1970's. Closer examination of the data, however, reveals that the net outflow of people from the SE and W Midlands is the result of a considerable out-migration from the two major conurbations of these regions (Greater London and Birmingham). This is clear from figure 3.2. The net loss of people from the SE and the W Midlands to adjacent regions is explained by the overspill of population from the two major conurbations. This enormous overspill is partly the result of deliberate rehousing policies, but is also the consequence of a long-established tendency for jobs and population to decentralise. The net inflow of migrants into the SW shown in table 3.1 is more easily explained: the SW has traditionally attracted substantial numbers of retired persons.

On the surface, the recent migration flows between the UK regions offer some tentative support for the classical theory of migration. When overspill from the major conurbations and when flows of retired persons are taken into account, the traditionally less prosperous regions are seen to be net exporters of people whilst the more prosperous regions are net importers. As table 3.1 shows, the size of these net migration flows may not be large, and many of the net migration losses are offset by natural increase, but at least they do seem to be roughly in the expected direction.

An examination of *gross* migration flows between the standard regions of the UK, however, throws considerable doubt on this conclusion. The net migration statistics of table 3.1 conceal the important, and often forgotten, fact that in most cases gross migration between regions far exceeds the resulting balance of net migration. In particular, a substantial amount of apparently 'perverse' migration occurs from the more prosperous to the less prosperous regions. Thus the SE simultaneously imported 64,000 people *from* Scotland and exported 46,000 people *to* Scotland during 1966-1971. In other words, the gross flow from the SE to Scotland was more than twice as great as the net loss of migrants from Scotland to the SE (see table 3.2).

These apparently perverse flows into the less prosperous regions should not, of course, be surprising. After all, classical migration theory assumes that labour is a homogeneous factor of production, whereas the gross

Table 3.2 *Intraregional and interregional gross migration in Great Britain 1966-1971* (in thousands, all persons aged 1 and over)

Origin	Destination SE	E Anglia	SW	W Mids	E Mids	Yorks/ Humbs	NW	North	Wales	Scotland
SE	5030	110	194	63	73	48	65	34	37	46
E Anglia	53	374	10	6	13	8	5	3	3	4
SW	134	9	931	23	12	10	15	8	14	11
W Mids	76	9	41	1401	36	15	32	10	21	10
E Mids	57	16	19	26	822	35	16	10	6	8
Yorks/Humbs	63	11	17	19	40	1363	40	36	7	11
NW	84	9	27	30	19	35	1865	19	34	15
North	48	6	11	13	14	32	22	947	4	15
Wales	43	3	20	18	7	6	18	4	643	4
Scotland	64	6	13	14	14	14	22	16	4	1644
Balance of inward and outward movements	-47	+74	+116	-39	+35	-42	-36	-26	+6	-42

Note:
Errors due to rounding.
Source: Census of Population 1971, Migration Tables, Part I (10% sample).

migration statistics of table 3.2 are an aggregate of workers of all skills as well as including non-workers. It is quite possible that what is a high wage region for one occupation may be a low wage region for another, giving rise to flows of workers in both directions.

There is, however, another explanation of the 'perverse' migration into the less prosperous regions which is not so charitable to the classical model. The difficulties faced by migrants in their new locations may be so great that they return to their regions of origin. Gross migration flows include a large element of return migration of this type, particularly during recessions (Vanderkamp 1971). Estimates suggest that up to 1 in 4 migrants return to their region of origin within two years, many within only a few months (Kiker and Traynham 1976).

Finally, the interregional population movements in table 3.2 suggest that two of the crucial assumptions of the classical model are unlikely to reflect reality. There is evidence of a significant distance decay factor in operation. Contiguous regions show a greater interchange of migrants than do pairs of regions separated by long distances. The Northern region, for example, dispatched some 32,000 migrants to Yorkshire and Humberside between 1966 and 1971. Only 13,000 migrated to the more distant West Midlands from the North, in spite of the fact that the West

Midlands was both more populous and more prosperous than Yorkshire and Humberside. This suggests that the assumptions of zero migration costs and perfect information are in serious error. Distance is apparently a severe barrier to migration.

3.2 Interregional Capital Movements

A simple classical theory of capital migration
The effect of capital mobility on interregional differences in factor returns can be examined by retaining all the original assumptions given at the beginning of the previous section, with the exception that it is capital which is assumed to be the perfectly mobile factor and labour is assumed to be immobile.

We saw in figure 3.1 that a fall in the labour supply in the East led to the emergence of a higher real wage of R_2 in that region compared to the real wage of R_1 in the West. Capital can be expected to flow towards the low wage West since the capital owner will expect a higher rate of return on his capital in regions where wages are lower (assuming a simple two-factor model). The real wage differential in favour of the East is therefore mirrored by a capital rental differential in favour of the West. Since we have assumed that labour cannot migrate from the West to the East, these differentials induce a flow of capital from the East to the West. The abundance of capital relative to labour in the East has therefore been removed through the equilibrating movement of capital from the East to the West. Notice that, in this illustration, the movement of capital not only leads to the equalisation of real capital rentals in each region, but also to the equalisation of real wage rates. The perfect mobility of labour on its own would also equalise *both* sets of factor prices. In reality, where both labour and capital show some mobility, the two types of factor mobility will mutually reinforce each other to bring about factor price convergence.

The movement of industry in the UK, 1966-71
Unlike labour migration, information on movements of capital is extremely scarce, with the result that we have to rely upon scanty and inadequate data in order to obtain a picture of interregional capital flows in the UK. Some data on the interregional flows of funds can be extracted from

regional social accounts (see Brown 1972) but the accuracy of such estimates is unknown, and in any case it includes public as well as private transfers. The most complete and up-to-date information available on interregional capital flows in the UK is that relating to the *number* of manufacturing establishments actually set up in a sub-region in which the firm involved did not previously have any producing units. The inadequacies of these data are obvious. First, measuring capital flows by counting the number of establishments moving from one sub-region to another is likely, at best, to produce only a very rough approximation to the actual pattern of capital movements. Second, data are confined to the manufacturing sector. Third, many capital flows are ignored since the transfer of productive capacity from an existing plant located in one sub-region to an existing plant (of the same firm) located in another sub-region is simply not recorded. Fourth, the capital flows resulting from labour migration, including both liquid capital and remittances back to the region of

Table 3.3 *The interregional movement of manufacturing industry in the United Kingdom, 1966-71* (number of moves).

Destination Origin	SE	E Anglia	SW	W Mids	E Mids	Yorks/ Humbs	NW	North	Wales	Scot- land	N Ire- land
SE	285	120	75	3	49	12	33	58	87	68	32
E Anglia	3	13	1	—	—	2	—	4	2	5	1
SW	3	—	15	2	2	—	2	2	11	4	1
W Mids	7	3	6	90	17	1	19	15	56	12	3
E Mids	3	1	5	3	20	12	5	18	16	10	7
Yorks/Humbs	—	3	1	2	12	23	5	18	2	9	6
NW	3	—	—	4	2	2	73	21	17	11	7
North	2	1	—	—	2	4	2	15	1	7	1
Wales	3	—	—	—	1	—	5	4	35	1	—
Scotland	2	—	—	—	1	—	2	1	1	44	1
N Ireland	—	—	—	—	—	—	—	—	1	—	6
Total inflow	26	128	88	14	86	33	73	141	194	127	59
Total outflow (exc. intra-regional moves)	537	18	27	139	80	58	67	20	14	8	1
Net movement (inflow minus outflow)	-511	+110	+61	-125	+6	-25	+6	+121	+180	+119	+58

Source: Unpublished data supplied by Department of Industry and made available to us by Ross Mackay and John Rhodes. Brian Ashcroft assembled the interregional flow data.

origin, are ignored. Finally, capital investment by wholly
indigenous firms (whether already in existence or entirely
new) which is financed by savings inflows from other
regions, is ignored.

In spite of these formidable limitations, the industrial
movement data are of some interest since they do at least
provide us with a broad picture of the pattern of
interregional capital movements within the UK
manufacturing sector. Table 3.3 shows the interregional
flow of manufacturing establishments between UK regions
during 1966-71.

Inspection of the net capital flows in table 3.3 indicates
that capital has certainly moved out of the two most
prosperous regions, the SE and the W Midlands. In addition,
capital has flowed into the less prosperous regions of N
Ireland, Scotland and the North. As with the labour
migration data, a superficial inspection of the capital flows
suggests that at least some of the capital flows are in the
expected direction. But this completely ignores the fact that
the interregional movement of industry in the UK during
1966-71 was strongly influenced by government policy. The
expansion of manufacturing establishments was severely
curtailed, particularly in the SE and the W Midlands, by
stringent controls on the extension of existing buildings and
plant. In addition to this, attractive investment incentives
were available to firms willing to extend their productive
capacity in the Development Areas (N Ireland, Scotland,
Wales, the Northern region and parts of the NW and SW).
Finally, much of the movement of industry to East Anglia,
the SW and the E Midlands was the consequence of the
policy of restricting industrial expansion in the cities of the
SE and the W Midlands. The classical assumptions can
hardly be said to be a relevant basis for predicting the
interregional movement of industry in the UK during 1966-
71.

In view of the influence of government policy on
interregional flows of industrial capital, the lack of a
negative relationship between net capital migration and net
labour migration (see figure 3.3) should not surprise us.
Movements of capital and labour may not conform to the
classical predictions for many reasons. This is supported by
the absence of a negative relationship between net labour
migration and net capital migration in the UK even for the

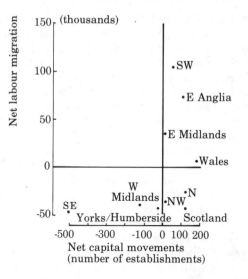

Notes:
1. Net labour migration = gross inflow minus gross outflow (see table 3.2)
2. Net capital movements = gross inflow of manufacturing establishments minus gross outflow (see table 3.3)

Figure 3.3 *The net migration of capital and labour in the GB regions, 1966-71*

period 1952-59, which is generally regarded as a period of inactivity as far as regional policy is concerned.

3.3 Relaxing the Assumptions of the Simple Classical Model of Migration

The simple classical theory of migration predicts that labour will move from low wage regions to high wage regions and that capital will move in the opposite direction, the effect being to reduce regional differences in factor prices. Once the highly restrictive assumptions of the classical model are relaxed, however, we find that capital and labour movements may not in fact be equilibrating.

One of the strongest assumptions of the classical model of factor migration is that migration is costless. Migrants clearly have to incur many costs, some of which are pecuniary whilst others are distinctly non-pecuniary or 'psychic' (see Sjaastad 1962). The pecuniary costs include those resulting from household removals, such as the costs of buying and selling non-movable assets and the costs of transporting movable assets. In addition, the migrant may have to forgo income temporarily whilst he searches for a job in a new location. The non-pecuniary costs result from the uprooting of families and from the difficulties of settling into an unfamiliar location. These non-pecuniary costs are difficult, if not impossible, to quantify but are likely to be more important than the money costs of migration.

The significance of migration costs in restricting the movement of labour is reflected by the strong negative influence of distance on migration as is evident from table 3.2. Since both the pecuniary and non-pecuniary costs of migration can be expected to increase with the distance moved by the migrant, we would expect interregional exchanges of labour to diminish as distance increases. This 'friction of distance' effect on migratory flows is, however, quite complex. There seems to be a kind of threshold beyond which extra distance has only a small effect on migrants.

The importance of migration costs is reflected in other ways. One very widely observed phenomenon is that gross migration flows are frequently considerably higher between pairs of prosperous regions than between a depressed and a prosperous region. One explanation of this may be the greater ability of higher income groups to bear the pecuniary costs of migration. A more likely explanation may lie in the previous success of prosperous regions in attracting migrants. People who have migrated once, and have already broken social and family ties, face fewer non-pecuniary costs in subsequent moves Individuals who have migrated once are much more likely to undertake further moves.

Whether or not distance is an impediment to labour migration because of the pecuniary and non-pecuniary costs it imposes, or because information on job opportunities in more distant regions is less readily obtainable, remains debatable. That there may be some truth in both points of view is suggested by the tendency of migrants to follow in the footsteps of previous generations of migrants. This is the well-known 'migrant stock' effect. The existence of a community of earlier migrants in the destination region not only opens up a channel of information on job opportunities and other relevant aspects of life in their new location for friends and relatives 'in the home town', but may also reduce both the pecuniary and the non-pecuniary costs for new arrivals.

The assumptions of zero migration costs and perfect information seem more appropriate to capital than to labour migration. The interregional movement of capital is certainly less restricted than the movement of labour. National capital markets are highly integrated, and capital suffers few of the barriers and costs standing in the way of would-be labour migrants. It is important, however, not to over-estimate the mobility of capital. It is *investment* capital rather than the existing capital *stock* which is mobile. Furthermore, the assumption that investors possess perfect information is equally erroneous. Investment location decisions are taken on the basis of remarkably little information in most cases. This is a theme to which we will return later in the chapter.

A second major weakness of the simple classical model of migration is the assumption that factor prices are perfectly flexible. As far as labour is concerned, we know that factor prices are not perfectly flexible in a downwards direction and the predictions of the model are accordingly affected. Consider a very simple example. Suppose the real wage is initially equal in our two hypothetical regions, the East and the West, but that excess supply subsequently appears in the West and this is exactly matched by the appearance of excess demand in the East. (Note that in a more realistic situation there would be no guarantee that the total demand for labour in all regions would equal its supply.) Since wages are flexible only in an upwards direction, the excess supply in the West will not lead to a fall in the real wage in that region with the result that unemployment will appear. The excess demand for labour in the East may or may not lead to an increase in the real wage in that region, depending on the speed at which labour migrates from the West to the East to fill the new jobs that have appeared. In view of the many frictions to labour mobility already examined, it is likely that migration from the West to the East will be so desultory that it will be only partially successful in eliminating the excess demand. We therefore find ourselves in a position where the East has a higher real wage than the West and that there is also a persistent unemployment differential between the two regions. By relaxing the assumption of perfectly flexible real wages, regional unemployment differences are given a central role alongside regional wage differentials as determinants of labour migration.

Simply to assume that wage rates are downwardly inflexible may not be enough. It will be argued in Chapter 6 that wages may not only be downwardly inflexible, but may also tend towards equality in different regions in spite of substantial regional differences in the excess demand for labour. There are several possible explanations of why this may occur. The national, rather than regional, negotiation of wage rates is a good example of the circumstances in which workers may receive a similar wage, regardless of their location. Situations such as this indicate the irrelevance of the assumption of perfect competition in regional labour markets. The implications of this for factor migration are obvious and severe. To the extent that the necessary factor price 'signals' to migration fail to appear, it is regional differences in unemployment and not wages which are likely to be the driving force behind labour mobility. The adoption, in excess supply regions, of national wage settlements will exacerbate regional unemployment problems.

The tendency of the bargaining process to lead to the equalisation of wage settlements for similar groups of workers in different regions is more typical of the British labour market than elsewhere, such as Canada and the USA. In the USA, for example, there is evidence that differing degrees of unionisation between the South and the North, and differing degrees of monopsonistic power of firms, may be a powerful influence on regional wage differentials (see Perlman 1969).

There is considerable evidence supporting the assertion that regional unemployment differences are an important determinant of regional labour migration. These results should, however, be interpreted cautiously. The fact that low wage regions are often high unemployment regions means that it is not always possible to distinguish between the effect of regional differences in real wages on labour migration and the effect of regional unemployment differences. Nor should we make the mistake of thinking that it is those actually unemployed who predominate amongst migrants. Indeed, the longer a person is unemployed the less likely he is to migrate. In other words, it may be the 'pull' of the job opportunities associated with low unemployment rather than the 'push' of unemployment which causes workers to move.

3.4 An Alternative Model of Labour Migration: the Human Capital Approach

We have argued that the simple classical explanation of the interregional movement of factors of production, particularly labour, is inadequate. A more realistic approach is offered by the human capital model of labour migration. The supreme advantage of this model is that it does not assume the existence of a timeless world in which workers respond instantaneously to *current* regional differentials in real wages. Instead, the migrant is assumed to respond to the higher earnings he can expect to obtain from migration over his full *lifetime*. Migrants, like all other members of society, exhibit a positive time preference. In other words, the sooner the benefits of migration accrue, the more attractive will the move appear to the potential migrant. For this reason the lifetime of higher earnings which the migrant can expect to enjoy is expressed in human capital models as a present value, with a discount rate being used to incorporate the influence of the migrant's time preference. This can be written as:

$$R_{ij} = \sum_{t=1}^{T} \frac{y_{jt}}{(1+d)^t} - \sum_{t=1}^{T} \frac{y_{it}}{(1+d)^t}$$

where:

R_{ij} = gross present value of the lifetime increment to earnings expected to result from the migration from region i to region j.

T = number of years of working life remaining to the migrant.

$1/(1+d)^t$ = discount factor where d, the discount rate, measures the time preference of migrants.

y_j = expected earnings of the migrant in region j (destination region).

y_i = expected earnings of the migrant in region i (origin region).

Notice that it is the earnings that the migrant *expects* to obtain and not those *actually* obtained which are important, and available evidence indicates that the migrant's expectations are shaped by the previous performance of regions (Greenwood 1970). A more rigorous model would also allow for uncertainty, a factor which undoubtedly plays a crucial role in migration decisions. The existence of uncertainty stems partly from poor information about existing economic and social conditions in other regions, and partly from the dangers of subsequently becoming unemployed. Uncertainty will prevent migrants from accurately assessing how worthwhile it is to migrate, and the greater the uncertainty, the less attractive a proposition will migration become.

Another enormous advantage of human capital models over the classical theory of migration is their ability to incorporate all the costs and benefits of migration. There is no attempt to assume away any of the many costs of migration as in the classical model. Potential migrants are assumed to weigh *all* the costs and benefits of migration. The net present value of migrating from one region to another can be expressed as follows:

$$PV_{ij} = R^*_{ij} - C_{ij}$$

where:

PV_{ij} = net present value of migrating from region i to region j.

R^*_{ij} = gross present value of the time stream of expected benefits of migrating from i to j.

C_{ij} = gross present value of the expected costs of migration.

If PV is positive, the discounted value of the benefits exceeds the discounted value of the costs, making migration a worthwhile venture. The benefits of migration, as we have seen, consist principally of a time stream of higher earnings, but they may also include non-pecuniary benefits such as better working conditions in the destination region, or a superior social and environmental milieu. The overspill from the densely populated conurbations reflects attempts by migrants to exploit this kind of psychic benefit, as does the migration of retired persons to the SW of England, to Florida and California in the USA and to British Columbia in Canada. The costs of migration comprise both substantial cash outlays as well as psychic costs.

Human capital models should not be used too mechanically. In a world of imperfect information and great uncertainty, migrants will not weigh up the pros and cons of migration in anything more than the most intuitive fashion. The greater realism of the assumptions underlying human capital models, however, does mean that they offer a more acceptable explanation of many observed features of migration than is obtained from the simple classical model. Consider, for instance, the apparently perverse migration from prosperous to depressed regions. Such migration can be accounted for in several ways by the human capital approach. As well as allowing for the fact that depressed regions may be high wage regions for certain occupational groups, it is also possible that the expectations of migrants may favour what is currently a depressed region. The human capital approach is even capable of explaining situations where migrants in the same occupational category, and receiving the same wage, move in opposite directions. This will occur if different migrants attach different weights to the non-pecuniary costs and benefits of migration.

Finally, the human capital approach is eminently suited to explaining the observed selective nature of migration. Migrants are inevitably drawn disproportionately from the ranks of the young, the skilled, and the highly educated. The bias towards younger workers is explained by the longer remaining working lifetime over which the cost of migrating can be recouped. Younger workers have more time to recoup any additional costs that have to be borne, for example, when a change of job necessitates an element of retraining. Both skilled workers and more highly educated workers also tend to exhibit greater mobility. There may be several reasons for this, one of them being the existence of greater earnings differentials between regions for these groups. Another reason may be that these workers have better access to information about job prospects and living conditions in other regions or, more simply, their higher incomes may enable them to meet the cash outlays involved in migration. A more obvious explanation is that it is the skilled and educated who migrate because they are also the *younger* members of society.

3.5 Factor Mobility: Equilibrating or Disequilibrating?

The prediction of the simple classical theory of migration that the movement of factors between regions will reduce regional differences in factor prices is open to question. We have already seen how the introduction of more realistic assumptions about factor movements may destroy the simple classical prediction. It is necessary, however, to go further than this. As we saw in the previous chapter, it is essential to look at the dynamic implications of factor movements, since in a dynamic framework factor movements may not always be equilibrating.

In the case of labour migration, there is some evidence that the net interregional flows of labour are in the expected direction — towards the prosperous regions. But whilst this may have some immediate beneficial effects in reducing interregional real wage and unemployment differentials, over the longer run the effects could be just the opposite. First, the selective nature of migration may not only make it harder for depressed regions to attract the investment necessary for their regeneration, but will simultaneously improve the prospects of the prosperous regions. Second and perhaps more important, is the distinct possibility that the inward flow of migrants into the prosperous regions will have a cumulative expansionary effect on output, employment and incomes in the destination regions whilst simultaneously having the opposite effects in the original regions. By contributing to the growth of market demand in prosperous regions, migrants enhance the attractiveness of those areas for further expansion of productive capacity. As a region's population increases, and as income levels rise, new industries emerge to satisfy the growing demands for locally produced goods and services. This process is a cumulative one. Those employed by the market-orientated industries themselves add to the demand for locally produced goods and services.

Even in the short run, it is by no means certain that immigrants to prosperous regions will add more to the supply of labour than to its demand. New workers and their families will require accommodation, schooling, medical services, transport facilities and a whole range of other locally produced goods and services. This demand for locally produced goods and services is likely to be high in the first instance, the demand for housing and places in schools being the primary examples. This 'lumpiness' of the migrant's initial expenditures and the consequent multiplier effects may lead to an increase in the demand for labour far greater than the increase in supply resulting from the immigration. The immediate consequence of inward migration may therefore be the precise opposite of that predicted by the classical model, and labour migration may actually stimulate further inflationary pressures rather than reduce them.

In the case of interregional capital movements, of which we have very little information, they may even be in the 'wrong' direction, with the high wage regions attracting the lion's share of new capital formation. Many reasons have been advanced for this perverse flow of capital. One is that the rate of return on capital is not simply a function of wage costs. A great weakness of the classical model is the assumption of constant returns to scale. Dynamic, expanding regions may offer superior investment opportunities because the size of their markets allows internal economies to be exploited, and because external and agglomeration economies also emerge. In other words, the rate of return on capital is not only a function of the proportions of labour and capital employed but also of the scale of production. Furthermore, labour and capital are not the only factors of production. Immobile reserves of raw materials, for example, may attract capital from other regions in spite of having higher labour costs than elsewhere. The returns to capital are determined by all factor costs, not simply the costs of labour.

Not only does the possibility of returns to scale open the way towards disequilibrating capital and labour movements, so too does the relaxation of the crucial assumption of a single commodity in all regions. Where there are many different industries, for example, high wage regions may still be the most profitable locations for mobile capital investment. Thus a region specialising in the production of commodities whose export demand is buoyant may prove to be an attractive location for capital even if it is a high wage region (Borts 1960). High wages would therefore be perpetuated, attracting subsequent 'rounds' of both labour and capital in-migration.

Even if low wage regions were the most profitable locations for mobile capital, several factors would still prevent an equilibrating flow of capital towards them. Firms are more likely to plough their profits back into existing plant rather than search for more profitable locations elsewhere in the economy. The movement of firms from existing locations tends to respond very much to 'push' factors, such as the refusal by the planning authorities to grant permission for further extensions to existing plant or the high costs of land and labour at existing locations. There is very little empirical evidence to support the view that firms seek out a profit-maximising site or that they even undertake a comprehensive survey of alternatives when considering a site for an extension to their productive capacity. According to empirical surveys of industrial movement in the UK, firms exhibit 'satisficing' behaviour rather than 'maximising' behaviour, searching outwards from existing sites for a satisfactory alternative until one is found (Loasby 1967, Townroe 1972). This may account, at least in part, for the apparent reluctance of firms to even consider the possibility of moving from the prosperous to the declining regions.

The centralised nature of the capital market may also prevent equilibrating capital flows by syphoning-off the savings of peripheral areas. Funds flow into the central capital market through the normal savings channels, from all parts of the economy. Whether this inflow from peripheral areas is matched by a return flow of funds in response to regional differentials in the rate of return will depend upon whether central capital markets operate with any bias or with imperfect knowledge of regional opportunities for investment (Morgan 1973).

There may be a similar bias in public investment. The need for social infrastructure such as roads, schools and hospitals largely depends on the size and growth of population, commerce and industry in a region. There is therefore a built-in tendency for social overhead capital to become concentrated in rapidly expanding regions, especially if substantial economies of scale exist in the provision of social overheads. This will encourage a greater concentration of public spending in specific geographical locations.

Finally, the development of large, oligopolistic and multinational firms in modern economies may result in the diversion of capital to low labour-cost locations in underdeveloped *countries* rather than to low labour-cost locations within the national boundary. Such a policy has many advantages for the multinational firm. The depressed regions of advanced countries are high labour-cost locations by world standards. In addition, a multinational investment programme offers the advantage of allowing a company to exploit different tax requirements in each country through 'transfer pricing' (Holland 1976b). This involves adjusting the prices of their inter-plant transactions so that profits are declared in countries where taxes are lowest. International capital movements may therefore preclude equilibrating interregional capital movements.

Conclusion

The simple classical theory of migration argues that the migration of labour from low wage regions to high wage regions, and the mobility of capital in the opposite direction, will help to remove regional differences in real wages and returns to capital. The real world, of course, is more complicated. There are significant frictions within the economic system preventing the classical equilibrating forces from working efficiently, hence the fact that interregional wage differentials have exhibited a remarkable long-run persistence and stability in spite of considerable interregional migration (see Perlman 1969, Goldfarb and Yezer 1976). More controversially, we have argued that interregional movements of factors may actually cause regional differences in factor prices to increase rather than diminish.

One thing at least is clear. We cannot rely on the inherent equilibrating mechanism within the economic system to correct regional differences in living standards.

Selected references

Brennan (1967); Greenwood (1975); Hart (1975); Okun and Richardson (1961); Sjaastad (1962); Weeden (1973).

4
Interregional Trade

In spite of an almost total absence of reliable data, there is no
doubt that regional economies are very open. Regions sell
most of what they produce to buyers in other regions or in
other countries. Similarly, they purchase most of their
consumption and other requirements from producers outside
the region.

The openness of regional economies can be illustrated by
drawing upon UK examples. Northern Ireland, the only
region for which reliable trade statistics exist in the UK,
exported goods and services to the value of £843m in 1971.
Comparing this with Northern Ireland's GDP of £991m in
1971, the ratio of exports to GDP was 0.85, which is
remarkably high compared to the corresponding ratio of 0.25
for the UK as a whole. Recent work on the Scottish input-
output table indicates a ratio of 0.69 for Scotland in 1973
(Scottish Council Research Institute). Two-thirds of Scottish
exports, in fact, were sold to other regions in the UK. Earlier
estimates by Brown (1972) indicate that the propensity to
export was at least 0.7 in all UK regions.

Part of the reason for the openness of regional economies
lies in their small size compared to national economies.
Small, industrially specialised regions are inevitably forced
to rely heavily on trade. But specialisation and size provide
only part of the answer. The great distances involved
between many regions in North America, for example, do
not prevent close trading links between them. The openness
of regional economies can be more easily explained by
factors such as the absence of tariff and non-tariff barriers
between regions, the existence of a single monetary regime

within which all regions operate, and the absence of many barriers found in international trade as a result of the economic sovereignty of nations. Of course, many frictions to trade continue to exist even at the regional level. Regional policy itself, for instance, distorts interregional trade through the provision of subsidies to industries located in assisted areas. But there is simply not the plethora of barriers found in international trade. Ironically, the fewer frictions that exist to interregional trade compared to international trade means that the theory of international trade may be more suited to explaining transactions between regions than transactions between nations.

The trading relationships between regional economies undoubtedly have a profound effect on their economic performance. The significance of trade for regional economies, for example, has already been demonstrated in our earlier discussion of why regions grow at different rates. The economic activity of individual economies is closely tied to the competitive position of a region's export sector in national and world markets. The competitive position of a region will also have an effect on the extent to which it can ride the storms of short-run cyclical fluctuations and the extent to which it can adapt to fundamental changes in consumption and production techniques. In view of the importance of interregional trade to regional economies, this chapter examines the theoretical basis of trade between regions. In addition, the implications of chronic deficits or surpluses in a region's balance of payments are also examined.

4.1 The Basis of Interregional Trade

Interregional and international trade have much in common. Indeed, international trade theory was initially developed with interregional as well as international trade in mind, the common link being the principle of comparative advantage. Consider the simple example shown in table 4.1. There are two regions, East and West. In the initial pre-trade (or autarky) position, each produces only two commodities, textiles and steel. The East is more efficient relative to the West in the production of *both* commodities. Hence in the East it takes 2 man-days to produce a unit of textiles and 20 man-days to produce a unit of steel, whereas in the West it takes 5 man-days to produce a unit of textiles and 125 man-

Table 4.1 *Regional comparative advantage: a hypothetical example*

| Commodity | Number of man-days required to produce one unit of each commodity | |
	East	West
Textiles (1 unit)	2	5
Steel (1 unit)	20	125

Note:

Each number in the table is the *inverse* of the average product of labour. If it takes 2 man-days to produce one unit of textiles, 1 man-day will produce half a unit of textiles.

days to produce a unit of steel. The East can be said to have an absolute advantage in the production of both commodities.

Absolute differences in efficiency, however, are irrelevant as far as trade is concerned. Provided a region has a *relative* advantage in the production of a commodity, trade will be advantageous. The East, for example, is relatively more efficient at producing steel whilst the West is relatively more efficient at producing textiles. To see why this should be so, we must look at the opportunity costs of producing steel and textiles. If the East were to produce one more unit of steel, it would have to transfer 20 man-days from the production of textiles, thereby losing 10 units of textiles (since each unit of textiles requires 2 man-days for its production). The opportunity cost of a unit of steel in the East is 10 units of textiles. In the West, 125 man-days must be transferred from textiles to produce an extra unit of steel, which means that 25 units of textiles will have to be forgone (since each unit of textiles requires 5 man-days for its production). It follows that the East is relatively more efficient in steel production than the West.

The existence of comparative advantage creates the possibility of mutually advantageous trade between the East and the West provided there are no barriers to trade. We have seen that one extra unit of steel 'costs' 10 units of textiles in the East, whereas an extra unit of steel 'costs' 25 units of textiles in the West. With these internal exchange ratios of 1:10 in the East and 1:25 in the West, it is clear that the East can obtain more textiles per unit of steel by selling steel to the West than by transferring resources into textile production at home. The East will therefore specialise in steel and export it to the West. The West will do the opposite.

With steel flowing from East to West, and with textiles flowing from West to East, we cannot expect the exchange ratios to remain the same. The exchange rate of 1 unit of steel = 10 units of textiles in the East will rise as the supply of steel falls and the supply of textiles increases. The exchange rate of 1 unit of steel = 25 units of textiles in the West will fall as the supply of steel increases and the supply of textiles falls. Suppose the new 'world' exchange ratio settles at 1:15. The gains from trade to both the East and West can be seen by comparing the initial exchange ratio with the newly established 'world' exchange ratio. The East can buy 15 units of textiles from the West for each unit of steel it produces whereas it can only produce 10 units of textiles by giving up the production of 1 unit of steel. The West reaps similar gains. To produce an extra unit of steel, the West has to give up 25 units of textiles, whereas it can obtain an extra unit of steel by selling 15 units of textiles to the East.

The analysis so far has been very much in the Ricardian tradition. In its most basic form it is labour productivities that are the cause of comparative cost differences. These are shown in table 4.1 as the number of man-days required to produce a unit of output. Since labour is assumed to be the only factor of production in the Ricardian model, the view that differences in labour productivity determine comparative costs is not perhaps surprising. Furthermore, Ricardian theory offers no explanation of *why* labour productivities differ between regions. The modern view is that in the light of the many restrictive Ricardian assumptions the only possible cause of differing labour productivities is differences in production technology between regions.

Attempts have been made to test the Ricardian view at both regional and international levels. Dixon (1973), for instance, has used United Kingdom data to test whether regions which have high labour productivity per worker in a given industry in the region (relative to national productivity per worker) specialise in that industry. Deriving a measure of regional specialisation is difficult. Most researchers have favoured the use of location quotients (LQ) which are defined, using employment data in this case, as:

$$LQ_i = \frac{e_i/E_i}{\sum_i \dot{e}_i / \sum_i E_i}$$

where:

e_i = regional employment in industry i
Σe_i = regional employment in all industries
E_i = national employment in industry i
ΣE_i = national employment in all industries

A region is said to specialise in the production of commodity i if it has a location quotient greater than unity. Hence if a region has more than 2% of the nation's workforce for industry i, and if the entire regional workforce is only 2% of that of the whole nation, regional specialisation in industry i is said to exist. Not surprisingly, Dixon's results for the UK regions offer little support for the explanation of comparative advantage based on regional differences in labour productivities. More realism can be added to the basic Ricardian view by allowing for regional differences in money wages, which may offset regional differences in labour productivity. Once again, Dixon found little support for this modified view.

Rejection of the Ricardian explanation of comparative advantage leads on naturally to the general equilibrium approach developed by Heckscher and Ohlin. Whilst Ricardian theory focuses on differences in labour productivities as the basis of comparative advantage and can only hint at the causes of these differences, the Heckscher-Ohlin theorem attempts a succinct explanation of the *causes* of comparative advantage as part of a 'thorough theoretical integration of commodity prices, factor prices, and the comparative static adjustments towards interregional equilibrium' (Moroney 1972). According to this more modern theory, two broad causes of comparative advantage are possible. These are, firstly, regional differences in technology and, secondly, regional differences in the availability of factors of production. In the Heckscher-Ohlin theorem, regional differences in technology are assumed away and the focus is placed on different regional factor endowments as the cause of comparative advantage.

Let us again assume a simple two-region economy in which the East is capital-abundant whilst the West is labour-abundant. In the pre-trade situation, both regions produce steel and both produce textiles. Production of steel is capital-intensive relative to textiles and production of textiles is labour-intensive relative to steel in both regions. The Heckscher-Ohlin theorem predicts that the capital-

abundant East will specialise in the production and export
of steel, which is capital intensive. Similarly, the labour-
abundant West will specialise in the production and export of
textiles, which is labour-intensive.

The Heckscher-Ohlin theorem has a powerful intuitive
attraction. One would expect the capital-abundant East to
have relatively low capital prices as the result of its
endowment of capital. This in turn should give it a
comparative advantage in steel. An identical argument
would lead us to expect the West to specialise in textile
production. This seductive logic, however, rests on the
following highly restrictive assumptions:

(i)   Production functions are identical in both regions.
       (This assumption removes the possibility that
       comparative advantage will arise from regional
       differences in technology.)
(ii)   Production functions exhibit constant returns to
       scale.
(iii) Perfect competition exists in both the commodity
       market and the factor market.
(iv)   Trade is free from all obstructions — such as tariffs
       or transport costs.
(v)   Factors of production are qualitatively similar in
       both regions.
(vi)   Each region's endowment of capital and labour is
       fixed at any instant of time and supply is inelastic.
(vii) Production of steel is capital-intensive and
       production of textiles is labour-intensive at all
       possible sets of factor prices (i.e. there exists 'strong
       factor intensity').
(viii) Tastes are identical in both regions and do not vary
       with regional income levels.

Quite obviously, some of these assumptions are more
restrictive than others in a regional setting. Most restrictive
of all are the assumptions of perfect competition and
constant returns to scale, and of fixed supplies of labour and
capital. We have already noted the importance of external
and agglomeration economies of scale in regional economic
growth. There is also, as we have seen, a substantial degree
of interregional migration of labour and capital which
violates the assumption of fixed factor supplies.

The basic elements of the Heckscher-Ohlin theory of
interregional trade can be illustrated by extending our

earlier example. In the East, where labour is scarce relative
to capital, the price of labour is high compared to the price of
capital. The East will therefore use less labour per unit of
capital in producing steel than is the case in the West, where
the relative abundance of labour means that labour is cheap
compared to capital. Hence, as shown in figure 4.1, to

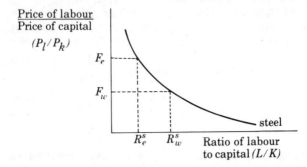

Figure 4.1 *Factor abundance and factor prices: the steel industry*

produce one unit of steel, the East selects a factor mix of R_e^s
whereas the West selects a factor mix of R_w^s. The East
therefore produces steel using a low labour/capital ratio
since labour is relatively expensive, and the West does the
opposite because labour is relatively cheap.

A similar argument applies to the production of textiles.
To produce one unit of textiles, the East selects a
labour/capital ratio of R_e^t whereas the West selects the
higher labour/capital ratio of R_w^t (see figure 4.2). Notice,
however, that textile production remains more labour-
intensive than steel in both regions. The function relating

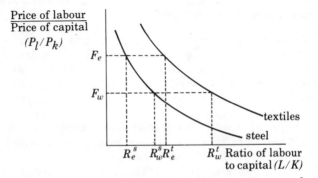

Figure 4.2 *Factor abundance and factor prices : steel and textiles*

factor prices (P_l/P_k) and factor combinations (L/K) in the textile industry is therefore further from the origin in figure 4.2 than in the case of the steel industry. Textile production is assumed to require a greater labour/capital ratio than steel at any given price of labour relative to capital. (We shall consider below the situation where this 'strong factor intensity' assumption is dropped.)

Finally, we need to establish the relationship between factor prices and product prices. If labour is abundant relative to capital, the price of labour will be low compared to the price of capital. This will give the labour-intensive commodity an advantage over the capital-intensive commodity. Thus, in the present example, if labour is cheap (because of its abundance) and capital is expensive (because of its scarcity), the price of steel will be high relative to the price of textiles. But as labour becomes more expensive and as capital becomes cheaper, the labour-intensive commodity (textiles) will become more expensive compared to the capital-intensive commodity (steel): the P_s/P_t ratio will therefore fall as the P_l/P_k ratio rises. This relationship is shown in figure 4.3. Hence, if labour is scarce and capital is

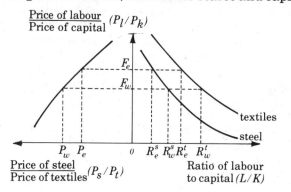

Figure 4.3 *Factor abundance, factor prices, and commodity prices*

plentiful, labour-intensive commodities will have a high price and capital-intensive commodities will have a low price. In terms of the two regions in our example, the price of labour will be high relative to the price of capital in the labour-scarce East, and this will be associated with a price of steel that is low compared to the price of textiles. The opposite occurs in the West. The labour-abundant West has a low labour/capital price ratio, which is associated with a high price of steel compared to the price of textiles.

We have therefore seen that in a simple world of two regions, two factors of production and two commodities, the labour-abundant region can be expected to have a comparative advantage in the production of labour-intensive commodities, and the labour-scarce region can be expected to have a comparative advantage in the production of capital-intensive commodities. In our example, the labour-abundant West emerges with a high price of steel relative to the price of textiles; and the labour-scarce East ends up with a low price of steel relative to the price of textiles. It is precisely this difference between the pre-trade commodity price ratios that creates the possibility of gains from trade, as indeed is the case in the simpler Ricardian theory of comparative advantage. A basis for mutually beneficial trade is therefore established.

The assumptions of the Heckscher-Ohlin model have been subject to extensive criticism. This is particularly true of the assumption of 'strong factor intensity', which asserts that an industry exhibiting, say, labour-intensity at one factor price ratio will exhibit labour-intensity at *all* factor price ratios. Thus, in our two commodity example, textile production was seen to be more labour-intensive than steel production at *all* levels of the P_l/P_k ratio. But if labour and capital happen to be highly substitutable in the production of textiles, we may see textiles becoming highly capital-intensive when the price of labour becomes very high relative to the price of capital.

This situation is illustrated in figure 4.4, which shows that textile production is more labour-intensive than steel when the P_l/P_k ratio is low, but that a complete reversal occurs

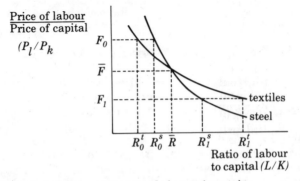

Figure 4.4 *The case of weak factor intensity*

when the P_l/P_k ratio rises above $\bar{F}$. When the price of labour is high relative to the price of capital, textiles become the capital-intensive product as textile producers switch into more capital-intensive methods of production. The possibility of this 'reversal' of factor intensities has received considerable attention in the trade literature. Fortunately, there is little evidence that such reversal takes place in regional trade (Moroney 1972).

So well-accepted is the 'law' of comparative advantage that most of the empirical testing of trade theory at both regional and international levels is not concerned with establishing whether it is comparative or absolute advantage which is the basis of trade, but rather with testing the various alternative explanations of what causes a region to have a comparative advantage in certain commodities (see McCrone 1969 for a dissenting view).

A number of regional tests of the Heckscher-Ohlin theorem have been carried out. Almost all have followed the pioneering work of Moroney and Walker (1966), who have tested the model in the context of North-South trade within the USA. Since the South is relatively well-endowed with labour (relative to capital) for historical reasons, one would expect the South to specialise in the production and export of commodities the production of which requires high labour/capital ratios. In practice this so-called 'static equilibrium' test involves correlating labour/capital ratios of industries in the South against measures of regional trade specialisation.

There are many practical difficulties involved in this kind of test. To begin with, measuring labour/capital ratios for individual industries is a notoriously difficult task (Smith B. 1975). Newer capital stocks, for example, frequently embody recent technological advances. In addition, both labour and capital are far from homogeneous factors of production. Problems are also posed by the absence of reliable regional trade statistics. Researchers are forced to use measures of *production* specialisation such as the location quotient, rather than measures of *trade* specialisation. This does, however, have the advantage of neatly side-stepping any problems caused by regional differences in tastes. For example, if the South exhibited an intense demand for labour-intensive commodities, it is possible that it could specialise in the production of such commodities, but *not* their export, given the high local demand. The assumption of identical regional tastes is an integral part of the Heckscher-Ohlin model (Greytak 1975).

Surprisingly, the Moroney and Walker study obtained apparently perverse results, implying that the South was actually specialising in *capital-intensive* industries. The reason for this apparent failure of the model seems to arise from the over-simple focus on only two factors of production — labour and capital. Eight 'rogue' industries are identified which exhibit low labour/capital ratios. Some of these rogue industries were found to be *raw material-intensive,* such as chemicals, pulp and paper, and oil refining. They exploit the raw materials of the South, but also happen to be capital-intensive. The failure to incorporate raw materials as a third factor invalidates their results. This is borne out by more favourable results using a three-factor test incorporating raw materials as well as labour and capital (Moroney 1975). Favourable results have also been obtained for New England. Like the South, New England is labour-abundant, but it has few natural resources (Klaasen 1973, Estle 1967).

The 'static equilibrium' test is not the only possible test of the Heckscher-Ohlin theory of interregional trade. Again, following Moroney and Walker, regional tests have included a 'comparative static' approach. This involves calculating the direction in which regional specialisation is changing over time. As a region moves towards equilibrium in its trade and specialisation, the output of commodities in which the region has a comparative advantage should grow the fastest. Rates of change of location quotients should therefore be positively correlated with labour/capital ratios in the labour-abundant region. These 'comparative static' tests have provided much stronger support for the Heckscher-Ohlin theorem than have the 'static equilibrium' tests. Natural resource endowment seems to affect only initial industrial structure and not subsequent rates of development.

4.2 Regional Trade and Factor Price Equalisation

An important extension of the Heckscher-Ohlin model is the factor price equalisation theorem (Samuelson 1948) which argues that trade will tend to equalise regional factor prices.

Earlier, we showed that the labour-abundant West had a comparative advantage in the production of textiles, whilst the capital-abundant East had a comparative advantage in the production of steel. This is reflected in figure 4.5 by the high price of steel relative to textiles in the labour-abundant West, and by the opposite situation in the East.

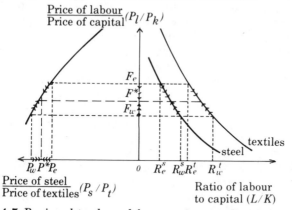

Figure 4.5 *Regional trade and factor price equalisation*

Once trading begins between these two regions we find that the West concentrates on the production and export of textiles whilst the East concentrates on the production and export of steel. The effects of this are far-reaching. The run-down of steel production in the West releases more capital than labour, steel production being capital-intensive. The growing textile industry in the West, however, requires relatively more labour than capital. Since we have assumed factors of production to be in fixed supply in both regions, the West is forced to substitute capital for labour in its production. This is indicated in figure 4.5 by a fall in labour/capital ratios in the West (as shown by the arrows marked on the diagram). In other words, the switch to textile production in the West resulting from trade creates a demand for labour which cannot be met fully by labour released from the declining steel industry. Inevitably, the price of labour in the West will tend to rise relative to the price of capital. In the East, a reverse process occurs as the East switches production from textiles to steel. Here, the price of labour falls relative to the price of capital. The result will be an eventual equalisation of the factor price ratio in both regions at F^*, and of the commodity price ratio at P^*. Although we have shown the equalisation of *relative* factor prices, it can be shown that *absolute* factor prices too will be equalised (Krauss and Johnson 1974).

This relationship between trade and regional factor prices is an important one, at least in theory. In each region, specialisation of production for export effectively increases the *derived demand* for the previously abundant factors, and simultaneously decreases the derived demand for scarce factors. The result is a tendency, *even in the absence of factor migration,* for regional factor price differences to narrow, and 'commodity trade thus serves as a perfect substitute for factor mobility, since such trade implies the equalisation of factor prices even under conditions when factors of production are immobile' (Krauss and Johnson 1974).

We should be careful not to expect too much of the factor price equalisation theorem. Its assumptions are many and restrictive. The partial success of the regional tests of the Heckscher-Ohlin theorem shows, however, that many of the apparently restrictive assumptions held in common by the Heckscher-Ohlin and factor price equalisation theorems may not be wildly at variance with reality.

4.3 Regional Trade and Factor Migration

The assumption of zero factor migration is a major weakness of interregional trade theory. Interregional migration may be far from perfect, but it is also far from insignificant.

The existence of substantial capital and labour migration poses problems of *causality* for the Heckscher-Ohlin theorem. In our earlier example, we argued that it is the relative abundance of labour in the West that gives it its comparative advantage in textile production. If labour and capital are mobile, however, it is quite possible that textile production would be attracted to the West for other reasons, such as access to markets or to non-mobile raw material supplies. Local labour supplies become unimportant if they can be supplemented by in-migration. In other words, the West may *become* labour-abundant *as a result of* its specialisation in textile production. The direction of causality would be the reverse of that postulated by the Heckscher-Ohlin theorem.

The erratic results of regional tests of the Heckscher-Ohlin theorem in the UK seem to bear this out (Dixon 1973, Smith B. 1975). Distances are so small between UK regions that labour and capital are quite mobile. Labour-abundant regions do not always specialise in the production of labour-intensive commodities except where there exist distinct barriers to labour migration, such as the geographical separation of N Ireland from the rest of the UK.

4.4 Regional Balance of Payments Problems

Balance of payments problems figure prominently in government policymaking at the national level. Yet at the regional level, balance of payments problems are conspicuous by their absence. The government does not deliberately intervene to correct regional balance of payment problems in their own right. We do not find governments using fiscal or monetary policies to correct the payments deficits or surpluses of individual regions, nor are there tariff or quota restrictions on regional trade (with the exception, for example, of those resulting from regional variations in the liquor laws in Canada and the USA!). The reason for this lack of concern is simple. Regional balance of payments problems exist, but they are not perceived as such.

A number of automatic adjustment mechanisms exist which in the short run effectively hide, and in the longer run rectify, any regional balance of payments problems that may arise. Imbalances that would emerge as balance of payments crises at the national level take quite a different form at the regional level. This automatic adjustment to balance of payments problems results from the institutional framework within which regional trade operates. Regional trade, unlike international trade, occurs within the framework of a single currency area in which a rigidly fixed exchange rate of 1:1 exists between regional currencies. None of the uncertainties of international exchange rate fluctuations occur. Add to this the fact that there is usually an integrated national capital market and banking system and the stage is set for an extremely liberal system of trading.

The freedom of trade and the automaticity of balance of payments adjustment may seem a rosy state of affairs. This view is misleading. The openness of regional economies means that any economic instability is rapidly transmitted from region to region. At the same time, regional economies are unable to protect themselves as their national counterparts can. Regional economies do not have the power to use contractionary or expansionary macro-policy to correct payments imbalance, nor can they vary the exchange rate or restrict imports into the region.

Balance of payments disequilibria may not be perceived, but that does not mean that they somehow magically disappear at the regional level. They are merely hidden beneath the veneer of a single currency area and an integrated banking system. The role of the banking system is crucial (Ingram 1959). Commercial banks located in a deficit region suffer a net outflow of money to surplus regions. With a regional banking system as in the USA, the process of adjusting to a regional deficit is quite complex. Regional banks in the deficit regions quickly find their reserve ratios under pressure, unless they have some 'slack' in these reserve ratios. Normally this would lead to a multiple credit contraction in the deficit region, but in the short run the response is likely to be rather different. If the deficit is not expected to be a persistent one, the banks of the deficit region will react by selling from their portfolio of 'readily transferable claims', which consist of government and other securities readily acceptable to banks in surplus regions. In effect, an equilibrating short-run capital inflow into banks of the deficit region enables multiple credit contraction to be avoided. All kinds of financial claims can constitute this pool of 'readily transferable claims'. Mortgages, for example, fulfilled this role in the American West during the nineteenth and early twentieth centuries. A secular growth in these 'generalised securities' has occurred in most countries. With a UK-style system of national banks, the mechanism is simpler. Reserve ratios are calculated at the national level and the banking system merely hides regional trade surpluses and deficits within its structure.

To the role of the banking system in responding to short-term deficits and surpluses we must add two further mechanisms with similar effects. Firstly, the growth of 'multiregional' firms, as distinct from purely local firms, means that many interregional trade transactions between regional branches of the same firm simply by-pass the banking system and do not even enter banking accounts. Secondly, trade credit is a most important mechanism whereby firms in a deficit region can avoid immediate payment for inputs from other regions. Trade credit is effectively a short-term loan to firms in deficit regions from firms in surplus regions.

None of these responses to an immediate regional balance of payments deficit, however, is capable of protecting the deficit region from the effects of a persistent imbalance. Moreover, since the region shares a common currency with the remainder of the nation it cannot look to depreciation of the exchange rate to remedy a continuing loss of funds through its banking system. Over the longer term, a contraction of credit in the region will inevitably occur.

This long-term contraction of credit within deficit regions bears some superficial resemblance to adjustment under the classical gold standard system. The contraction of the money supply over time should place a downward pressure on regional prices, thereby restoring competitiveness. Unfortunately, as we pointed out earlier, regions are very open economies. Even if factor and commodity prices were flexible downwards, which they are not, they are established in national markets and the scope for regional variation is small.

A more likely effect of a long-term deficit is to cause downward multiplier effects on income and employment in the deficit regions. Exports represent an injection to and imports a withdrawal from a region's circular flow of income. The deflationary effects of a chronic deficit, like deflationary fiscal policies, will be a painful but effective method of reducing the deficit. The adjustment is painful because regional income falls and unemployment rises. It is effective because regions are open economies, and as regional demand falls there will be a sharp reduction of imports in response to the fall in income.

Great controversy surrounds the role that long-term capital movements play in regional balance of payments problems. We argued in the previous chapter that prosperous regions attract the bulk of long-term capital movements because of factors such as the bias in the geographical allocation of funds by financial institutions and the 'ploughing back' of profits by firms located in prosperous regions. In addition, Scitovsky (1958) has argued that the greater level of economic activity and investment in prosperous regions will generate capital inflows. The need for investment and working capital will lead to an excess of new issues in prosperous regions. This will eventually force up interest rates and yields on securities in prosperous regions, thus resulting in capital inflows since 'if the capital market is sufficiently well-organised and integrated to permit and promote such capital flows, they will easily respond to, and thus eliminate, regional differences in prospective yields' (Scitovsky 1958).

How likely it is that regional differences in interest rates and security yields will emerge is open to doubt. A more likely explanation of the flows of long-term private capital into prosperous regions is that these regions may offer distinct locational advantages. External economies, agglomeration economies, and market access may outweigh the low-wage and labour supply advantages of depressed areas for mobile capital. Following Whitman (1967), it is possible to conceptualise these advantages as an outward shift of the marginal efficiency of capital schedule in prosperous regions. As noted in the two previous chapters, such locational advantages in prosperous regions may cumulatively reinforce one another.

Whether or not these long-term private capital movements will remove regional balance of payments problems is difficult to assess. To begin with, it is impossible to be sure which type of region is likely to have a balance of payments deficit. Whitman has developed a series of 'scenarios' in order to determine the conditions under which prosperous regions will have a balance of payments deficit. If a region's prosperity is export-led, the initial surplus is likely to be reinforced by capital inflows for investment purposes. This may be followed by a deficit as imports of investment goods increase. Finally, the region may move back into surplus as new capacity created in the export sector comes into operation. Deficits will only occur in this final stage if debt repayment and profit repatriation is large.

The propositions that prosperous regions may run balance of payments deficits and that capital movements will be equilibrating are controversial. The traditional argument is that the decline of export demand in depressed regions has meant that regional recession and regional balance of payments deficits are synonymous. If this is so, long-term capital movements will have disequilibrating effects on regional balance of payments problems. In the absence of reliable data, all that can be said is that the effects of capital movements will depend on the particular situation in each region.

The role played by interregional labour migration is also

controversial. As we have seen, net migration tends to be in the direction of prosperous regions. This will have an equilibrating effect provided it is the depressed regions that are in deficit, since the movement of labour will reduce imports in depressed regions and increase imports in prosperous regions. If it is the prosperous regions that are in deficit, however, the movement of labour will have disequilibrating effects on the balance of payments. We must, however, be careful not to jump to excessively simple conclusions. Even if it is the depressed regions that are in deficit, the movement of labour from depressed to prosperous regions may still not be equilibrating. Labour migration, as we have seen, is selective. It is the young and the skilled who migrate. Their loss may substantially reduce the attractiveness of depressed regions as suitable locations for investment, and may therefore hinder long-term equilibrating *capital* movements to those regions. Migrants may also take mobile assets with them when they migrate to other regions, or they may send remittances back to families who remain in depressed regions. The net balance of these flows of funds may or may not be equilibrating.

Finally, we should note that government financial transfers help regions to achieve an equilibrium in their balance of payments. Depressed regions automatically obtain positive net transfers from prosperous regions. On the one hand, they reap the benefits of unemployment assistance and other welfare payments. This is clear from table 4.2, which indicates that the per capita expenditure on social security tends (as expected) to be higher in regions of high unemployment. On the other hand, depressed regions contribute less in taxation (per capita) to the Exchequer. There is no doubt that depressed regions obtain substantial automatic fiscal transfers (King 1973). In addition, regional policy itself results in *discretionary* fiscal transfers to depressed regions which will have an equilibrating effect where a balance of payments deficit exists. Work by Bowsher *et al.* (1957) in the USA has shown that rural areas lose funds to local and national centres. In return, there are partially offsetting flows from national centres back to the rural areas, some of which take the form of regional aid from the Federal government.

Whether or not the various long-term adjustment processes are equilibrating remains a matter of controversy. What is certain, however, is that regional balance of

Table 4.2 *Regional distribution of social security payments in GB 1969/70-1973/74*

Region	Social security payments (1969/70-1973/74 average at 1974 prices)			Per cent registered wholly unemployed
	£m	£'s per capita	Index (GB = 100) of £'s per capita	1969-73 average
SE	1751	102	94	1.8
E Anglia	169	101	93	2.4
SW	427	113	104	2.9
W Midlands	507	99	91	2.5
E Midlands	344	102	94	2.4
Yorkshire and Humberside	544	114	93	3.3
NW	788	117	107	3.5
N	405	123	113	5.3
Wales	349	128	117	4.2
Scotland	600	115	106	5.0
GB	5886	109	100	2.9

Source:
Short (1977); *British Labour Statistics Yearbook* 1973.

payments problems do not magically disappear. They reappear in the form of unemployment or net outward migration rather than as problems in their own right.

Conclusion

The reasons for the emergence of regional imbalances remain shrouded in controversy. The extremely open nature of regional economies means that the fate of any one region is often, to a substantial extent, beyond its powers to control. As we have shown, regional factor movements and regional trade play a vital role in regional development, and an understanding of the many and complex determinants of migration and trade is clearly crucial if we are to isolate the major causes of regional imbalance.

Selected references

Dixon and Thirlwall (1976); Ingram (1959); Moroney (1972); Smith B. (1975); Whitman (1967).

5
The Case for Regional Policy: The Problem of Regional Unemployment

Elsewhere in this book we have argued that regional policy ought to be concerned with more than just regional differences in the rate of unemployment. Policymakers have relied far too heavily upon the unemployment rate as an indicator of the economic and social well-being of regions in their efforts to remove the problems arising from regional imbalance. Certainly, regional policy must be concerned with more than just regional differences in unemployment. But having said this, it is perfectly clear that regional differences in unemployment have, nonetheless, resulted in serious economic and social problems. It is perhaps stating the obvious to say that regional differences in unemployment will continue to have a major impact on shaping regional policies — and in our view rightly so.

As far as regional unemployment is concerned, the problem facing the policymaker is to construct a policy package that will efficiently bring unemployed labour into use. But the construction of such a policy will depend, at least in part, upon the nature of the unemployment problem. All regions are unlikely to have the same type of problem, and the more we understand about the nature of the problem, the more appropriate are the policy measures likely to be. Regions, for example, with an out-dated and inefficient industrial base may experience a slow growth of employment opportunities. Government action to stimulate employment growth by inducing newer industries to move into such regions or by encouraging existing industries to expand would seem appropriate. Other regions, however, may be faced not with a dearth of employment opportunities, but with a labour force ill-equipped to fill the jobs already available. Unemployment could be reduced in this case by policies to retrain labour.

The crucial point is that an understanding of the nature of the regional unemployment problem is an essential prerequisite to the construction of regional policies. If the problem is misunderstood, we will end up with inadequate and inappropriate policies. It is the purpose of this chapter to explore the nature of the regional unemployment problem. After a brief overview of the issues, the chapter examines the basic causes of regional unemployment. This is followed by a detailed investigation of the use of U - V analysis in identifying the different categories of unemployment. Finally, some of the main limitations of regional unemployment statistics are outlined. In particular, the existence of substantial 'hidden' unemployment — and especially of female labour — is demonstrated.

5.1 The Regional Unemployment Problem: An Overview

The regional unemployment problem is a complex phenomenon. It is dangerous to oversimplify the issues. This is the case, for example, with the traditional structural hypothesis which, in its crudest form, argues that regions with an 'unfavourable' industry mix will experience higher unemployment rates than regions with a 'favourable' industry mix. There is very little support for this explanation, however, as far as the UK is concerned (Cheshire 1973). Table 5.1 compares actual regional unemployment rates (at June 1963) with the rates that *would* have occurred if the region had experienced the national average unemployment rate in each of its industries. In other words, national unemployment rates are applied to a region's industrial structure to produce a hypothetical unemployment rate. The difference between the actual and the hypothetical unemployment rate would be small if the region's industry mix had been instrumental in determining its overall unemployment experience.

The results indicate that the reverse has been the case. There are substantial differences between the actual and the hypothetical unemployment rate. In other words, regional differences in unemployment would have been very small if each regional industry had experienced the same

Table 5.1 *Actual and hypothetical unemployment rates in the GB regions, June 1963*

Region	Male unemployment rate:			Female unemployment rate:		
	actual	hypo-thetical	differ-ence	actual	hypo-thetical	differ-ence
	u_r	u_{rn}	$u_r - u_{rn}$	u_r	u_{rn}	$u_r - u_{rn}$
SE	1.37	2.13	-0.76	0.60	1.14	-0.54
E & S	1.31	2.16	-0.85	0.69	1.14	-0.45
Midlands	1.45	1.98	-0.53	0.81	1.23	-0.42
SW	1.70	2.25	-0.55	0.85	1.14	-0.29
Yorks & Lincs	1.64	2.09	-0.45	-0.90	1.24	-0.34
NW	2.83	2.11	0.72	1.70	1.25	0.45
N	4.33	2.34	1.99	2.38	1.16	1.22
Wales	2.70	2.10	0.60	2.03	1.13	0.90
Scotland	4.35	2.37	1.98	2.69	1.16	1.53

Notes: *Source:* Cheshire 1973, p. 6.
1. u_r = actual unemployment rate (in region r)
2. u_{rn} = hypothetical unemployment rate (in region r)

$$= \sum_i \left[\left(e_{ir} / \sum_i e_{ir} \right) u_{in} \right]$$

3. e_{ir} = regional registered workforce in industry i
4. u_{in} = national unemployment rate in industry i

unemployment rate as its national counterpart. The influence of a region's industry mix is small. Apparently, to understand regional differences in unemployment we have to explain why, ostensibly, the same industry behaves differently in different regions. Why is the unemployment rate in, say, the engineering industry high in one region and low in another? It may be the case that the composition of individual industries varies markedly between regions, with the result that the more vulnerable parts of particular industries are concentrated in specific geographical areas. The Northern region of Britain, for example, tends to specialise within the engineering industry on heavy capital goods (Northern Region Strategy Team 1976a). This may help to explain part of the relatively high unemployment rate experienced by the engineering industry in this region compared to elsewhere in the country. A region's industry mix may, however, have more subtle effects on its overall unemployment rate, as we shall explain below. The structural hypothesis may therefore have more to its credit than is implied by the results in table 5.1.

Another conventional, but analytically more useful, approach to the regional unemployment problem divides regional unemployment into two distinct parts.

Unemployment may be due to a deficiency in the *aggregate* demand for goods and services, or to a fundamental *mismatching* between the demand and supply for labour. All regions, of course, suffer from short-run fluctuations in the aggregate demand for goods and services, and hence in their unemployment rates. It is clear, however, from even the most superficial analysis of regional unemployment data that these fluctuations in aggregate demand do not fall evenly on the regions of an economy, with the result that the impact of

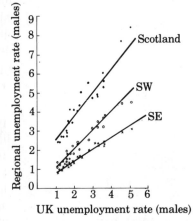

Figure 5.1 *Relationship between regional and national unemployment rates in selected regions, 1951-74*

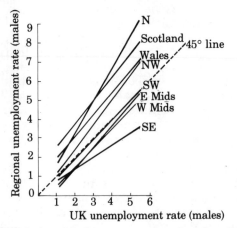

Figure 5.2 *Relationship between regional and national unemployment rates in the GB regions, 1951-74*

business depressions varies markedly between regions. That some regions are more cyclically sensitive than others can be seen from figures 5.1 and 5.2. The slope of each regression line in figures 5.1 and 5.2 reflects the cyclical sensitivity of each region — the steeper the line, the greater the cyclical sensitivity. Scotland, for example, has experienced an increase of about 1.2% in its unemployment rate for each increase of 1% in the national unemployment rate, whereas the corresponding figure for the SE is only 0.6%.

The second aspect of the regional unemployment problem is that marked differences in regional unemployment continue to exist even during periods of high aggregate demand. An expansion of the UK economy towards full employment would probably reduce the national male unemployment rate to a minimum of around 3%, which implies a rate of 2% in the SE and a rate of 5% in Scotland if previous experience is anything to go by. An examination of regional unemployment rates at each post-war peak in the business cycle suggests that there exists a substantial problem of 'non-deficient-demand' unemployment in the UK (see table 5.2). If labour were perfectly mobile between different occupations and different geographical areas,

Table 5.2 *The rate of registered unemployment in UK regions at business cycle peaks, 1951-73*

Region	Peaks in the business cycle (i.e. troughs in the unemployment rate)					
	1951	1955	1961	1965	1970	1973
SE	} 0.9	0.7	1.0	0.9	1.6	1.5
E Anglia				1.3	2.1	1.9
SW	1.2	1.1	1.4	1.5^c	2.8	2.4
W Midlands	0.4	0.5	1.0^b	0.9	2.0	2.2
E Midlands	} 0.7	0.6	1.0	0.9	2.2	2.1
Yorkshire & Humberside					2.9	2.9
NW	1.2	1.3^a	1.6	1.6	2.7	3.6
N	2.2	1.5^a	2.5	2.6	4.7	4.7
Wales	2.7	1.8	2.6	2.6	3.9	3.5
Scotland	2.5	2.4	3.1	2.9^d	4.2	4.6
N Ireland	6.1	6.4^a	6.7^b	6.1	6.9	6.4
UK	1.3	1.2	1.6	1.5	2.6	2.7

a = 1956; b = 1960; c = 1964; d = 1966
Source: Historical Abstract of Labour Statistics and British Labour Statistics.

unemployment in all regions would fall to zero provided the demand for labour were at least equal to the supply of labour. The unemployment rate never falls to zero, of course, because there are always some workers in all regions who are in the process of changing their jobs. This is a natural feature of all labour markets and is usually referred to as frictional unemployment. More important, however, as far as the regional unemployment problem is concerned, is the persistence of substantial regional differences in unemployment due to a fundamental mis-matching between the demand and supply for labour. There exists either a geographical mis-matching between the demand and supply for workers or an occupational mis-matching, or more usually a combination of both. This type of unemployment is termed 'structural'.

All regions experience both frictional and structural unemployment to some degree. Their relative importance, however, varies between regions.

5.2 The Causes of Regional Unemployment: Demand-Deficiency

The close synchronisation of regional business cycles, as reflected in unemployment statistics, suggests that individual regions are strongly integrated into the national system of economic activity. Any expansionary or contractionary tendencies are rapidly transmitted from one region to another because of the extensive trading links that tie regions together. In view of these close trading links, it is not surprising that the export base of a region is regarded as a main determinant of short-run movements in regional income and employment.

It is primarily through the export sector that business fluctuations are transmitted from one region to another. If we think in terms of a system of regions, with each region relying upon a large number of other regions in the system to purchase the output of its export sector (and this is the natural outcome, of course, of regional specialisation), it becomes clear that the fortunes of regions are interrelated. Suppose, for instance, that the government decides to reduce the level of demand in the economy by raising income taxes. As incomes fall, the demand for goods and services will fall. Individual regions will consequently experience a reduction in the demand for their export commodities, though the extent to which demand falls will depend upon the income elasticity of demand for each region's exports.

It is obvious that the effect of a change in the demand for a region's exports on the total level of regional income will depend upon the size of the region's export sector. But this is not the only factor of importance, since the impact of a change in the demand for a region's exports will also depend upon the inter-industry linkages within the region. If the region's export industries purchase inputs from other regions rather than from other industries in the same region, the effects of the reduced demand for the region's exports will be transmitted elsewhere. (But note that there may eventually be feedback effects as these changes in demand work their way through the economic system.) The majority of regions, however, will have an export sector that depends heavily upon local households for labour services. In turn, households purchase goods and services from the non-export sector of the region. Hence the transmission of impulses from the export sector to the non-export sector will depend upon the purchasing habits of the households of a region.

The export-base explanation of regional cyclical sensitivity is not adequate, however, in its simplest form. In particular, it needs disaggregating. Some commodities have a high income elasticity of demand whilst other commodities have a low income elasticity. It follows that regions will vary in their cyclical sensitivity according to the extent to which they specialise in different export commodities. The heavy engineering industry, for example, tends to be much more sensitive to income fluctuations than the food processing industry, with the result that a region specialising in heavy engineering is likely to suffer more severe fluctuations than a region specialising in food processing. Heavy engineering, being part of the capital goods sector, is of course subject to large fluctuations in demand because the demand for capital goods is highly sensitive to fluctuations in aggregate demand. Even within an industry group, there may be large differences in cyclical sensitivity. The production of heavy chemicals, for example, tends to be more sensitive to the business cycle than the production of pharmaceuticals. In other words, a region's industry-mix should provide us with a guide to its cyclical sensitivity. Indeed, if we know how sensitive individual industries are to changes in income, and we know the composition of industry in each region, we should presumably be able to predict the overall sensitivity of each region to national fluctuations in business activity. Empirical work, however, indicates that a region's sensitivity to fluctuations in business activity can be only partly explained by its industrial structure (Thirlwall 1966). Other factors are apparently at work as well.

The reason why a region's industry mix does not provide us with a totally accurate guide to the cyclical sensitivity of a region is that the cyclical sensitivity of the *same* industry varies between regions. An industry may be more cyclically sensitive in one region than in another. One of the reasons for this is to be found in the relationship between the export sector of a region and the service sector. The service sector is defined to consist of those industries that supply goods and services to households within the region. But many of these households rely for their income upon the region's export sector. It follows that the demand for locally produced goods and services will depend, in the main, upon income earned by households in the export sector. The obvious implication of this is that the cyclical sensitivity of industries serving the local market will reflect the cyclical sensitivity of the export sector (Vining 1948).

Consider two regions, A and B, each with an export sector and a service sector. A's exports are assumed to be highly cyclically sensitive; B's exports are assumed to be the opposite. The demand for services is assumed to be largely dependent upon income earned in the export sector. A's service sector is therefore likely to be more cyclically unstable than B's service sector because it depends upon a cyclically more unstable export sector. Even though the service sectors in A and B may be very similar in their organisational and market characteristics, there could nevertheless be a substantial difference in their cyclical sensitivity. This argument suggests the interesting hypothesis that regions with highly cyclically sensitive export sectors will be even more cyclically unstable than their industry-mix would lead us to expect (because of the transmission of income changes to local service industries). Tests on the US economy lend some support to this hypothesis, but only for periods of time when business fluctuations have been severe (Borts 1961). Alternative explanations must consequently be sought.

Another explanation of the observed regional differences in cyclical sensitivity is that although firms within an industry may produce very similar products, their organisational and market characteristics may differ quite considerably, and these differences may have an effect upon their cyclical sensitivity. The steel industry in one region, for example, may sell to cyclically more stable markets than the steel industry in another region.

Or we may find that the steel industry in one region is dominated by less efficient units than the steel industry in another region because its capital equipment is of an older vintage. Since the less efficient parts of an industry are likely to suffer more severely during cyclical downturns, regions with more than their 'fair share' of less efficient plants will be cyclically more unstable. Just as an individual firm will tend to draw upon its less efficient stand-by machinery when demand is high, and will tend to lay-off its stand-by machinery when demand falls, it may also be the case that regions possessing the least efficient parts of an industry will be able to compete with the most efficient parts only when demand is high. Fluctuations in demand will therefore tend to be absorbed by the regions with the less efficient parts of the industry. As capacity constraints become operative at high levels of demand, the existence of short-run diminishing returns in the most efficient parts of the industry will force costs of production up and help the less efficient parts of the industry to compete more effectively; but only if demand remains high. The converse will occur during recessions.

Finally, fluctuations in the level of employment may vary for the same industries between different regions depending upon supply conditions in local labour markets. A firm in a labour-scarce area may decide to hoard its labour rather than release it on a cyclical downturn, provided the firm expects a subsequent recovery in demand. Releasing skilled and experienced workers may be more costly than temporarily hoarding labour, which involves the firm in paying for more manhours than it actually needs to produce its output. The other side of the picture is that firms in labour-abundant areas will be less reluctant to lay-off workers if they believe that adequate labour will be available when demand recovers. Thus, the excess supply position in the local labour market will affect the extent to which workers are likely to be laid-off during cyclical downturns.

5.3 The Causes of Regional Unemployment : Structural Mis-matching

Earlier, it was pointed out that a high level of *national* demand does not necessarily guarantee a low level of unemployment in all regions. Full employment may exist in the sense that there is an adequate number of job opportunities to provide work for all those searching for jobs (at going wages and prices). Yet there may still be considerable amounts of unemployment in particular areas and in particular occupations — even allowing for frictional unemployment. In brief, the demand and supply for labour may be equal *in aggregate,* but a mis-matching may exist. For one reason or another, the skill structure of the demand for labour may not exactly match the skill structure of the supply of labour. And even if these two skill structures match up exactly, there remains the possibility that the demand for labour could be located in a different geographical labour market from the supply of labour. In either case (and both cases can, of course, occur at the same time), there will exist unemployment — namely structural unemployment.

Structural unemployment has two fundamental dimensions, a skill dimension and a geographical dimension. It occurs not because of inadequate demand at national level (though this can make structural problems more intractable), but because of inadequate demand for specific types of labour in specific labour markets. The basic causes of structural unemployment can be traced to factors such as a change in the pattern of demand, a change in production methods, the discovery of a new source of a raw material or the exhaustion of an old source. Structural unemployment arises because the movement of labour out of contracting occupations, industries and regions and into expanding occupations, industries and regions takes time, thus resulting in a temporary mis-matching between the demand and supply for labour. Furthermore, as a result of geographical specialisation, there will be a locational bias in structural changes such that some regions are more severely affected than others. The growth in the demand for labour will therefore vary, often substantially, between regions.

Turning to the supply side of the labour market, there are two reasons why regional differences in the growth of the labour supply will be relatively small in most cases: first, the natural growth rate of the population is usually similar between regions, and second, there are many barriers to the geographical mobility of labour. Together, these two factors explain why regional differences in the growth of the labour supply often vary less than regional differences in the growth of labour demand. It follows that the divergence between the growth in the supply of labour and the growth in the demand for labour will vary between different regions. This is the basis of the locational aspect of the structural unemployment problem.

5.4 The Division of Unemployment into Separate Categories

Different methods are available for distinguishing between the deficient-demand and non-deficient-demand categories of unemployment. Earlier, we adopted a fairly crude 'rule of thumb' distinction between these various types of unemployment. Deficient-demand unemployment was defined to be the unemployment that would disappear if the economy were to be run such that the aggregate demand for labour at least equalled the aggregate supply of labour (e.g. as at some business cycle peaks). Non-deficient-demand unemployment was therefore treated as a residual. It is the unemployment that would remain even if there existed an adequate demand for labour *in aggregate.* Thus, the persistence of regional differences in unemployment rates at cyclical peaks (see table 5.2) was taken as a rough indicator of the magnitude of non-deficient-demand unemployment.

The amount of non-deficient-demand unemployment may change markedly over time, of course, and more sophisticated methods are required to isolate it from the deficient-demand component (Brechling 1967). Essentially, it is necessary to allow for shifts in the relationship between regional and national unemployment rates, which is usually achieved in empirical work by including a time trend in the regression of regional on national unemployment rates. The distinction between deficient-demand and non-deficient-demand unemployment becomes extremely tenuous once we move from a static world into a dynamic world. During periods of high demand, and therefore labour scarcity, there will be more opportunities for labour to retrain; and more firms are likely to move to areas where labour is less scarce. A persistently high level of aggregate demand will therefore lead to a reduction in the mis-matching between the demand and supply for labour.

In spite of such problems, we shall see that it is nevertheless convenient to retain the distinction between deficient-demand unemployment and non-deficient-demand unemployment. It would also be useful to derive more accurate measures of the various categories. If appropriate and efficient policy measures are to be devised to deal with the regional unemployment problem, the initial step of identifying the nature of the problem and measuring its magnitude is an essential one. It is to this measurement problem that we now turn.

The components of unemployment: U-V analysis
A far more ambitious method of identifying and measuring the various types of unemployment than the 'rule of thumb' approach described above is the U - V method. This relies on detailed data of both unemployment and unfilled job vacancies. Fundamental to this method of subdividing the unemployed into categories is the proposition that both unemployment (U) and vacancies (V) are a function of aggregate product demand. As demand rises (relative to supply), unemployment falls and job vacancies increase. A plausible relationship between U and V is traced out in figure 5.3 (see Hansen 1970 for a theoretical treatment). Provided the U-V relationship is stable, we can take the point where $U = V$ as the benchmark for extracting deficient-demand unemployment from total unemployment. Given a level of unemployment of U_1 in figure 5.3, for instance,

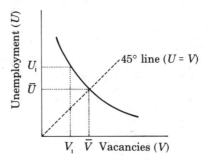

Figure 5.3 *The U - V relationship*

deficient-demand unemployment is the difference between U_1 and $\overline{U}$, where $\overline{U}$ is the level of unemployment at which there are apparently sufficient jobs in total for the unemployed since $\overline{U} = \overline{V}$. The remaining unemployment of $\overline{U}$ is treated as a residual: it is the non-deficient-demand component of unemployment. If actual unemployment were to fall to $\overline{U}$ or below, deficient-demand unemployment disappears completely.

The most immediate problem is the measurement of $\overline{U}$. It is only rarely that we find situations where vacancies equal (or exceed) unemployment. In most cases unemployment exceeds vacancies (as at U_1 and V_1 in figure 5.3). Consider table 5.3, for example. This shows that over the period 1958

Table 5.3 *The ratio of unemployment to vacancies in GB 1958-1972*

Year	Ratio of unemployment to vacancies	
	Males	*Females*
1958	4.04	1.94
1959	3.47	1.49
1960	1.87	0.93
1961	1.70	0.86
1962	4.06	1.36
1963	4.86	1.40
1964	2.07	0.71
1965	1.53	0.53
1966	1.87	0.55
1967	4.38	1.04
1968	4.59	0.78
1969	4.22	0.72
1970	4.73	0.88
1971	9.06	1.72
1972	8.41	1.81

Source: Hughes 1974, tables 2 and 3.

to 1972 at no time did male vacancies exceed male unemployment in Great Britain as a whole. The position for females is somewhat more favourable, with vacancies exceeding unemployment in eight of the 15 years. In such circumstances, $\overline{U}$ can be estimated only approximately and with difficulty (see Cheshire 1973, Thirlwall 1974). Estimates of $\overline{U}$, the non-deficient-demand component of unemployment, vary. Over the period of the 1960s and early 1970s, $\overline{U}$ appears to have been of the order of 200,000 to 250,000 (Hughes 1974). Deficient-demand unemployment by definition, varies over the cycle, but during the same period averaged around 500,000.

The value of U-V analysis can be greatly extended by disaggregating non-deficient-demand unemployment into its main constituent parts. Ideally, four distinct components can be identified and measured. First, there are the frictionally unemployed. These are defined as unemployed workers who are 'qualified to fill an existing vacancy'. By this we mean that an unemployed person is in the same occupational category as an existing vacancy (i.e. has appropriate skills) and is in the same region as an existing vacancy (i.e. is within reasonable travelling distance of the vacancy). Consider the simple two-region, two-occupation

Table 5.4 *A hypothetical U-V analysis for a two-region, two-industry economy*

Occupation	North		South		Total
	U	V	U	V	
Engineering	250	150	250	100	$U_E = 500$ $V_E = 250$
Clerical	250	150	250	600	$U_C = 500$ $V_C = 750$
Total	U_N=500	V_N=300	U_S=500	V_S=700	$U = 1000$ $V = 1000$

Notes:
1. U = numbers unemployed
2. V = number of unfilled job vacancies
3. Deficient-demand unemployment = 1000-1000 = 0
4. Frictional unemployment = 150 + 100 + 150 + 250 = 650
5. Structural unemployment = 1000-650 = 350

example shown in table 5.4. For simplicity, deficient-demand unemployment is excluded, that is aggregate vacancies equal aggregate unemployment at 1,000 each. Since frictional unemployment includes all unemployed who are 'qualified to fill an existing vacancy', we see from table 5.4 that there are 150 unemployed engineering workers in the North and 100 unemployed engineering workers in the South who could fill existing vacancies. As for clerical workers, the 150 vacancies in the North could be filled by unemployed clerical workers from within this region. The situation in the South is rather different: vacancies for clerical workers exceed unemployed clerical workers, which means that vacancies exist for all the 250 unemployed clerical workers in the South. Total frictional unemployment is therefore as follows:

    150 unemployed engineering workers in the North
    100 unemployed engineering workers in the South
    150 unemployed clerical workers in the North
    250 unemployed clerical workers in the South
    ───
    650

The second, third and fourth components of unemployment can be considered together under the general heading
of structural unemployment. The structurally unemployed
are those unemployed workers who are 'not qualified to fill
an existing vacancy'. In our example, since deficient-
demand unemployment is zero, and frictional
unemployment is 650, structural unemployment must be
350. The existing vacancies for these 350 structurally
unemployed workers are all clerical vacancies in the South.
Unfortunately, the unemployed workers are not qualified to
fill these vacancies. Failure to qualify, however, occurs for
three distinct reasons. Firstly, unemployed workers may not
have the appropriate occupational skills. This gives rise to
an *occupational dimension of structural unemployment*. In
our example, the 150 structurally unemployed engineering
workers in the South fall into this category. Secondly,
unemployed workers may have the appropriate
occupational skills, but may be located in the wrong region.
The 100 structurally unemployed clerical workers in the
North fall into this category. They have the appropriate
skills, but are not in the right region to fill the clerical
vacancies going begging in the South. These represent a
locational dimension of structural unemployment. Thirdly,
100 structurally unemployed engineering workers in the
North are not only occupationally mis-matched but are
locationally mis-matched as well.
    In summary, then, it is possible to identify four distinct
types of non-deficient-demand unemployment. In our simple
example, these are:

Frictional unemployment   = 650
Structural unemployment
    (occupational mis-matching)   = 150
Structural unemployment
    (locational mis-matching)   = 100
Structural unemployment (occupational and
    locational mis-matching simultaneously)   = 100
                                        Total = 1,000

Estimation of the various components of non-deficient-demand unemployment for Britain have yielded interesting results. About one-half of the 200,000 to 250,000 non-deficient-demand unemployment over the 1960s and early 1970s consists of structural unemployment, the remainder being frictional. More importantly, a large majority of the structurally unemployed are the result of occupational and not locational mis-matching.

There is one further way in which U-V analysis can be utilised to throw light on the regional unemployment problem. This involves applying the U-V method to individual regions. This allows the various causal categories of unemployment to be isolated for each region in turn and not simply aggregated together to give national totals. In other words, each region is regarded as a separate economy

Table 5.5 *A hypothetical U-V analysis for a specific region*

Occupation	North Unemployed	Vacancies
Engineering	250	150
Clerical	250	150
Total	$U = 500$	$V = 300$

Notes:
1. Deficient-demand unemployment = $500 - 300 = 200$
2. Frictional unemployment = $150 + 150 = 300$
3. Structural unemployment = $500 - 500 = 0$

in its own right. Table 5.5 shows the results of this exercise for the North (using the previous example). As can be seen, a deficiency of *regional* demand for labour of 200 is now revealed even though sufficient vacancies exist in the South for these unemployed workers (i.e. even though *aggregate* demand and supply for labour are in balance). By treating each region as a separate economy, those who were formerly regarded as structurally unemployed workers in the North (since vacancies exist for them in the South) are now regarded as unemployed due to a regional demand-deficiency.

Several regional applications of U-V analysis have now been carried out in Great Britain (see Cheshire 1973, Thirlwall 1974). Table 5.6 reproduces some of Thirlwall's results, which clearly demonstrate that on average during the period 1963-1972 the regions which have suffered from relatively high unemployment rates have done so because of

Table 5.6 *Types of unemployment in the GB regions, average experience 1963-72*

Region	Deficient-demand unemployment	Frictional unemployment	Structural unemployment	Total
(a) *males*				
SE	44.0	37.9	18.1	100
E & S	26.9	46.8	26.3	100
SW	68.4	22.6	9.0	100
Mids	53.6	27.2	19.2	100
Yorks/Humbs	65.2	18.4	13.5	100
NW	78.7	15.3	6.0	100
N	88.5	9.0	2.5	100
Wales	81.0	11.2	7.8	100
Scotland	90.3	8.1	1.6	100
GB	67.3	22.5	10.2	100
(b) *females*				
SE	0	88.2	11.8	100
E & S	0	91.2	8.8	100
SW	2.8	71.7	25.5	100
Mids	13.9	64.0	22.1	100
Yorks/Humbs	10.4	65.6	24.0	100
NW	18.1	56.9	25.0	100
N	55.8	30.8	13.4	100
Wales	58.3	30.6	11.1	100
Scotland	65.6	24.2	10.2	100
GB	10.0	67.5	22.5	100

Note:
As was shown in figure 5.3, frictional and structural unemployment should be measured when deficient-demand unemployment is zero (i.e. when $U = V$). Not all regions have experienced a situation in which $U = V$, however. Strictly, the U-V data should be adjusted so that frictional and structural unemployment are estimated at the (hypothetical) point where $U = V$ so that frictional and structural unemployment are not underestimated.
Source: Thirlwall 1974.

a fundamental deficiency in the *regional* demand for labour compared with the typically low unemployment regions. For some of the workers unemployed as a result of deficient regional demand, vacancies exist in other regions. For most, however, there are insufficient vacancies in other regions.

Some problems with U-V analysis
Attractive though the U-V method may seem at first sight, it is by no means free from problems and the results of all applications of this method must be interpreted with the

utmost caution. This certainly applies to applications of the *U-V* method at the standard region level since these regions are far too large to be considered as labour market areas. One may find, for instance, unemployed engineering workers in West Cumberland and engineering vacancies 150 miles away in Teesside. Both areas lie within the same region — the North. Yet to classify such unemployed engineering workers in West Cumberland as part of frictional unemployment is unrealistic. They are 'qualified' in the sense of having appropriate skills, but not in the sense of being located in close proximity to the vacancies. Unfortunately, even if appropriate data were available, it is by no means clear just what the appropriate sub-regions are for *U-V* analysis. How far workers are prepared to travel to take up vacancies varies with the type of worker (married women, for instance, being unwilling to travel as far as men) and with the quality of local transport. Nor should we disaggregate too far. With very small areas we would classify many unemployed workers as structurally unemployed due to a locational mismatching when in fact the unemployment is frictional.

Similar comments also apply to the occupational categories used in *U-V* analysis. An unemployed engineering worker is assumed to be 'qualified' to take a local engineering vacancy and therefore classified as being frictionally unemployed. But if an unemployed worker is skilled in marine engineering, for example, whilst the vacancy is for a worker with electronic engineering skills, the unemployment is hardly frictional — it is structural. Again there is no obvious disaggregation of occupations which can be regarded as 'correct' for *U-V* analysis, though the detailed classification provided by the Department of Employment in the UK is probably quite adequate for this purpose.

In addition to these difficulties with the geographical areas and occupational categories used, the *U-V* method assumes that any excess of total unemployment over total vacancies is due to a demand deficiency. There are two problems with this assumption. First, we do not know the accuracy of either registered unemployment data as a measure of unemployment, or of the vacancy data as a measure of job vacancies. We cannot therefore rely on the assumption that deficient-demand unemployment will equal zero when $U = V$. The second problem is more fundamental. The *U-V* method is based upon the proposition that both U and V are a function of excess product demand. As demand increases (relative to supply), unemployment falls and job vacancies increase. The proposition that vacancies are a function only of excess demand may be reasonably plausible, but care must be taken to check that institutional changes in the way in which vacancies are notified and collected have not occurred when the various components of unemployment are being compared over time.

More serious problems arise on the unemployment side of the U-V relationship. Unemployment may change not only because of changes in the demand for labour, but also because of changes on the supply side of the labour market. It has been argued, for example, that higher unemployment benefits relative to earnings have induced unemployed workers to spend more time searching the market for a suitable job. Hence, we may find the U-V relationship shifting its position — upwards in this particular example as shown in figure 5.4.

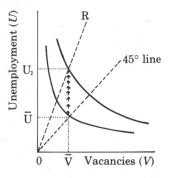

Figure 5.4 *An upward shift in the U - V relationship*

Assuming that unemployment rises because of an increase in the time spent by the unemployed searching the market for a job, a higher unemployment rate would be associated with each level of the pressure of demand. If we also assume that the vacancy-excess demand relationship remains unchanged, we would see an upward shift in the U-V relationship similar to that depicted in figure 5.4. Before the upward shift in the U-V relationship occurred, deficient-demand unemployment was zero when $U = V$ (i.e. at combination $\overline{V}, \overline{U}$ on the 45° line). But after the upward shift in the U-V relationship, deficient-demand unemployment is at zero when $U > V$ (i.e. at combination $\overline{V}$, U_2 on the ray OR). In this case, unemployment has increased from $\overline{U}$ to U_2 not because of a fall in demand, but because the unemployed are spending more time searching for a suitable job. The possibility of such shifts in the U-V relationship make it highly dangerous to regard the difference between U and V as an accurate measure of deficient-demand unemployment. Essentially, a model capable of predicting such shifts in the U-V relationship is required if this particular problem is to be overcome.

5.5 Some Limitations of Regional Unemployment Data

The accuracy of registered unemployment data as a measure of unemployment has long been in doubt. Most analyses of the regional unemployment problem — such as U-V analysis — are cast in terms of regional differences in the registered unemployment rate. The investigation of the regional unemployment problem, however, would be incomplete without considering the limitations of the registered unemployment rate, and in particular the problem of hidden unemployment. To understand the meaning of hidden unemployment and why it occurs, three supporting concepts are required: namely, the concepts of 'full employment', 'secondary workers' and 'discouraged workers' (Taylor 1974).

First, a brief discussion is required of the term 'full employment'. Full employment exists when there is sufficient aggregate demand in the economy such that jobs are available for all those searching for work at current wages and prices. For simplicity, we assume a linear relationship between the aggregate demand for *goods* and the aggregate demand for *labour*. The higher the demand for goods, the higher will be the level of employment (subject to the constraint that there is an adequate supply of labour available to meet the increase in demand). If we now assume that the supply of labour is inelastic in the short run with respect to the aggregate demand for goods, demand and supply can be considered simultaneously and full employment can then be defined in terms of the aggregate demand for goods.

Turning to figure 5.5, we can see that full employment will be achieved when aggregate demand is at D^*. If aggregate

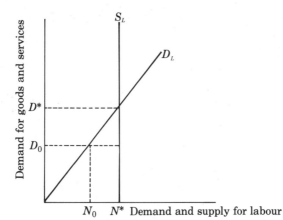

Figure 5.5 *Demand and supply for labour as a function of the aggregate demand for commodities.*

demand falls below D^*, say to D_0 ,the employment level will fall to N_0 from N^*. The gap between the actual level of employment and N^* indicates how much deficient-demand unemployment exists in the economy. Hence with aggregate demand at D_0, unemployment will be N^*-N_0. In addition to this 'deficient demand' unemployment, of course, there will exist a certain amount of frictional and structural unemployment.

The second concept we require in order to understand the nature of hidden unemployment is based upon the division of the workforce into two broad categories. There are those persons who are permanently attached to the workforce and who will remain there until the normal retiring age, apart from unplanned withdrawals due to illness; and there are those who are only temporarily attached to the workforce and who may join it or leave it several times during their working life. Those persons permanently attached to the workforce are termed 'primary workers'; those persons who are only temporarily attached to the workforce are termed 'secondary workers', the latter consisting mainly of married women, students and those who have retired from full-time work and seek only casual (usually part-time) employment.

The discouraged-worker hypothesis, which is the final part of the jigsaw, utilises both the notion of full employment and the distinction between primary and secondary workers. It argues that secondary workers move out of the *registered* workforce when the labour market is 'slack'.

When jobs are scarce and unemployment is high, secondary workers tend to disappear from the registered workforce. Diagrammatically, this can be represented by altering the slope of the labour supply curve (see figure 5.6). Instead of

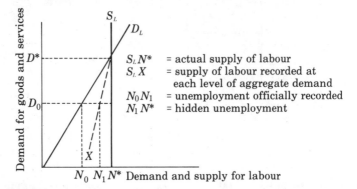

$S_L N^*$ = actual supply of labour
$S_L X$ = supply of labour recorded at each level of aggregate demand
$N_0 N_1$ = unemployment officially recorded
$N_1 N^*$ = hidden unemployment

Figure 5.6 *Graphical illustration of hidden unemployment*

being perfectly inelastic with respect to aggregate demand, the supply of labour apparently falls as aggregate demand falls — as indicated by $S_L X$ in figure 5.6. As aggregate demand falls from D^* to D_0, for instance, the level of employment falls from N^* to N_0. Of this increase in unemployment of $N^* - N_0$, however, only the portion $N_1 - N_0$ is recorded in the official count of the unemployed. $N^* - N_1$ simply disappears from the registered workforce for reasons we will now examine.

There are three ways in which secondary workers can disappear from the registered workforce: (1) secondary workers who lose their jobs may fail to register as unemployed; (2) secondary workers who *would have* joined the workforce if jobs had been available may fail to register as unemployed; (3) secondary workers on the unemployment register may stop registering their unemployment when they see no prospect of getting a job. Yet we may still ask why secondary workers who are unemployed fail to register their unemployment. The reason is unambiguous. There is no incentive to register for those not entitled to unemployment benefit, which is the case for most married women workers (i.e. about 75%) in the UK since their national insurance payments do not cover them for unemployment. Even if a person is not entitled to unemployment benefit, however, that person may still be likely to register as unemployed provided there is a reasonable chance of obtaining an acceptable job through the local Job Centre. But as the prospect of finding a job diminishes, more and more of those not entitled to unemployment benefit will cease to register their unemployment. To summarise, the discouraged-worker effect becomes stronger as job prospects decline.

Earlier in this chapter, unemployment was divided into two separate causal categories, a deficient-demand category and a residual (or non-deficient-demand) category, the latter being partly attributed to a fundamental structural mismatching between the demand and supply for labour. The distinction was made on the grounds that the type of policy action required to solve the regional unemployment problem is dependent upon the nature of unemployment in a region. This is equally true of hidden unemployment since there is reason to expect both a deficient-demand and a non-deficient-demand dimension to the hidden unemployment problem. Indeed, two empirical facts suggest that both types of hidden unemployment exist, at least in the UK:

(1) The registered female workforce is subject to marked pro-cyclical fluctuations about its long-run trend, as can be seen from figure 5.7. The registered female

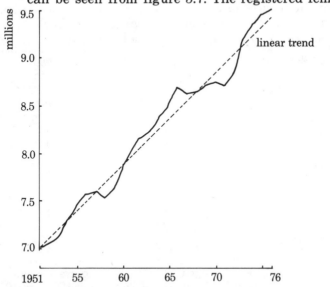

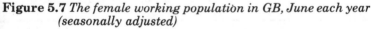

Figure 5.7 *The female working population in GB, June each year (seasonally adjusted)*

workforce rises to a cyclical peak immediately following the point in the business cycle where the pressure
of demand is at its highest.

(2) The female activity rate differs considerably
between regions, and more so between localities
within regions, even when the economy is at the peak
of the business cycle. (An activity rate is the proportion of persons of working age who are either
employed or registered as unemployed.)

The pro-cyclical fluctuations in the female activity rate
strongly confirm that a discouraged-worker effect has been
operating in Britain during the post-war period. A
slackening of the job market, as occurred for instance during
the 1952, 1958, 1963, 1967 and 1971 recessions, caused the
registered female workforce to fall (or rise very slowly) in
spite of a steep long-run upward trend. As predicted by the
discouraged-worker hypothesis, secondary workers do
appear to drift out of the labour market when the market is
slack. This implies the existence of a deficient-demand
variety of hidden unemployment.

Differences in the female activity rate between regions,
and more importantly between labour market areas,
indicate that a non-deficient-demand variety of hidden
unemployment may exist in addition to the deficient-
demand variety. Even at the peak of the business cycle,
considerable differences in female activity rates exist

Table 5.7 *Female activity rates in the UK regions, 1966 and 1971*

Region	Female activity rate[a]	
	1966	*1971*
SE	44.3	44.8
E Anglia	36.8	38.7
SW	36.9	37.6
W Midlands	45.6	45.4
E Midlands	42.6	43.3
Yorks/Humberside	41.4	41.7
NW	44.7	44.4
N	37.8	40.0
Scotland	41.2	42.4
Wales	33.4	35.7
N Ireland	33.5	36.0
UK	42.0	42.6

[a] Percentage of females aged 15 and over who are economically
active (as defined in the Censuses of Population 1966 and 1971).
Source: Abstract of Regional Statistics.

between labour market areas. At the peak of the mid-1960s boom, for example, the female activity rate varied between 33.4% in Wales and 45.6% in the West Midlands, with the other nine UK regions scattered fairly evenly between these two outer limits (see table 5.7). Even though there are considerable differences in the female activity rate between regions, these regional averages do, in fact, conceal much of the geographical dispersion that exists in Britain.

Yet we cannot say to what extent these geographical differences in female activity rates indicate the existence of non-deficient-demand unemployment until the influence of basic supply factors has been accounted for. We should also note that if we are to use geographical differences in female activity rates as a guide to the amount of the non-deficient-demand variety of hidden unemployment, it is important to select a point in time when the economy is operating at a full employment level of aggregate demand. If the economy is not operating at a full employment level of demand, geographical differences in the female activity rate will partly reflect cyclical problems, since the cyclical sensitivity of different areas can vary considerably.

As far as the influence of supply factors is concerned, there may be reasons on the supply side of the labour market why the activity rate is high in some areas and low in others. Areas with a high percentage of their female population in either the 20-34 or 55 and over age groups would be expected to have lower activity rates than areas with a high percentage of their working population in the 15-19 and 35-54 age groups. Explicit allowance must therefore be made for differences in the demographic structure of areas. Other influences from the supply side, such as the socio-occupational status of the local population, must be taken into account before the differences in the female activity rate between labour market areas can be used to approximate hidden unemployment.

We end on a further note of caution concerning unemployment data. It is sometimes forgotten that differences in the rate of unemployment *within* regions are considerably more severe than differences *between* regions. A few examples of *intra*regional differences in unemployment are given in table 5.8, which is self-explanatory. A statistical analysis of the geographical variation in unemployment rates (using 177 employment exchange areas in the UK) revealed that only about one

Table 5.8 *Intraregional differences in unemployment rates (November 1975): some examples*

Low unemployment localities	%	Region	%	High unemployment localities	%
Hertford	1.7			Colchester	3.8
Crawley	1.9	SE	3.5	Oxford	3.9
St Albans	2.2			Luton	4.6
Aldershot	2.6			Canterbury	4.8
Cambridge	2.3	E Anglia	4.2	Norwich	4.2
Taunton	3.8			Swindon	6.0
Salisbury	4.4	SW	5.9	Plymouth	6.5
Bristol	4.7			Torbay	10.5
Stoke	3.3			Coventry	6.2
Dudley	3.6	W Mids	5.2	Wolverhampton	6.3
Burton-on-Trent	3.7			Birmingham	6.5
Coalville	2.1			Chesterfield	4.9
Loughborough	2.8	E Mids	4.2	Leicester	5.1
Northampton	3.2			Corby	5.3
York	3.3			Scunthorpe	6.1
Huddersfield	3.4	Yorks & Humbs	4.8	Doncaster	6.2
Sheffield	3.6			Hull	7.3
Crewe	3.4			Wigan	6.5
Bury	3.8	NW	6.2	Widnes	7.4
Oldham	3.8			Liverpool	10.0
Neath	5.0			Shotton	7.3
Swansea	5.3	Wales	6.9	Ebbw Vale	9.3
Cardiff	6.9			Wrexham	9.5
Aberdeen	2.2			Glasgow	6.6
Perth	3.8	Scotland	5.9	Dunbarton	7.4
Hawick	3.9			Irvine	8.0
Belfast	6.5			Londonderry	14.0
Craigavon	7.2	N Ireland	9.4	Newry	24.3
Ballymena	8.6			Strabane	27.2

Source: Department of Employment *Gazette,* December 1975.

third of the variation in unemployment rates between localities is explained by the unemployment of the region within which a locality is situated. In other words, two-thirds of the variation in unemployment rates between localities is explained by factors other than the regional variation in unemployment rates. Apparently, there is much more to the *geographical* variation in unemployment rates than is reflected by *regional* differences in unemployment.

Conclusion

Persistently high unemployment rates in certain regions of an economy constitute a powerful argument in favour of regional policy. Indeed, marked regional differences in the unemployment rate remain the main driving force behind regional policy in those countries, such as Britain and Canada, in which sophisticated regional policy instruments are being developed.

The economic losses resulting from high unemployment rates are obvious. The full *social* costs resulting from high unemployment rates are considerably less obvious, however, since it is impossible to quantify the personal hardship and the sense of deprivation that arises from long-term unemployment and the feeling of job insecurity.

By tracking down the causes of interregional differences in unemployment, it can be shown that the problem of regional unemployment emanates from two main sources: a deficient demand for labour in aggregate (at national level) and a deficient demand for particular types of labour. The existence of high unemployment rates in particular regions indicates either that these regions suffer more severely during periods of national recession, or that these regions suffer from basic structural problems. More commonly, the relatively depressed regions suffer from both ailments at the same time. This division of regional unemployment (into a deficient-demand component and a structural component) is valuable in so far as it isolates the underlying causes of the regional unemployment problem and should therefore be helpful in the construction of appropriate policy measures.

Selected references

Bowers (1975); Cheshire (1973); Gordon (1970); Hughes (1974); Perlman (1969), Chapter 8; Rees (1973), Chapters 6 and 7; Taylor (1974), Chapter 3; Thirlwall (1974).

6
The Case for Regional Policy: Inflation, Agglomeration and International Economic Integration

We began the previous chapter by drawing attention to the considerable economic costs that can result from persistently high unemployment in certain regions of the economy. In this chapter, we examine three further arguments in favour of having a regional policy. The first of these is a corollary of the regional unemployment problem: the existence of regional imbalance may have adverse consequences on national price stability. Regional differences in the pressure of demand are often seen to result in the simultaneous existence of an excess supply of labour in some regions and an excess demand for labour in others. It may therefore be possible to reduce inflationary pressures by diverting demand away from areas of excess demand and towards areas of excess supply.

The second argument in favour of regional policy examined in this chapter is that regional policy is required in order to counteract the excessive concentration of population in the major conurbations. Serious concern over the excessive concentration of population, particularly in Greater London, can be traced to the Barlow Report in 1940, which recommended a policy of 'decentralisation or dispersal, both of industries and industrial population, from such areas' (White Paper 1940).

Finally, this chapter turns to a more recent, and still very controversial, case for regional policy: the integration of nations into larger economic units, through the removal of trade barriers and barriers to factor mobility, may exacerbate the problems of regional imbalance. One of the problems with international economic integration is that it tends to reinforce the geographical polarisation of economic development, resulting in adverse consequences for the peripheral parts of the new economic community — unless specific policy measures are taken to prevent this from happening. The consequence of integration may therefore be to impose additional unemployment, inflation and urbanisation costs on certain member nations of the economic community, such as may be the case for Britain and other 'peripheral' economies within the EEC.

6.1 The Inflationary Consequences of Regional Imbalance

The inflationary consequences of regional imbalance are still largely an unknown factor. Yet in spite of not knowing exactly how regional differences in the pressure of demand actually affect the rate of inflation in practice, an appealing theoretical case can be made which contends that regional imbalance makes inflation worse than it otherwise would be. Regional policy may therefore offer the policymaker an additional way of fighting inflation. We begin with a brief overview of the widely accepted excess demand theory of inflation.

The excess demand theory of inflation

A vast range of theories exist which attempt to explain the inflationary process (see Trevithick and Mulvey 1975). The consensus view amongst economists, however, is that inflation is strongly influenced by the pressure of demand. As product demand rises relative to product supply, inflationary pressures will emerge and prices will rise. This proposition is the basis of the excess demand theory of inflation.

One way of modelling the process of inflation is to divide the economy into two markets: a factor market and a product market. Thus, an increase in the demand for goods is transformed into an increase in the demand for factor inputs, such as labour, and the consequence is an increase in production costs as the competition for scarce factor inputs forces up their price. Consider a hypothetical economy in which the only factor of production to have a variable price is labour. Assuming a simple mark-up relationship between the price of a product and labour costs, and assuming that labour costs will rise if there exists an excess demand for labour, we can write:

$$\dot{W} = f(X)$$
$$\dot{P} = a\dot{W}_{-l}$$

where:

$\dot{W}$ = wage inflation (i.e. the rate of change of money wages over time)

$\dot{P}$ = price inflation

X = excess demand (i.e. aggregate demand for labour minus aggregate supply of labour)

a = a given proportionate mark-up of prices on money wages

l = a time lag (determined empirically)

A problem with this simple model of inflation as it stands is that it ignores the possibility of feedback effects from prices to wages. It argues that an increase in wages emanating from an increase in the demand for labour will be transmitted to the goods market through the mark-up formula. But if workers expect prices to rise between the present wage settlement and the next one, they will aim to build this *anticipated* inflation into the negotiated wage increase. Hence, workers will want to make sure that the negotiated wage increase allows for future price increases. Wage changes are therefore likely to be determined by the expected rate of inflation as well as by the pressure of demand. The wage inflation part of the model is therefore modified as follows:

$$\dot{W} = f(X) + b\dot{P}^e$$

where:

$\dot{P}^e$ = the expected (anticipated) rate of inflation

b = a coefficient which equals unity if anticipated inflation is fully incorporated into the negotiated change in wages.

This explanation of wage inflation argues that there will be upward pressure on wages even in the absence of an excess demand for labour if future price inflation is expected to be positive. Similarly, there will be downward pressure on wages if future price inflation is expected to be negative (i.e. if prices are expected to fall). These relationships are more easily seen by plotting wage inflation against excess demand (which can be either positive or negative) for all different expected rates of inflation. Figure 6.1 shows the relationship between wage inflation and excess demand for

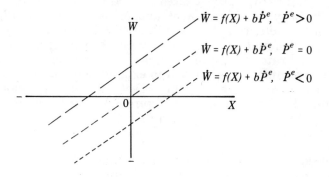

Definition of variables
$\dot{W}$ = wage inflation
X = excess demand for labour
$\dot{P}^e$ = expected rate of price inflation

Figure 6.1 *The relationship between wage inflation and the excess
demand for labour*

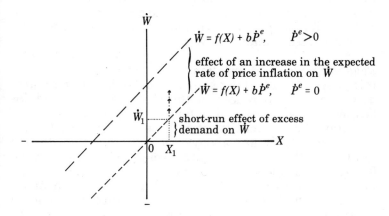

Definition of variables
$\dot{W}$ =   wage inflation
X =   excess demand for labour
$\dot{P}^e$ =   expected rate of price inflation

Figure 6.2 *The effect of an expansionary policy on wage inflation*

three different expected rates of inflation.

The way in which wages and prices interact and 'feed upon each other' is shown in figure 6.2. Suppose the level of excess demand is initially at zero ($X = 0$) and that the expected rate of inflation is zero ($\dot{P}^e = 0$). Suppose also that the government has decided to expand demand in order to reduce unemployment. The effect of the expansion in demand from zero to X_1 in figure 6.2 is to force up wage inflation from zero to $\dot{W}_1$ and this is likely to occur fairly quickly. In the absence of offsetting increases in labour productivity, this increase in production costs will subsequently cause prices to rise, which in turn leads to an increase in the *expected* rate of inflation. If the government is determined to hold the level of excess demand at X_1, this will lead to a situation of persistent inflationary pressure. The consequent rise in prices will not be ignored by workers in their subsequent wage discussions with employers. The expected price inflation will become positive and wage inflation will begin to rise above $\dot{W}_1$, a situation depicted diagrammatically (in figure 6.2) by an upward shift in the wage inflation/excess demand relationship. We thus move into a situation of a permanent — and possibly increasing — rate of inflation if the government is determined to hold the level of excess demand above zero.

Regional policy and inflation

It is possible to adapt our simple model of inflation to show how regional differences in the pressure of demand for labour can give rise to inflationary tendencies in an economy. For simplicity, it will be assumed that price expectations ($\dot{P}^e$) are always zero. In other words, the tendency of the wage-price spiral to magnify inflation will be ignored; this allows us to concentrate on a single wage inflation/excess demand relationship as shown in figure 6.3, in which $\dot{P}^e = 0$. It is also assumed that the economy represented in figure 6.3 consists of two regions, A and B, each of which has an identical wage inflation/excess demand relationship. Labour is initially assumed to be of homogeneous quality so that there is no possibility of structural unemployment emerging as a result of an *occupational* mis-matching between the demand and supply for labour. Finally, frictional unemployment (i.e. workers in the process of changing jobs) is initially assumed to be zero. These latter two assumptions will be relaxed shortly. They enable us to construct a relationship between

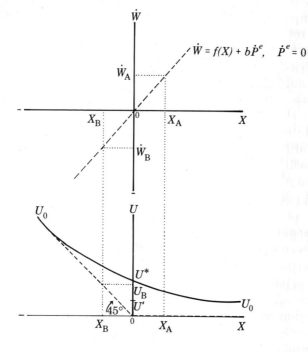

Definition of variables
$\dot{W}$ = wage inflation
$\dot{P}^e$ = expected rate of price inflation
X = excess demand for labour
U = unemployment

Note:
The position of the unemployment/excess demand relationship $(U_0 U_0)$ is determined by (i) the extent of the dispersion of excess demand between regions; (ii) the extent of the occupational mismatching between the demand and supply for labour; and (iii) the frictional unemployment arising as a consequence of workers changing their jobs. See text.

Figure 6.3 *Wage inflation, excess demand and unemployment*

unemployment and excess labour demand, as shown by the broken line in the lower part of figure 6.3. An excess demand for labour gives rise to zero unemployment whilst an excess supply of labour (e.g. X_B) gives rise to deficient-demand unemployment (i.e. U_B).

Consider a situation in which there exists an excess demand for labour in region A and an excess supply of labour in region B in our simple two-region economy.

Assuming the excess demand in region A and the excess supply in region B exactly offset each other, we see from figure 6.3 that aggregate wage inflation will be zero. The same result does not occur for unemployment, however, since the deficient demand for labour in region B gives rise to unemployment U_B whilst region A has zero unemployment. The result is a national average unemployment of *U' even though the aggregate demand for labour equals the aggregate supply*. The regional mis-matching in the demand and supply for labour creates unemployment even though excess demand is zero, and even though wage inflation is zero. The effect of the regional dispersion of demand is to shift the aggregate unemployment/excess demand function upwards so that it has a positive intercept of U'. Moreover, it is easily seen that average unemployment will rise as regional differences in excess demand increase.

In reality there are two other reasons to expect a positive rate of unemployment when aggregate demand equals aggregate supply. Firstly, the pressure of demand may vary between occupations as well as between regions giving rise to further structural unemployment when $X = 0$. Secondly, the existence of frictional unemployment has the same effect. As a result, the unemployment/excess demand function will resemble the function $U_0 U_0$ in figure 6.3. The unemployment of U^* is the sum of structural and frictional unemployment at the point where the aggregate demand for labour and the aggregate supply of labour are equal. Notice that the relationship between unemployment and excess demand is assumed to be non-linear. This results from the fact that as unemployment falls, it becomes more difficult to draw those who are still unemployed into jobs. Even at very high levels of excess demand, some frictional unemployment will persist.

The implication for the policymaker of regional differences in excess demand is clear. If the government attempts to reduce unemployment below U^* by expanding *aggregate* demand, it will generate an increase in money wages, which is subsequently likely to trigger-off a wage-price spiral. By operating regional policies designed to shift some of the demand for labour from region A to region B, however, it may be possible to reduce unemployment below U^* without generating any inflationary pressures. Policies designed to retrain labour will have a similar effect.

Unfortunately, the model developed so far is unrealistic in

an important respect. It assumes that workers will be
prepared to accept cuts in their money wages in those
regions in which there exists a deficient demand for labour.
In reality, we may find that workers are reluctant to accept
cuts in their money wage. If this is the case, the linear
relationship between wage inflation and excess demand
shown in figures 6.1 to 6.3 has to be amended to reflect the
resistance of workers to wage cuts (see figure 6.4). The

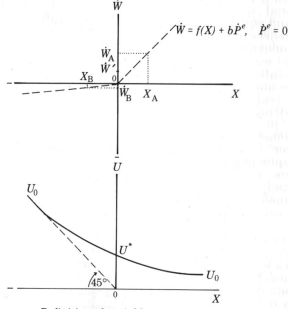

Definition of variables
$\dot{W}$ = wage inflation
$\dot{P}^e$ = expected rate of price inflation
X = excess demand for labour
U = unemployment

Figure 6.4 *Wage inflation, excess demand and unemployment
with downward wage rigidity*

resulting kink in the relationship between wage inflation
and excess demand plays an important part in the argument
that reducing regional differences in the pressure of demand
may help to reduce inflationary pressures.

Consider again the case where aggregate demand equals
aggregate supply but where there is an excess demand of X_A
in region A and a deficient demand of X_B in region B. Wage
inflation of $\dot{W}_A$ is generated in region A. (Notice that once

again we ignore the possibility of a wage-price spiral.) The resistance to wage cuts in region B, however, means that the negative wage inflation of $\dot{W}_B$ is very small and could even be zero if there is total resistance. The result is a positive national wage inflation of $\dot{W}'$ even though aggregate demand equals aggregate supply. In other words, regional differences in the pressure of demand not only give rise to unemployment when aggregate excess demand is zero, the rate of wage inflation is also positive ($\dot{W}'$ in figure 6.4); the wage inflation/excess demand function shifts upwards, just as the unemployment/excess demand function does, when some regions experience excess demand whilst others are experiencing excess supply. (More generally, this upward shift in the aggregate wage inflation/excess demand relationship will occur whenever the slope of the function is steeper for low-unemployment regions than for high-unemployment regions. See Archibald 1969.)

This analysis suggests that raising the pressure of demand in high-unemployment regions and reducing it in low-unemployment regions will have a beneficial effect on the inflation/unemployment trade-off facing the policymaker. Such a policy will allow the policymaker either to reduce inflation without increasing unemployment, or to reduce unemployment without increasing inflation, or to reduce both unemployment and inflation at the same time.

A major drawback of expanding the demand for labour in regions of high unemployment, however, is that there are likely to be substantial leakages of expenditure into regions where there already exists an excess demand for labour. Since these leakages will exert inflationary pressures in the low-unemployment regions, it will be necessary to reduce the demand for labour in the low-unemployment regions at the same time as demand is expanded in the high-unemployment regions. The reduction in the demand for labour in the regions of low unemployment will have to be sufficient to exactly offset the inflationary effects of expenditure leakages flowing into these regions. Attempts at such 'fine tuning' of fiscal policies would pose immense problems for the policymaker.

The foregoing explanation of the inflationary process has a further weakness. An examination of the rate of wage inflation in different regions of an economy quickly reveals that regardless of the unemployment rate, wage inflation tends to be very similar across all regions. A typical example

Table 6.1 *Wage inflation and unemployment rates in the UK regions, 1971-73*

Region	$\dot{W}$ (1971-72)	U (1971)	$\dot{W}$ (1972-73)	U (1972)
	1971-72		1972-73	
SE	13.3	2.0	13.5	2.1
E Anglia	20.0	3.1	11.6	3.2
SW	13.8	3.4	15.2	3.3
W Midlands	14.3	2.9	10.3	3.0
E Midlands	15.0	2.9	13.7	2.9
Yorks and Humberside	13.8	3.8	16.2	3.9
NW	15.0	3.9	13.4	3.9
N	12.8	5.7	12.4	5.8
Wales	13.1	4.7	13.6	4.5
Scotland	15.4	5.8	13.0	5.9
N Ireland	12.8	7.8	12.6	8.0
UK	14.1	3.4	13.2	3.5

Source: British Labour Statistics Yearbook 1973.
Note:
$\dot{W}$ = rate of change of average hourly earnings
U = percent unemployed

of this phenomenon is given in table 6.1, which shows the rates of wage inflation and unemployment in each standard region of the UK during a period of rapid wage inflation (1971-73). Wage inflation is seen to be high in all regions regardless of the unemployment rate in each region. Indeed, regional rates of wage inflation are unrelated to regional unemployment rates, which is not surprising since inflation is essentially a *national* phenomenon. The assumption that the rate of wage inflation is set within each region independently of events in other regions is totally unrealistic and must be discarded. Furthermore, empirical tests have so far been unable to detect a firm relationship between wage inflation and the regional dispersion of unemployment rates (Archibald *et al.* 1974), which implies that reducing regional differences in excess demand will not help to reduce inflationary pressures in the economy at large. But this conclusion may be unnecessarily pessimistic as we shall see.

There are, of course, a number of very plausible reasons why wage inflation tends to be similar in different regions even though the pressure of demand may be quite dissimilar between regions. First, regional economies are open. They trade extensively with other regions within the same national economy and will therefore be importing a large part of their price inflation from elsewhere. Since we have argued that workers will take careful note of any expected price inflation in their wage negotiations, it is likely that the price of traded goods will be an important element in transmitting expectations about price inflation from one region to another. A wage increase occurring in a region of labour scarcity will therefore be transmitted to regions of high unemployment if the wage increase in the labour-scarce region causes the price of imports into the labour-abundant region to rise.

Secondly, the process of centralised collective bargaining gives rise to wage increases in all regions simultaneously. The setting of wage rates for individual industries at national level through collective agreements between national employers federations and national trades unions means that wage bargains struck at national level are automatically implemented in all regions at the same time — regardless of local demand and supply conditions. Nationally negotiated wage rates are not necessarily adhered to at local level, however, in so far as employers in labour-scarce regions may have to pay 'over the odds' in order to acquire the workers they need. The fact that labour is scarce in at least some regions of the economy may therefore be enough to generate inflationary pressures which lead to the upward adjustment of wage rates in *all* regions through the national bargaining framework. If this argument is correct, it means that wage inflation is being transmitted from labour-scarce regions to labour-abundant regions through the medium of national wage bargaining. Cost-push theorists, of course, would deny that excess demand has any effect on nationally negotiated wage rates, in which case regional policy would be irrelevant in the control of inflation — unless the cost-push elements were regionally concentrated.

A third explanation of the regional transmission of wage inflation arises from the tendency of wage differentials to become ossified. If workers in labour-scarce regions gain a wage rise, workers with similar skills in labour-abundant regions will seek to re-establish parity with their fellow workers in the labour-scarce regions. Perhaps this phenomenon is seen most clearly within the operations of a single firm which has plants in a number of regions. A labour shortage at one of the plants will put upward pressure on wages not only at the plant that is short of labour but also at the other plants since workers within the organisation are often keen to maintain traditional differentials (or perhaps even to remove differentials completely). Inflation may therefore begin in a relatively small number of labour markets — inflation leaders — and may then be transmitted through the complex set of institutional linkages which tie labour markets together (MacKay and Hart 1975).

Finally, the interregional transmission of wage inflation may simply arise from the fear by employers that they will lose their skilled workers to their competitors in other (labour-scarce) regions unless they raise their wage rates in unison.

Whatever the mechanism by which inflation is transmitted from one region to another, the implications are the same. The *indirect* consequence on national wage inflation of a wage increase for a relatively small group of workers may be considerably more substantial than the *direct* consequence. In figure 6.4, for example, the direct consequence of excess demand in region A is to generate wage inflation of $\dot{W}_A$. If this is then transmitted to region B the national rate of wage inflation is no longer $\dot{W}'$, but becomes $\dot{W}_A$ itself. This being so, reducing inflationary pressures in labour-scarce regions could be of considerable help in the control of inflation. Unfortunately, there is no easy way to test the validity of this theory. And even if the theory is sound, we have still to face the problem that a policy of reducing demand in labour-scarce regions relative to labour-abundant regions would be exceedingly difficult to implement, as we shall see in Part 2 of this book.

6.2 The Urban Consequences of Regional Imbalance

It is often suggested that one of the unfortunate consequences of regional imbalance is the excessive concentration of residential, industrial and commercial activity in the major urban complexes. This concentration of economic activity is said to be excessive in that it results in an unnecessary increase in social costs in the form of congestion, pollution, noise and other urban problems. The removal of urban problems would therefore seem to require a serious attempt to plan the geographical distribution of the nation's population and industry. A case can therefore be made for regional policy on the grounds that serious social costs can be avoided by preventing the major cities from growing either too large or too quickly. The fundamental elements of the urbanisation case for regional policy can be illustrated by considering the example of traffic congestion.

The urbanisation case for regional policy rests on the existence of negative externalities (or external costs) as urban areas expand. Welfare theory adopts a twofold definition of an externality. Firstly, for an externality to exist there must be *interdependence*. Four distinct types of interdependence can exist. There may be interdependence between the utility functions of individuals such that the utility which one individual obtains from the consumption of a commodity is influenced by the consumption of commodities by other individuals. Road congestion is a particularly vivid example of this kind of externality, where the consumption of the road transport service by one road user causes disutility to other road users who suffer traffic congestion. Urban residents also suffer disutility from road users in the form of noise, vibration, air pollution and visual intrusion. Similarly, interdependence also occurs between the production functions of firms. An example of these producer-producer externalities is water or air pollution by one firm which adversely affects the production costs of other firms. Finally there may be producer-consumer externalities resulting, for example, from industrial pollution; or consumer-producer externalities such as the effects of road congestion by private motorists on commercial hauliers.

Secondly, the interdependence between the utility functions of consumers and the production functions of producers is only a necessary, not a sufficient, condition for the existence of an externality. For an externality to occur, not only must there be interdependence, the externality must also be *unpriced*. If firms compensate those suffering from any externalities, or if they are 'bribed' by the sufferers to stop the nuisance, the interdependence is internalised and the externality ceases to exist by definition.

The existence of externalities leads to a mis-allocation of resources and is a cost to society which can only be avoided by some kind of government intervention. Consider the following illustration. Motorists using urban roads face two distinct types of direct cost: their vehicle operating costs and the costs of their time spent in travelling. Suppose that a particular stretch of urban road can absorb up to 1,000 vehicles an hour without there being any congestion. Let us also assume that the basic time and vehicle operating costs of using this uncongested stretch of road is £1 per vehicle. When more than 1,000 vehicles an hour use this road, however, congestion begins to occur, the effect of which is to increase the cost per vehicle as both operating costs and time costs rise.

Suppose that the traffic flow increases by 100 vehicles an hour and that as a consequence the *total* costs increase from £1,000 (£1 per vehicle x 1,000 vehicles) to £1,210 (see figure 6.5). This marginal increment to the traffic flow has raised

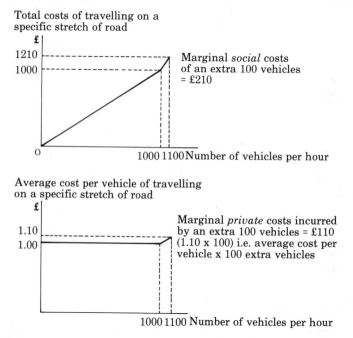

Figure 6.5 *The difference between marginal social costs (MSC) and marginal private costs (MPC) : an illustration*

total cost by £210 and this represents the extra (or marginal) *social* costs of the extra 100 vehicles. Notice that the marginal social cost *per vehicle* has now risen to £2.10 from its original level of £1. But whilst the marginal social cost per vehicle has risen to £2.10, this is not the cost that the additional 100 motorists are forced to pay. The resulting congestion falls on all vehicles equally and all 1,100 vehicles pay an *average* cost of £1.10 (£1,210 ÷ 1,100). There is a distinct external diseconomy here, for the extra 100 vehicles meet only £110 of the extra £210 of social costs which they impose. The remainder is borne by the other 1,000 road users in the form of lower speeds and higher operating costs. This illustration leads us directly to the crucial difference between *marginal social costs* and *marginal private costs* (Walters 1961). In this simple illustration, the marginal social cost of the extra 100 vehicles is £210 whereas the marginal private cost is only £110.

The more general case of the difference between the social and private costs of road congestion is shown in figure 6.6.

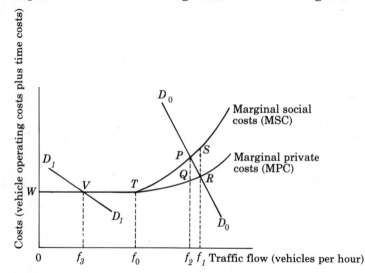

Figure 6.6 *A negative urban externality : road congestion*

The marginal private cost function (MPC) shows additions to private costs borne by motorists as the traffic flow increases, and includes time costs as well as vehicle operating expenses. It can be seen that up to a vehicle flow of f_0, marginal private costs remain constant at OW and there is no congestion. Only at traffic flows beyond f_0 do we reach the point where additional vehicles begin to impede each other, and marginal private costs begin to rise. Not only do private costs begin to rise, but each addition to the traffic flow imposes social costs on other motorists over and above the marginal private costs. There is a clear negative externality beyond f_0. Hence, at a flow of f_1 the marginal motorist faces private costs of $f_1 R$, but by his presence on the road he in fact imposes additional costs of SR on other motorists.

That externalities such as road congestion cause a misallocation of resources can be easily demonstrated. Given a typical demand schedule for road users (e.g. $D_0 D_0$ in figure 6.6), the demand for road space rises as the costs of motoring fall. The demand schedule reflects what individual motorists are willing to pay to use the road. Clearly, the flow along this road will stabilise at f_1 for at this point the private cost (to the marginal motorist) is $f_1 R$ and this just equals what he is willing to pay to use the road. Beyond f_1 the private cost exceeds the private benefit of extra trips. Unfortunately, a flow of f_1 represents an over-allocation of vehicles to the road. At f_1 the social cost of the marginal trip is $f_1 S$ and exceeds the benefit obtained from it (as shown by the demand schedule). This over-use of the road results from the existence of an externality. Additional motorists impose costs on society as shown by the marginal social cost function but in fact only pay marginal private costs. From the point of view of society, a flow of f_2 would be more desirable, for at f_2 the benefit from the marginal trip just equals its social cost of $f_2 P$.

There is an obvious case for government intervention in some form to reduce the traffic flow from f_1 to f_2. Notice that this does not imply the complete elimination of road congestion, which would require a reduction of the flow from f_1 to f_0. It is worthwhile for society to put up with the externality generated between f_0 and f_2. In addition, where demand fluctuates, as with road use, between peak and off-peak periods of the day, government intervention may only be justified at peak periods. In the case of figure 6.6, an off-peak demand of $D_1 D_1$ results in a flow of f_3 and no externality is generated.

Many urban externalities appear to exhibit social cost functions of the form shown in figure 6.6. Typically there is some threshold below which no externality occurs. In this case, the threshold is at flow f_0 and arises from the physical capacity of the road. In the case of externalities, such as air and water pollution, a certain limited amount of waste disposal has no externality effect because of the ability of natural air and water systems to cleanse themselves. Beyond these thresholds, however, externalities often exhibit a rapid, non-linear increase (Pearce 1976).

Superficially, the view that regional policy is justified as a means of preventing urban development from over-running itself in the rapidly growing regions is an attractive one. No one would deny that economic development is primarily an urban phenomenon. Nor can it be denied that urban growth brings with it substantial external diseconomies for both firms and households. The example of road congestion in figure 6.6 is a very obvious one, as are the various environmental costs of urban growth. In addition, it is possible, though not likely, that rapid urban growth may pose problems in the use of urban social infrastructure and the provision of urban public services. Where urban growth and in-migration is particularly intense there may be problems of short-run over-utilisation of urban social infrastructure and public services (with under-utilisation in the urban areas of depressed regions). Over longer run periods the provision of public services can respond to the excess demand, but excessive urban growth can still pose economic costs if there are diseconomies of scale in the provision of public services. The empirical evidence on economies of scale in the provision of urban public services has not provided a conclusive answer to this question (Alonso 1971).

Unfortunately, a closer examination of the urbanisation case for regional policy reveals many flaws. An obvious one is that no mention has so far been made of positive as distinct from negative externalities. It is not a coincidence that urbanisation and economic development go hand-in-hand (Pred 1966). The external benefits arising from the existence of urban industrial complexes can be classified into localisation economies and agglomeration economies (see Chapter 2). Briefly, localisation economies are the result of firms within the same industry locating in the same geographical area, whereas agglomeration economies are more general. Localisation economies therefore accrue from factors such as the emergence of specialist subsidiary activities within an industry. Agglomeration economies are more general in the sense that they result from the geographical concentration of many different types of activity, such as access to large and well-organised labour markets, access to specialist commercial facilities and access to common transport requirements. Private households too may enjoy substantial benefits from urban life, with its wider range of job choice and its many social and recreational benefits.

Urban development can only be said to be excessive if there exists some 'optimum' city size beyond which increments to the size of the city generate social costs in excess of social benefits. Since it is impossible to quantify most of these costs and benefits, it is also impossible to show that the existing polarised nature of regional development is excessive. Indeed, the whole concept of an optimum city size remains vague and imprecise. Whether a city is greater or smaller than its optimum size depends not only upon the social costs and benefits generated within the city, but also on the position and role of the city in the whole urban hierarchy. The system of urban centres must be looked at as a whole and what may be an optimum size for a city at one level of the hierarchy need not be optimum at some other level (Richardson 1973).

There are other flaws in the urbanisation case for regional policy. Whilst regional development and urbanisation go hand in hand, this does not necessarily mean that the rapid growth of a region will lead to an excessive expansion of its largest cities. The growth of the region may be channelled into the smaller, medium-sized urban centres, thereby avoiding many of the costs of urban growth whilst simultaneously reaping the benefits of close proximity to a large conurbation.

This is admirably demonstrated by the pattern of employment and population growth in South East England. Figure 6.7 shows that between 1961 and 1971 the fastest rates of population increase occurred in areas of the South East away from the large urban centres. Indeed, many of the central areas of Greater London and other cities such as Portsmouth have experienced *absolute* reductions in population. Much of the responsibility for this rests on the enormous net migration flows away from the London conurbation. These are shown in figure 6.8 for the period 1966-1971. The small and medium-sized towns of the South East have been recipients of migrants both from Greater London and from the other regions of Britain even though the South East as a whole was a net loser of migrants to the rest of Great Britain over this period.

A similar picture emerges when employment changes between 1966 and 1971 are considered. Employment is increasingly concentrated in urban centres away from Greater London as figure 6.9 shows. This is borne out by

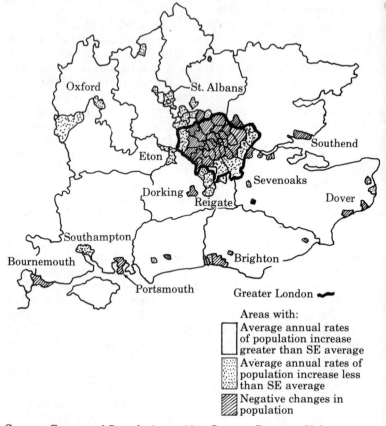

Source: Census of Population, 1971, County Reports, Volume 1,
     Table 2.

Figure 6.7 *Population changes in South East England, 1961-71*

table 6.2 which shows the sub-regional movement of
manufacturing firms within the South East between 1966
and 1971. The metropolitan area has not only lost large
numbers of manufacturing firms to other regions (partly as
the result of regional policy), but has also consistently shed
firms to the peripheral less-urbanised areas of the region and
to East Anglia.

This tendency of population and employment to migrate
out of the large urban centres is a long-term phenomenon
and is partly the automatic response of households and
firms to the disadvantages of central city locations. In the

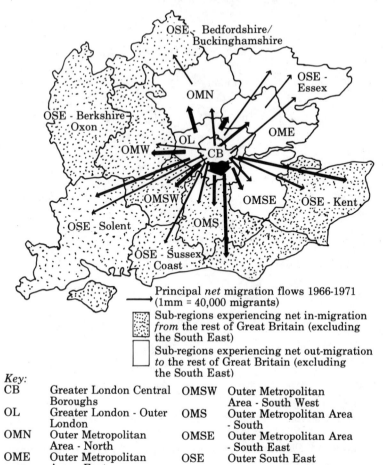

Principal *net* migration flows 1966-1971
(1mm = 40,000 migrants)

Sub-regions experiencing net in-migration
from the rest of Great Britain (excluding
the South East)

Sub-regions experiencing net out-migration
to the rest of Great Britain (excluding
the South East)

Key:

CB	Greater London Central Boroughs	OMSW	Outer Metropolitan Area - South West
OL	Greater London - Outer London	OMS	Outer Metropolitan Area - South
OMN	Outer Metropolitan Area - North	OMSE	Outer Metropolitan Area - South East
OME	Outer Metropolitan Area - East	OSE	Outer South East
OMW	Outer Metropolitan Area - West		

Source: Census of Population, 1971, Regional Report, South East
    Region, Tables 1B and 2B.

Figure 6.8 *Net migration in the South East, 1966-71*

case of the South East, this automatic process of structural
change has been deliberately enhanced by a policy of
planned decentralisation. Urban externalities are not just a
simple function of population density, however, and the
growth of long-distance commuting back into city centres
has posed severe problems. Yet there seems little reason to
think that the South East is physically unable to handle a

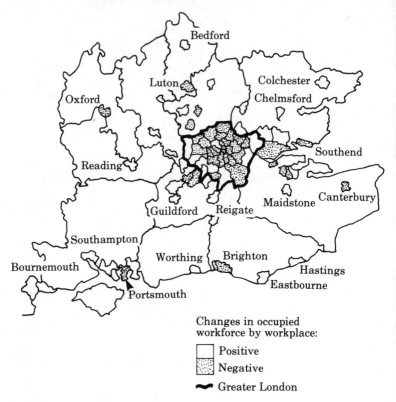

Changes in occupied
workforce by workplace:

☐ Positive
▨ Negative
〜 Greater London

*Source: Census of Population 1966 and 1971, Economic Activity
Tables, County Leaflets.*

Figure 6.9 *Changes in occupied workforce by area of workplace,
1966-71*

rapid expansion of economic activity without incurring
excessive urbanisation costs.

One further flaw in the urbanisation case for regional
policy should be mentioned. Even if regional imbalance
does lead to excessive urban growth, this does not
necessarily imply that an active regional policy is the best
response. There are other, perhaps more desirable policy
options for dealing with urban problems. As we have seen,
sub-regional planning offers one possibility. More efficient
pricing policies for urban public services and for the use of
urban infrastructure offers an alternative approach.
Congestion taxes on private vehicles fall into this category.

Table 6.2 *The movement of SE manufacturing establishments,*
1966-71

Sub-region	Gross movement within the sub-region	Net movement to E Anglia	Net movement to rest of SE	Net movement to other UK regions
Movement from:				
Greater London	124	+ 87	+ 221	+ 226
Outer Metropolitan	134	+ 23	– 60	+ 138
Outer SE:				
Essex	7	+ 1	– 28	+ 3
Kent	14	+ 1	– 42	+ 3
Sussex Coast	28	0	– 28	+ 5
Solent	54	+ 1	– 47	+ 15

Bedford ⎫
  Bucks ⎬
  Berks ⎪
  Oxfordshire ⎭
	11	+ 4	– 16	+ 4

Source: Unpublished Department of Industry data kindly made
available to us by Ross MacKay and John Rhodes. Brian
Ashcroft assembled the interregional flow data.

6.3 International Economic Integration and Regional Problems

The recent expansion of the European Economic
Community has raised the question of the effect of
international economic integration on the performance of
individual regions within member nations. Formal
membership of an economic community is not, of course, a
necessary condition for international economic integration.
Even countries which have resisted formal entry into the
European Economic Community, such as Norway and
Sweden, face a gradual process of *de facto* integration as the
result of improved methods of transportation and
liberalisation of international trade.

The term 'economic integration' covers a wide range of
practical possibilities. At one end of the spectrum are free
trade areas in which coordination is confined to ensuring
that trade is free from tariffs and controls. At the other end of
the spectrum is full economic and monetary union where
member nations form a fully integrated economy with a
single currency area and a common macroeconomic policy.
The European Economic Community lies between these two

extremes in that there exists free internal trade together with a common external tariff, free internal factor mobility, and a series of embryonic common policies such as agricultural policy, transport policy, social policy and a common regional policy. Economic and monetary union remains a longer term aim of the EEC with political union an even more distant possibility.

The effects of progressive international integration on regional problems are varied and profound. Some are detrimental, in the sense of leading to greater regional imbalance, whilst other effects may work in the opposite direction. It does seem, however, that in the absence of remedial policies the *net* effects are likely to be detrimental to the peripheral regions of an economic community. Moreover, as integration proceeds towards full economic and monetary union, these detrimental effects are likely to intensify. Integration therefore provides a supplementary case either for strengthening the individual regional policies of member states, or for creating a common regional policy for the whole community — but only if it is accepted that regional imbalance itself justifies a regional policy.

There are two main consequences of international economic integration for the depressed regions of member states. Firstly, progressive economic integration is likely to lead not only to a worsening of existing regional problems, but also to new types of regional problems. Secondly, integration will, paradoxically, reduce the effectiveness of certain types of regional policies operated by individual member states whilst simultaneously offering greater potential for improving the overall effectiveness of regional policies in member states. This potential for improvement arises where member states take the opportunity to orchestrate and coordinate their attack on regional problems.

Integration will have profound long-term effects on the geographical location of industry both within and between member states. Indeed, the whole rationale of economic integration implies a substantial degree of geographical relocation of industry. If the hoped-for benefits of integration are to be achieved, immense structural changes will have to occur. Apart from the effects of trade creation as tariff and other barriers are removed, there will be substantial diversion of trade amongst member states. The potential for longer-term exploitation of economies of scale and increased competition can also only be realised if there is a willingness to accept, and indeed encourage, changing geographical patterns of production.

Clearly, this process of structural change may have adverse effects on individual regions, but it is impossible to predict accurately which regions and which industries will be most severely affected. It has been argued that peripheral regions which rely heavily on small scale production units may be simply unable to reap the scale advantages of integration or face the competition posed by the large multinational producers (Holland 1976). All we can say for certain, however, is that structural changes are very likely to occur, and that the greater the degree of integration the more substantial the structural changes will be. Over time, member nations can expect to face changes in the industrial and geographical patterns of production; hence the development of policies within the European Economic Community to coordinate and smooth out the painful, but necessary, periods of adjustment. The rationalisation of the coal and steel industries under the auspices of the European Coal and Steel Community is an example of the way this can be done. But the changes are rarely so well monitored and controlled.

This process of long-run structural change carries with it two implications for regional policy. First, the regional strategies of individual member nations, such as Britain, must change. Regional policies must be flexible enough to meet unforseen regional problems — perhaps in regions not formerly regarded as in need of government assistance. Secondly, there is a case for a common regional strategy operated by the economic community as a whole, and which would be complementary to the individual regional policies of member nations. A common regional policy is, indeed, being developed within the European Economic Community. Its main role is to alleviate specific regional problems arising from structural changes that result from economic integration.

Perhaps the most obvious and distinct structural problem which will arise as economic integration proceeds is that concerned with border regions. The EEC defines two distinct types of border region — external and internal. External border regions, such as the Zonenrandgebiet along the West German/East German border, face the most severe problems of adjustment since they have close economic links with non-member states. The effect of integration is to impose a wall of tariff and other barriers with the result that the border regions are faced with the need to re-orientate their trade towards other member states. Internal border regions lie along the borders of member states of the community. In this case, the effects are likely to be more beneficial. Existing barriers to trade and factor mobility are reduced as economic integration occurs. The role for regional policy is not to protect and cushion these regions, but rather to encourage the internal border regions to exploit the opportunities offered by integration (Hansen 1977).

Little has yet been said which indicates that *existing* regional problems are likely to deteriorate as a direct consequence of international economic integration. Unfortunately, there is reason to believe that economic integration will lead to a widening of existing regional disparities. In Western Europe, for example, there is a heavy concentration of industrial growth in the belt stretching from the English Midlands down through the heart of the European Economic Community to Northern Italy (Lambooy 1973). As the EEC moves towards full economic and monetary union these agglomerative tendencies will probably be strengthened. Both demand and supply forces exert a stronger 'pull' on the location decisions of firms towards the central areas of Western Europe. On the demand side, there are the advantages of central locations in serving the entire Western European market (Clark *et al.* 1969). In addition, there may be substantial attractions for firms from the supply side of the market. As we suggested in our discussion of regional growth in Chapter 2, the geographical concentration of industry may be a cumulative process because of the existence of external and internal economies and because of possible 'perverse' effects of labour and capital migration. The reduction of barriers to trade and to capital mobility will encourage firms to respond to the 'pull' of central locations. Similarly, the deliberate reduction of barriers to labour mobility may encourage the community workforce to follow suit.

There are other reasons why economic integration may aggravate existing regional imbalance. Consider the case of a member nation which has several regions in which labour productivity is relatively low compared to the community as a whole. Britain is a typical example. Britain's low productivity regions can compete with the high productivity regions of Western Europe, however, through the medium of the exchange rate. If factor prices become too high in Britain, a downward adjustment of the national exchange rate will restore competitiveness to her exports, which consequently provides the depressed regions of Britain with a measure of protection. The effect of reducing domestic prices relative to world prices is, of course, equivalent to reducing the real wage. If full economic and monetary union is achieved, however, the existence of a single currency will destroy the protection afforded by flexible national exchange rates. With a single community currency (or at least 'locked' exchange rates) in existence, low productivity regions can only improve their competitive position by accepting lower *money* wages, or by forgoing wage increases when workers in high productivity regions obtain a wage increase. The onus of adjustment is therefore thrown upon factor price flexibility within individual economies. Unfortunately, there is likely to be a secular tendency towards greater equality of factor prices within an economic community. This is likely to occur with labour costs since common collective bargaining or some other wage transmission process will tend to equalise money wages across the community. In such circumstances, low-productivity regions will suffer the harsh consequences of their inferior competitive position (McCrone 1969).

These gloomy predictions are not without their critics and the contrary view ought to be aired. We have implicitly assumed that the depressed peripheral regions are the low-productivity regions, and reality is not as simple as this. We have also implicitly accepted a polarisation theory of regional growth. It is possible, however, that the relaxation of barriers to capital mobility may encourage the movement of industry to the peripheral regions. More importantly, however, it can be argued that common markets exist as a means of enhancing the growth of member nations through the exploitation of economies of scale and through the lower trade barriers which help to stimulate greater efficiency in domestic industries. All regions, depressed and prosperous alike, benefit from the faster rate of national growth. But whether the advantages for depressed regions will offset the disadvantages is an open question. If it is accepted that integration will worsen any existing regional problems, there is a strong case for constructing a regional policy.

Economic integration also has important implications for

the regional policies adopted by individual member nations, since the existing regional policies of member nations may become less effective in some cases and more effective in others. In the European Economic Community, member nations each have their own regional policies, which are mainly designed to redistribute capital internally from prosperous to depressed regions. In addition, member nations which are particularly depressed, such as Eire, have deliberately used cash grants and tax relief inducements to attract mobile international investment.

Economic integration tends to reduce the effectiveness of these regional policies in several distinct ways. One of the purposes of economic integration is to encourage the free movement of capital within the whole economic community, and any attempt by an individual member to use policy instruments, such as restrictions on the location of industry in prosperous regions, may drive firms not to depressed regions within the same nation but to other nations within the community. Firms prevented from expanding in South East England, for example, now have the option of locating elsewhere in the European Economic Community. The depressed regions of Britain may therefore face more competition for mobile investment than before the UK became a member of the EEC.

It is not only the use of the 'stick' instruments of regional policy (such as controls on industrial location) which suffer a loss of effectiveness as economic integration proceeds. The financial aids which make up the 'carrot' side of regional policy also suffer. In the EEC, for example, member states have deliberately used regional financial inducements to 'competitively bid' for mobile foreign investment. The response of the EEC to these problems has been to impose restrictions on the use of regional inducements for this purpose (Commission 1975b).

Finally, the effectiveness of certain types of regional inducements may have to be deliberately curtailed in an economic community. Many of the benefits of economic integration materialise only when free and unhindered trade is allowed to occur. Because of this, regional policy instruments tend to operate *against* integration either by giving the companies receiving them a competitive advantage, or by impeding the free movement of capital. The result is that certain types of regional policies, such as continuing labour subsidies, may have to be kept under strict control if the hoped-for benefits of integration are to be attained. Once again we see that the effectiveness of regional policies in individual member states is reduced.

Since economic integration may have undesirable effects on the depressed regions of at least some of the member nations and on the effectiveness of their own individual regional policies, the implications are clear. There must be a common regional policy for the community as a whole to tackle the problems caused by progressive integration. In addition, coordinated action is required by all nations within the community in the construction of regional policies. A community-wide regional policy must be developed rather than rely on a set of separate, possibly conflicting, regional policies. (See Armstrong 1978).

Conclusion

Of the many economic arguments that have been used to justify the existence of regional policies, the strongest are those of equity and regional unemployment. Few would deny that unemployment causes severe costs to society and efforts must be made to deal effectively with the regional unemployment problem. The principle of equity also provides a powerful argument for government intervention in the regional arena.

The other economic arguments for regional policy are less convincing. First, too little is known about the process of inflation for us to be able to say with any confidence that regional policy can help to reduce inflationary pressures to any significant extent. More empirical work is needed, particularly on the mechanism by which wage inflation is transmitted from one region to another, before we can hope to assess the potential role of regional policy as a means of fighting inflation. Secondly, the argument that regional policy is needed to avert the problems caused by excessive urban growth is not entirely convincing. It would certainly be wishful thinking to imagine that regional policies are capable in themselves of removing the problems caused by the expansion of the major cities.

Finally, it seems very likely that international economic integration (whether through the creation of economic communities or through greater specialisation and trade between all nations) will tend to increase regional disparities unless appropriate regional policies are constructed.

The policy instruments available to tackle these regional problems form the subject matter of the next section of this book.

Selected references

Archibald, Kemmis and Perkins (1974); Cameron (1974); Commission of the European Communities (1973a); McCrone (1969); MacKay and Hart (1975); Pearce (1976); Richardson (1973); Thirlwall (1969b).

PART 2

Regional Policy Options

*The purpose of regional policy is to achieve specified
objectives. To assume that regional policy is desirable* per
se *is simply not enough. We need to know why
regional policy is desirable and how the economy will
benefit from it. In the previous chapter we argued that
regional disparities cause problems. They cause problems
in the sense that they prevent the attainment of national
policy objectives — such as full employment, stable
prices, balance of payments equilibrium and the optimum
allocation of resources. Regional policy is thus needed in
order to facilitate the achievement of national policy
objectives. In this sense, we can regard regional policy as
an important component of a broader and more
comprehensive economic policy embracing the whole
economy.*

*Regional policy is just like any other economic policy
in one important respect: the policymaker has to face up
to the existence of trade-offs. Any single policy
instrument may affect the achievement of several
objectives at the same time — not necessarily in the
desired direction. The application of any single policy
instrument will usually have 'bad' effects as well as
'good' effects. Two regional examples may help to clarify
this important point.*

*First, regional policies which induce industry to move
from prosperous, fast-growing regions to depressed, slow-
growing regions may bring in new jobs for the
unemployed as well as reducing inflationary pressures.
But at the same time, costs of production may be
temporarily higher at the new location during the first
few years of production due to the high set-up costs for
the incoming firms. New labour may have to be trained
and it takes time before workers become familiar with
new jobs in new surroundings. The necessary linkages
with suppliers of raw materials and other factor inputs*

147

will have to be developed, and firms will expect to operate at relatively low levels of efficiency during the early years of production at a new location.

A second possible consequence of regional policy is a slower rate of capital accumulation due to the imposition of controls on the location of industry in the rapidly expanding regions. Firms refused permission to expand their existing factories or offices in Greater London, Birmingham, Bristol or Southampton, for instance, may decide not to expand at all. They may decide that an expansion of their capacity in one of the assisted areas may harm the efficiency of the firm so much that expansion is just not worthwhile. There is no guarantee that regional policy will not indeed have such 'bad' effects. Trade-offs are just as much a part of regional policy formulation as other areas of economic policy.

In the next three chapters, we aim to do three things. Chapter 7 discusses the problem of delimiting regions for policy purposes in some detail in order to reveal the complex nature of regional problems, and to show that the task of defining regional problems is not as simple as it may appear to be at first sight. We devote special attention to the effort made by the EEC to improve the process of defining regions for policy purposes. Chapters 8 and 9 divide regional policy instruments into two broad and rather cumbersome classes: macro-policy and micro-policy options. In spite of the overlap between these two broad types of policy option, it is analytically convenient to split the options up in this way. The macro-options encompass fiscal and monetary instruments whereas the micro-options encompass a wide range of individual subsidies, taxes and controls which have been devised for the purpose of inducing a reallocation of factors of production. The distinction is crude but useful.

7
The Delimitation of Policy Regions

Immense confusion still surrounds the use of the term
'region'. The delineation, or mapping-out, of areas to be
assisted by regional policies remains an arbitrary
procedure, more often the outcome of intense political
bargaining than of logical endeavour. The resulting map of
policy regions is inevitably the subject of fierce controversy
on the part of localities finding themselves on the 'wrong'
side of the boundary. Not surprisingly this often leads, as in
Britain, to the policy regions tending to expand until they
threaten to engulf the whole country.

In Chapter 1 it was argued that an ideal delimitation of
policy regions would require a set of precise, quantified
objectives for regional policy. This theme is explored a little
further in this chapter, which also looks at some recent
progress in the delimitation of policy regions in Europe.

7.1 Assisted Areas as the Outcome of Classification

The delimitation of assisted areas is simply a process of
classification (Tietz 1962). Localities are classified into two
sets or groups : assisted areas and non-assisted areas. There
is no unique way of carrying out this classification. Indeed,
there are as many distinct ways of dividing a geographical
area (such as a nation) into regions as there are reasons for
doing it. Which localities are chosen to be assisted and which
are not, obviously depends on the policy objectives.

Consider a simple example. Suppose we decided to delimit
areas for assistance solely on the basis of relative unemployment rates. In part (a) of figure 7.1, for example, each of

149

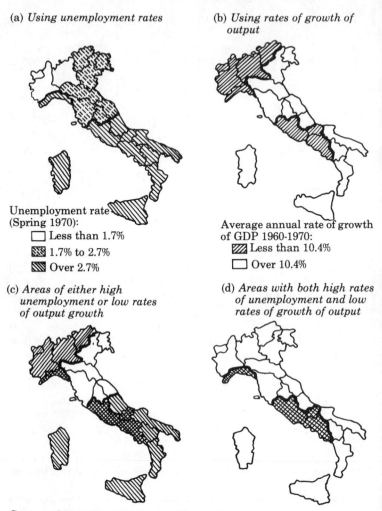

(a) *Using unemployment rates*

(b) *Using rates of growth of output*

Unemployment rate (Spring 1970):
☐ Less than 1.7%
▨ 1.7% to 2.7%
▧ Over 2.7%

Average annual rate of growth of GDP 1960-1970:
▧ Less than 10.4%
☐ Over 10.4%

(c) *Areas of either high unemployment or low rates of output growth*

(d) *Areas with both high rates of unemployment and low rates of growth of output*

Source: Office Statistique des Communautes Européenes (1972), Tables I-5, II-2.

Figure 7.1 *The delimitation of policy regions : an example*

Italy's 20 administrative areas is classified into one of three homogeneous regions on the basis of a simple differentiating characteristic, namely the percentage of the workforce unemployed. Administrative areas with an unemployment rate greater than some critical threshold value, in this case the 1970 Italian average rate of 2.7%, are grouped into one region. Those with an unemployment rate between 1.7 % and 2.7 % are grouped into a second region, and those with an unemployment rate less than 1.7 % comprise the third. This may seem, at first sight, an eminently suitable way of mapping out areas eligible to receive assistance from regional policies. Indeed, an almost identical procedure, differing only in the magnitude of the 'threshold' unemployment rate, was used to designate assisted areas in Britain from 1960 to 1966. It was argued in Chapter 1, however, that the unemployment rate may be quite a poor measure of economic welfare, and should therefore be supplemented by other measures such as per capita income, out-migration rates and activity rates. In other words, the choice of *which* differentiating characteristics to use is constrained by the need for them to adequately reflect the objectives of regional policy.

Knowledge of objectives is not only needed for the selection of differentiating characteristics. The objectives should ideally have quantified targets attached to them, otherwise the selection of the critical threshold values becomes impossible. Consider part (a) of figure 7.1 again. Here the threshold value is 2.7%. If 1.7% were chosen instead, then another seven administrative areas join the original ten as areas eligible for assistance. Unless a target unemployment rate for regional policy is set, it is impossible to choose threshold values objectively.

Clearly, if the many objectives of regional policy are to be taken into account in the mapping out of policy regions, a number of differentiating characteristics will have to be used. Unfortunately, this is likely to be an extremely difficult task. One of the problems is that an increase in the number and range of differentiating characteristics used could lead to a violation of a fundamental rule of classification (Grigg 1967), which states that a clear, unambiguous classification of areas is possible only if there is a single purpose for undertaking the classification. This objection may seem strange for, in general, it may appear to be only too obvious which regions are in need of assistance and which are not. But this is a dangerous and also a curiously old-fashioned view. It resembles the classical view in human geography, now discarded, that regions exist as distinct entities in a complete economic, cultural and physical sense and can be delimited as such. This idea underlay much of the French 'pays' school of thought and provoked a major controversy

in human geography (Harvey 1969). It was argued that
whilst the precise boundaries might be difficult to define, the
fundamental wholeness of such regions could not be denied.
If this were true of problem regions then it would hardly
matter which differentiating characteristic were used since
they would all give the same result. This view is erroneous.
Consider part (b) of figure 7.1, which sub-divides Italy into
two regions on the basis of geographical differences in the
annual percentage growth of output between 1960 and 1970.
The threshold value is 10.4 % which is the average for Italy
as a whole over this period. Putting the two pieces of
information on unemployment rates and output growth
together in part (c) of figure 7.1, it can be seen that all but six
of the 20 administrative areas experienced either slower
growth or a higher unemployment rate than the national
average.

If the objectives of regional policy encompass the
reduction of both regional unemployment differences and
regional growth differences, the regional problem in Italy
certainly becomes an extensive one since 14 of the 20
administrative areas fall into either a slow growth category
or a high unemployment category. The core area of
depression, that part which stands out as a depressed region
under *both* differentiating characteristics, consists of only
four of the 20 administrative areas and is shown in part (d) of
figure 7.1.

The example in figure 7.1 is an extreme one but shows just
how difficult delimiting policy regions may be when the
multiple objectives of regional policy cannot be adequately
represented by any single differentiating characteristic. Of
the 20 administrative areas of Italy, four had a growth rate
below average and an unemployment rate above average,
six had a growth rate and an unemployment rate above
average, four had a growth rate and an unemployment rate
below average, and six had a growth rate above and an
unemployment rate below average. The example was
deliberately selected because it gives such extreme results.
In reality there is probably some truth in the view that
depressed regions do stand out 'like a sore thumb' across a
whole range of differentiating characteristics.

Consider another example. Parts (a) and (b) of figure 7.2
again show administrative areas of Italy delimited using
two separate differentiating characteristics, namely out-
migration rates and unemployment rates. The only

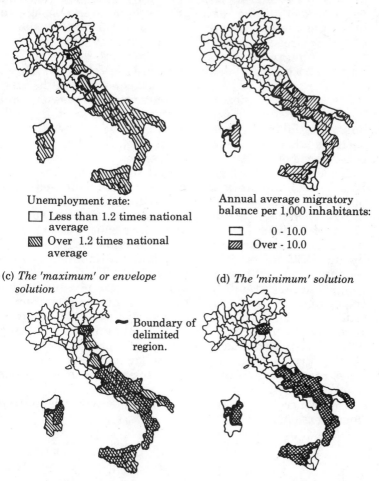

(a) *Using unemployment rates*

(b) *Using out-migration rates*

Unemployment rate:

☐ Less than 1.2 times national average

▨ Over 1.2 times national average

Annual average migratory balance per 1,000 inhabitants:

☐   0 - 10.0

▨   Over - 10.0

(c) *The 'maximum' or envelope solution*

(d) *The 'minimum' solution*

~ Boundary of delimited region.

Source: Commission of the European Communities (1973a), Carte 4 and Carte 8.

Figure 7.2 *The proposed delimitation of areas eligible for assistance from the European Regional Development Fund: areas suffering from structural underemployment*

difference from figure 7.1 is that more administrative areas are used, 92 instead of 20, and that the critical threshold for the unemployment rates is set at 1.2 times the national average instead of the national average itself. There is a much closer coincidence of regions delimited by unemployment and out-migration rates than by unemployment and output growth. Since out-migration is often in response to high local unemployment it is perhaps not surprising that 26 of the 38 areas with high unemployment rates also have high out-migration rates. Unemployment rates and out-migration rates may be said to be 'accessory characteristics'. Whilst there may be a kernel of truth, however, in the view that many differentiating characteristics are accessory and hence that distinct 'natural' depressed areas exist, it is still only a partial truth. Even with two closely related indicators such as unemployment and out-migration the resulting coincidence of areas is far from perfect.

If each separate indicator yields a different set of regional boundaries, how are assisted areas to be delimited? The objectives of regional policy are too diverse and too complex to rely upon a single differentiating characteristic, such as the unemployment rate, for delimiting policy regions. One way out of this apparent impasse is to follow the route set out by the EEC in its 1973 proposals for a Community-wide regional policy (Commission 1973b). These proposals, though never actually implemented, were notable in two important respects. First, the differentiating characteristics were derived from the objectives of the common regional policy. Second, no fewer than nine differentiating characteristics were used. Since the 1973 proposals were one of the first serious attempts to delimit policy regions objectively, it will be illuminating to examine them in some detail.

Two general characteristics were proposed for delimiting policy regions:

(i)   the areas must already be benefiting from the regional policies of member states of the EEC, and

(ii) the areas must have a GDP per head less than the EEC average.

These two general differentiating characteristics really spell out the objectives of EEC regional policy, if only in very broad terms. The delimitation of regions with per capita GDP values below the EEC average is the first step in the process of quantifying the efficiency and equity objectives of regional policy. Notice that GDP per capita is preferred to the unemployment rate as an indicator of economic welfare. That areas must also be benefiting from regional policies in member states reflects the objective that EEC regional policy must be complementary to regional policy in member states. This objective is included because the economic integration of member nations is likely to lead to a worsening of regional problems within these member states. This being so, there is a clear need for a *Community* regional policy in addition to the regional policies of each member.

In addition to these two very broad conditions, the 1973 proposals also required each eligible area to be at least one of three alternative types of problem region. They must be either:

(i)   regions heavily dependent upon agriculture and possessing few manufacturing activities, or

(ii) regions heavily dependent upon declining industries such as coalmining or textiles, or

(iii) regions suffering persistent under-employment due to fundamental structural problems.

Each of these different types of problem region was delimited by a distinct group of differentiating characteristics. Hence depressed agricultural regions (category (i)) were delimited using two characteristics: the percentage of the workforce employed in primary and secondary sectors respectively. Regions dependent upon declining industries (category (ii)) were delimited using three differentiating characteristics: the percentage of the workforce employed in coalmining and textiles, the unemployment rate, and the out-migration rate. Finally, regions characterised by structural under-employment (category (iii)) were delimited using three indicators : unemployment rates, out-migration rates and GDP per capita. The example already shown in parts (a) and (b) of figure 7.2 has in fact used the first two of the three characteristics employed in delimiting regions suffering from structural under-employment. The critical threshold values employed in figure 7.2 of 1.2 times the national average unemployment rate and a net out-migration rate of 10 per 1,000 inhabitants are also those of the 1973 EEC proposals. It is interesting to see how the EEC proposals resolve the problem of overlapping boundaries when more than one differentiating characteristic is used. The EEC proposals use a combination of two methods which we can perhaps call 'maximum' and 'minimum' methods. Returning to figure 7.2, it was noted earlier that using unemployment and out-migration to delimit policy regions

results in only a partial coincidence of eligible
administrative areas (i.e. 68% of the areas with high
unemployment also have high rates of out-migration). Parts
(c) and (d) show the two alternative solutions to this problem
of the failure of boundaries to coincide. In part (c), a
'maximum' or 'envelope' solution is adopted with eligible
areas encompassing those with *either* high unemployment
rates *or* high out-migration rates. Part (d) shows a
'minimum' solution. Eligible areas are designated only as
those administrative areas with *both* a high unemployment

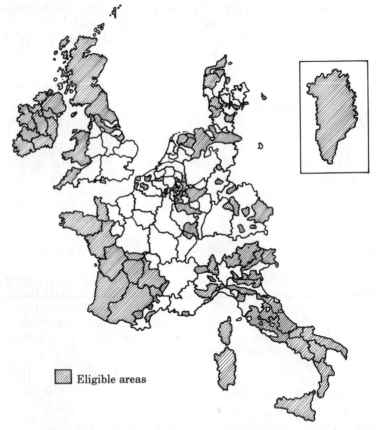

Eligible areas

Source: Commission of the European Communities (1973b).

Figure 7.3 *Areas eligible for assistance under the 1973 proposals
for an EEC Regional Development Fund: the
'Thomson Map'*

rate *and* a high out-migration rate. The 1973 EEC proposals adopt the envelope approach in most cases. Aggregating up from Italy to all nine member states, and incorporating all three types of eligible region results in a pattern of areas eligible for ERDF assistance under the 1973 proposals as shown in figure 7.3.

The (initially) separate delimitation of different types of problem region, such as agricultural problem regions, regions dependent on declining industries, and regions suffering structural underemployment, is an interesting procedure. In the end these were simply aggregated together to give the 'Thomson Map' shown in figure 7.3, but they do raise the possibility of having a series of different types of region, each delimited using different indicators, and each with a distinct set of regional policies designed specifically to tackle the problems of that particular type of depressed region. In addition to those identified by the EEC method, it is possible to add at least one more type of policy region: that with serious urban problems.

Assisted areas in Britain are not differentiated according to the type of problem they face. Policy regions are classified as either Special Development Areas, Development Areas or Intermediate Areas (see figure 1.4 in Chapter 1), the basis for this classification being the *extent* of a region's problems rather than the *type* of problem faced by a region. As yet, the policy package differs between these three types of policy region only in so far as the rates of the available incentives vary between them, reaching their maximum value in the Special Development Areas. As far as the future is concerned, it seems likely that there will be an increase in both the range of different types of policy region and the policies applied to them. It is also possible that more advanced statistical techniques may prove useful in this field. Principal components analysis (Miller 1972) has some potential as a means of reducing a large number of differentiating characteristics to a much smaller number, that is the principal components themselves, which in turn can be used to classify regions (Spence and Taylor 1970).

7.2 Policy Regions and Regional Policies

Regional policy objectives are certainly vital to the selection of the characteristics to be used to delimit policy regions. But this may not be sufficient, since the type of regional policies selected are also likely to have a significant bearing on the delimitation of policy regions. An example will help to clarify this link between the type of policy adopted and the way in which areas eligible for assistance are delimited. Suppose Britain decides to operate its regional policy by establishing a number of growth poles, with industries and services being induced to locate at only a handful of carefully selected urban locations. This is very different from traditional regional policy in Britain which, whilst it exhibits some elements of growth pole philosophy, has delimited very large policy regions and then offered incentives to firms expanding anywhere in these regions.

The delimitation of growth poles requires quite different indicators than would be used for delimiting problem regions using the traditional British 'blanket' approach. Since growth poles should be established at locations possessing considerable inherent growth potential, the differentiating characteristics must be capable of identifying locations with the greatest potential for growth. Thus, although regional policy based upon either the growth pole or the blanket approach is designed to achieve the same objectives, the differentiating characteristics used to delimit policy regions will be quite different in each of these two cases.

The policy regions which we have examined so far are *uniform* regions. Localities have been grouped into policy regions on the basis of their similarity or uniformity, as in the case of the Italian regions suffering from either high unemployment or high out-migration (see figure 7.2). Perroux (1950), however, distinguishes between several distinct types of region of which uniform regions are only one. The main alternatives to uniform regions are *nodal* regions, which are particularly appropriate for delimiting growth poles. In a nodal region, the constituent administrative areas are grouped together not on the basis of any similarities, but on the strength of interrelationships between them. For this reason, they are sometimes termed 'functional' regions.

Consider an example based on journey-to-work data. Figure 7.4 shows the journey-to-work catchment area for the town of Kendal in northern England. Nine administrative areas in the vicinity of Kendal send significant numbers of workers to the Kendal labour market each day. These nine

Key to areas:
1. Kendal MB
2. South Westmorland RD
3. Sedbergh RD
4. North Westmorland RD
5. Lakes UD
6. Windermere UD
7. North Lonsdale RD
8. Morecambe and Heysham MB
9. Lancaster MB

⟹1mm represents 800
   commuter movements

Source: Ball (1975).

Figure 7.4 *An example of spatial taxonomy: journey to work in
Cumbria, 1971*

administrative areas form a cohesive nodal region even
though they are exceedingly dissimilar: some are affluent,
others are not; some are urban, others rural; and so on. The
differentiating characteristic used in this case measures one
particular functional tie — total journey-to-work movements
— and has a critical threshold set at 500 person-trips. Only
those administrative areas sending 500 workers or more to
Kendal each day are grouped into the nodal region.

In this particular example, the administrative units are
contiguous with the exception of areas 8 and 9; that is, they
lie side-by-side geographically. With nodal regions,
however, it is frequently better to distinguish, as does
Perroux, between geographical space and economic space.

Economic space is best thought of in terms of economic linkages.

Consider another example. One of the more notable successes of British regional policy in the 1960s was the government-induced location of large motor assembly plants in Merseyside and Scotland. Such plants have strong input-output production linkages with a vast range of firms up and down the country. The assembly plants have maintained extensive linkages back to component and subcontracting firms in the Midlands and the South East (James 1964). These functional ties form a powerful nodal region in economic space even though the individual, linked plants of this nodal region are definitely not contiguous in geographical space.

It is information on functional ties such as forward or backward linkages in the production system, and access to local labour markets, as well as information on how such functional ties are changing over time, that is important to the selection of appropriate growth poles. These are, after all, the foci of such nodal regions. Unfortunately, both the theory and practice of growth pole policy remains in a confused and contradictory state (Hansen 1972). Since no one is certain of what exactly constitutes a growth centre, or around which industries they should be built, it is not surprising that the literature is so vague on the kinds of differentiating characteristics that should be used to identify them. What is clear, however, is that these differentiating characteristics, unlike those used to delimit traditional 'blanket' policy regions, will usually measure functional ties and not the degree of uniformity. Moseley (1974), for instance, argues that growth centres should have close ties not only to intraregional workforces as in figure 7.4, but also to intra- and interregional migrants, suppliers, markets and the like. In short, growth centres should be the foci of powerful nodal regions.

Furthermore, since growth centres are by definition inherently dynamic, the differentiating characteristics used to identify them are also likely to be of a more dynamic nature than those used for 'blanket' policy regions. Previous, or better still, potential growth rates of income, employment, population and so on will be the kinds of indicators required.

The growth pole and the blanket approach to delimiting assisted areas are fundamentally different from each other. Since the locations most likely to succeed as growth points do not necessarily lie inside the most depressed areas, the selection of growth centres involves a more painful choice for the policymaker than the blanket approach. The result in Britain has been that policymakers have opted for a compromise solution. New towns and industrial estates have been used to focus development at favourable sites within broadly defined assisted areas.

Conclusion

This chapter must end on a note of caution. Whilst there is certainly room for both a more precise approach to the delimitation of policy regions and a greater disaggregation of policy regions based on either the type of problem that exists or the severity of that problem, there are certain costs to be borne if this is taken too far; there is a trade-off between the complexity of regional policy and its effectiveness. A plethora of policy combinations designed to deal with a wide range of regional problems may seriously reduce their effectiveness by generating uncertainty and confusion. There is evidence that firms are less inclined to investigate the benefit of incentives the more complex they are (House of Commons 1973a). Finally, it may be an advantage not to change the boundaries of policy regions too frequently even though circumstances may change. Whilst this involves violating yet another rule of classification (that classifications may require frequent revision), it does have the advantage of allowing firms to take into account the possibility of obtaining *future* assistance when making a *current* location decision. In other words, reducing uncertainty may yield substantial benefits.

Selected references

Commission of the European Communities (1973b); Grigg (1967); Perroux (1950); Spence and Taylor (1970).

8
Regional Policy Options : Macro-Policy Instruments

The regional policymaker has a wide range of policy options at his disposal. In this chapter and the next, our intention is to appraise these policy options critically. This does not mean that we intend to investigate the effectiveness of individual policy instruments which have actually been used by regional policymakers. Our aim is more limited: we intend simply to examine the potential usefulness of the main policy instruments available to the regional policymaker.

Although regional problems do not fall into easily recognisable categories, it is nevertheless useful to adopt the traditional division of policies into macro-policies and micro-policies for the purpose of exposition. Policies principally designed to change aggregate income and expenditure imply a need for macro-policy instruments, whereas policies intended principally to affect resource allocation by influencing the behaviour of individual firms and households imply a need for micro-policy instruments.

It may seem strange that macro-policy instruments could be used for regional purposes, yet in practice macro-policies can be expected to have different effects in different regions. Devaluation of the national currency, for instance, will favour the regions most dependent upon international trade, and import controls will favour regions producing import substitutes. Similarly, expanding the national economy through fiscal or monetary policies will not necessarily have the same effect on output and employment in all regions. Different regions produce different commodities, and the demand for some commodities is more sensitive than others to changes in income. Macro-policies may thus induce quite

162

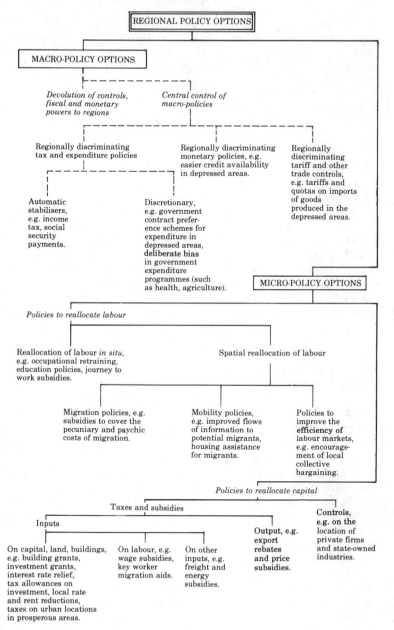

Figure 8.1 *Regional policy options : a simple typology with examples*

different changes in output and employment in different regions. This being so, it may be possible to introduce a regional component into macro-policies so that different changes in output and employment can be induced in different regions. At its most extreme, this could involve adding an entirely new dimension to macro-policy, namely the devolution of macro-powers to regional governments.

On the micro-policy side, it is possible to sub-divide policy options into two categories depending upon whether they are intended to induce a reallocation of labour or a reallocation of capital.

Figure 8.1 sets out a rough typology of regional policy options based on the macro/micro dichotomy. It is not a classification which should be used rigidly, however, since it violates several rules of taxonomy. In particular, the individual classes are not mutually exclusive in that it is quite possible, where substantial public expenditure is involved, for an individual micro-policy instrument to have both micro-effects and macro-effects at the same time, thus falling into both classes. In the present chapter, we concentrate on macro-policy instruments. Micro-policy instruments are discussed in the next chapter.

8.1 Fiscal Policy: Regional Aspects of Taxation and Government Expenditure

It is well known that fiscal policy instruments take two forms: automatic stabilisers and discretionary action. Many taxes and transfer payments are designed so that they will automatically stabilise employment and income by preventing large cyclical swings in business activity. For example, progressive income tax rates lead to an automatic increase in tax revenue as income rises and to a fall in tax revenue as income falls, which is the required effect if cyclical fluctuations are to be minimised. A similar role is played by unemployment benefits on the expenditure side of government fiscal policy. Benefits rise in recessions and so help to maintain expenditure at exactly the time that they are required. Automatic stabilisers, however, have not proved adequate *per se* to avert serious recessions or bouts of inflation, and governments have consequently developed a wide array of discretionary instruments which can be used if and when required. The most important discretionary instrument on the revenue side is the taxation of income and expenditure. The income tax yield can be altered by adjusting tax rates, or by adjusting the tax base of income earners. Taxes on goods and services can be adjusted similarly. The role of government expenditure as a discretionary instrument is obvious and needs no elaboration.

All these fiscal instruments, and many more, are available to the government in its efforts to control the level of demand *in the economy as a whole*. Unfortunately, the problem of under-utilisation of productive capacity in some regions and over-utilisation of productive capacity in other regions cannot be removed by simply expanding or contracting aggregate demand. The use of macro-policy instruments to solve regional problems is severely constrained by the existence of other policy goals. An expansion of aggregate demand, in an attempt to reduce unemployment in depressed areas, may cause inflation and balance of payments problems (unless the exchange rate is allowed to float downwards, in which case inflationary pressures are enhanced by rising import prices). Conversely, contracting aggregate demand to reduce inflation and balance of payments deficits may lead to the re-emergence of large-scale unemployment in the depressed regions. The existence of trade-offs between policy objectives means that regional problems cannot be solved by simply manipulating the aggregate level of demand in the economy.

One way out of this dilemma would be to replace the blanket approach to fiscal policy with one that is deliberately regionally discriminating. The central government could operate different tax and expenditure policies in different regions. In this way, any required contraction or expansion of demand could be concentrated in appropriate regions. Superficially, such 'regionalised' fiscal policies have much to recommend them. Indeed, they already exist in two important respects. First, the automatic stabilisers raise demand in regions suffering from a demand deficiency, and they reduce demand in regions suffering from an excessively high pressure of demand. This occurs, on the one hand, as transfer payments (i.e. unemployment benefits and other welfare payments) flow into areas of high unemployment. On the other hand, progressive income tax rates exert a restraining effect on regions experiencing a high level of income and employment.

The second way in which the government already operates a fiscal policy which discriminates between regions is through its role as purchaser of goods and services. The government has the power to affect the level of employment in specific regions by taking the geographical distribution of its purchases into account when drawing up its spending plans. An extremely wide range of goods and services are purchased from the private sector by state-owned enterprises and by government departments. The engineering, shipbuilding and vehicle industries, for instance, supply state-owned transport companies and government departments with a wide variety of capital goods, and they supply military equipment to the armed forces. The list of economic linkages between the government sector and the private sector is virtually infinite. Extensive cash grants have also been paid to particular firms in the shipbuilding and vehicle industries (e.g. Rolls Royce, Leyland, and Chrysler) to prevent bankruptcies and the consequent effects on local income and employment.

An excellent example of discrimination in the purchase of goods and services is the Contracts Preference Scheme operated in the UK Development Areas. Preference is given to assisted area firms tendering for contracts of government departments, nationalised industries and other public bodies. The dependence of a specific local economy on government contracts can be extremely pronounced. Consider the case of Barrow-in-Furness in the northwest of England. The Furness economy developed to its present size mainly as a result of the rapid growth of shipbuilding and marine engineering in the early twentieth century. The subsequent decline of the shipbuilding industry has seriously threatened male employment in the Furness economy, which is heavily dependent upon a single firm. This fact has meant that successive governments have been able to maintain employment levels in this locality by placing government contracts with the firm — in the face of an overall decline in the shipbuilding industry in Britain.

The government's expenditure on defence equipment is only one example of the way in which the government can discriminate between regions in its budgetary policy. Recent estimates of the regional distribution of government spending in Britain (Short 1977) indicate that a geographical bias occurs over a wide range of government expenditure. A programme-by-programme breakdown of

Table 8.1 Regional distribution of 'regionally relevant' public expenditure per capita (1969/70-1973/74)

Region	Agriculture, fisheries, forestry	Trade, industry, employment	Nationalised inds. capital expenditure	Roads and transport	Housing	Other environmental services	Law order and protection	Education and libraries	Health, personal services	Social security	Total
SE	56	64	91	96	126	100	121	107	110	93	100
E Anglia	278	61	83	87	78	117	82	102	91	93	95
SW	163	119	95	124	56	108	94	89	98	104	98
W Midlands	71	60	62	87	74	88	83	90	85	91	83
E Midlands	103	118	92	66	67	95	90	94	91	93	91
Yorkshire & Humberside	99	61	129	82	69	85	77	92	93	104	93
NW	37	111	84	105	88	97	96	95	94	107	97
N	120	210	122	129	111	93	97	93	89	113	112
Wales	174	151	159	125	79	121	88	102	103	117	115
Scotland	203	172	129	114	149	113	99	117	113	105	122
GB	100	100	100	100	100	100	100	100	100	100	100

Notes
1. Figures are average annual expenditure per capita over the period 1969/70-1973/74 and are expressed as an index (GB = 100).
2. Expenditure figures were calculated at 1974 prices.
3. 'Regionally relevant' expenditure is the public expenditure 'in and for a region'. It comprises "only those expenditures made in a region the purposes of which are for the benefit of that region" (Northern Region Strategy Team 1976b). Over the period 1969/70-1973/74 these regionally relevant expenditures comprised over 75% of total public expenditure.

Source: Short (1977).

certain categories of public expenditure indicates that a geographical bias has occurred in all categories of public expenditure (1969-73), the net effect being that regions such as Scotland, Wales and the Northern region have experienced much higher expenditures (per capita) compared to the West Midlands, the East Midlands and Yorkshire and Humberside.

A closer look at table 8.1 highlights some of the reasons for this geographical bias in public expenditure. A region may attract, or fail to attract, a high proportion of government expenditure for three main reasons. Firstly, it may be due to deliberate use of government expenditure to assist particular regions. Notice how Wales, Scotland and the SW have benefited from government agricultural policy, industry and regional policy, transport policy, and from capital expenditure by nationalised industries. Much of this represents a deliberate attempt to divert public expenditure

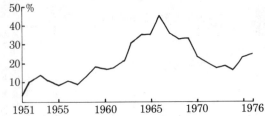

Source: Housing Statistics HMSO, *Reports of the Development Corporations.*

Figure 8.2 *Percentage of GB New Town housing completed in Scotland, 1951-76*

to depressed regions. The sharp increase in the percentage of GB New Town housing completed in Scotland during the 1960s is further evidence of the use of public funds to assist particular regions (see figure 8.2). Secondly, automatic stabilisers are in operation. The North, Wales, Scotland and the NW all benefit disproportionately from social security policies mainly because of relatively higher unemployment rates in these regions. Thirdly, government policies with non-regional objectives in mind may give rise to a regional bias in public expenditure. This is reflected by the high per capita expenditure in the SE on housing, environmental services, law and order, education and libraries. These are largely expenditures controlled by local governments and are high in the SE partly as a result of the peculiar significance of urban problems in that region.

The regional allocation of public expenditure in Britain provides us with a clear indication of the extent to which public expenditure can be regionally biased. In principle, there would seem to be considerable potential for extending the national planning of public expenditures by explicitly adding a regional dimension. The practical difficulties of such schemes should not, however, be ignored. Any attempt to expand demand in depressed regions relative to other regions in the economy will face the serious problem of spillover effects. An injection of expenditure into a depressed region will be transmitted into other regions through interregional trade, thus making it more difficult to expand selectively in one region. A similar argument holds for the policy of reducing inflationary pressures in regions of excess demand. Any withdrawal of expenditure from an inflationary region will lead to reductions in the demand for the products of depressed regions as well.

The available evidence on regional trading patterns tends to support the view that regional spillover effects are likely to be considerable. Direct evidence on regional exports and imports is scarce, but what there is indicates that regional economies are very open (see King 1973). Similarly, the empirical estimates of regional multipliers in Britain show most to be between 1.3 and 1.5 (e.g. Steele 1969) and these low values are primarily due to the high propensity of regional economies to import.

The policy implication is clear. Any attempt to expand output in problem regions through selective fiscal measures will be seriously impaired if interregional trade links are strong. Even if the industries of a region purchase most of their inputs from other industries within the region, the spillover effects are still likely to be significant. This is because a considerable proportion of a region's household expenditure is also likely to find its way into other regions. The extent of these spillover effects will depend upon the size of the region, its proximity to other regions and the diversity of the commodities produced by the region.

In addition to the problem of spillovers, there is a further reason for the reluctance of governments to rely upon 'regionalised' fiscal policies: the latter would generate intense political opposition. This is particularly true for tax policy. Regionally differentiated tax rates on income or profits, for instance, would immediately lead to claims of unfair treatment by those taxed the most heavily. The principle of 'horizontal equity' in taxation is quite widely held. This asserts that similar people ought to be treated similarly with respect to taxation and the provision of government services. If, for some reason, specific groups of people are receiving less than their 'fair share' of public goods relative to the taxes they pay, it is deemed to be the responsibility of the national government to correct such inequities through fiscal measures.

This section concludes on a cautious note. There is a clear need to extend fiscal policy by making it more sensitive to the needs of individual regions. But one of the problems with this approach is that there will be opposition to any policy that appears to violate the principle of horizontal equity. A further problem is that trade linkages between regions are such that attempts to change the level of demand in any one region will have repercussions on other regions, some of which will require the opposite of the 'shock' they receive. In principle, given sufficient information about trading linkages it might be possible to arrange fiscal action such that the 'right shocks' go to the 'right regions'. In practice, fiscal aggregates must be manipulated very much in the dark as far as the regional ramifications are concerned. The capacity for such fine-tuning of macro-policy just does not exist.

8.2 Regional Aspects of Monetary Policy

The main strand of monetary policy is control over the money supply. Put simply, expanding the quantity of money in an economy in which spare productive capacity exists will tend to cause an expansion of output and employment. A contraction of the money supply will have the reverse effect.

The use of monetary policy at the national level for regional policy purposes is strictly limited. Monetary instruments can be used to expand the economy during periods of high national unemployment in order to reduce unemployment in those regions where it is particularly high. But, as with fiscal policy, any expansion of aggregate demand by means of monetary policy will be limited by the effect that such a policy has on inflation and the balance of payments. Attempts to operate a centrally controlled, *but regionally discriminating,* policy of monetary expansion — such as the provision of easier credit facilities to firms and households located in depressed regions — will face similar problems. A large proportion of the increase in demand will leak away into other regions as imports into the depressed regions expand in response to the higher level of income. This will be an undesirable consequence to the extent that the leakage of expenditure into other regions leads to an intensification of inflationary pressures and balance of payments problems for the economy as a whole.

8.3 Regional Aspects of Import Controls

The third main group of macro-policies in addition to fiscal and monetary policy is the use of controls. One of the most commonly used methods of raising output in particular regions is to impose *national* import tariffs on the products of industries whose production is geographically concentrated. Tariffs are imposed in order to divert demand to home-produced goods. The objective is to provide sufficient time either for the industry to increase its efficiency so that it can compete with foreign suppliers, or to slow down the pace of decline of the industry to give factors of production (especially labour) time to be reallocated to other industries. The protection of cotton textiles in Britain against cheaper imports from India and Hong Kong during the postwar period is an excellent example of this type of policy. The purpose was to try to protect the jobs of textile workers in depressed areas such as Lancashire whilst the industry modernised itself, and whilst the excess supply of workers in the industry could be retrained and absorbed into other industries.

Tariffs and import quotas are a common device for protecting jobs in specific industries. There are, however, high costs to pay for such policies since protection (and the subsequent retaliation by other countries) denies a country the chance to exploit the potential gains from specialisation and trade. If these gains are to be fully reaped, the protection of declining industries (and hence the protection of regions in which they are located) must be regarded as a purely short-run measure.

A further problem with national protectionist policies which has not been given much consideration by economists is that the protection of individual industries not only prevents the economy as a whole from reaping the gains from trade, but also involves a geographical redistribution of income towards the areas dependent upon protected industries. This has been shown to be the case, for instance, in Canada (see Shearer *et al* 1971). Tariffs in Canada are directed against imported manufactured goods, which means that those regions specialising in the production of non-manufactured goods for export have to pay higher prices for manufactured consumption and capital goods than would be the case if there was free trade. The Province of British Columbia in Canada, for example, specialises in the production and processing of primary commodities for export, namely timber, minerals, fish and a number of agricultural goods. The manufacturing sector, apart from those industries involved in the processing of these primary commodities, is very small with the result that manufactured goods have to be imported into the region either from the eastern Provinces (mainly Ontario) or from abroad. Tariffs on manufactured imports have the harmful effect on British Columbia of shifting the terms of trade against it, since any given quantity of exports from the Province will purchase a smaller quantity of imports into the region than would be the case under conditions of free trade. This type of redistribution will occur in all countries with tariff policies and where regions specialise in the production of different commodities.

Removal of tariffs and other import controls would therefore have immediate benefits for regions such as British Columbia in addition to the longer-run benefits accruing to *all* regions as a result of freer trade.

8.4 Devolution and Regional Policy

So far it has been implicitly assumed that fiscal policies, monetary policies and import controls are under the direction of the central government. We have examined the possibility that the central government could deliberately use these macro-policies to help certain regions rather than others. An entirely new dimension is added to this debate, however, if devolution of macro-powers to *regional* authorities is considered. The term 'devolution' is unfortunately one of those general terms in the language which takes on different meanings in different contexts. In this section, devolution is defined as the transfer of *full* macro-powers to a regional 'authority'.

Devolution of central government powers to individual regions has been a perennial issue in countries with federal political systems such as Canada and the USA. In recent years, it has become an issue of major importance in Britain, ironically at a time of fairly rapid economic integration of the British economy with the other members of the European Economic Community. The full devolution debate is well outside the scope of this book. Indeed, the *economic* pros and cons of devolution may be of quite low importance in this wider debate. Scott and Breton (1975), writing about the Canadian case, argue that 'traditional ties to particular lands, language differences, historical enmities, race and sheer inertia combine in the rejection of complete unification' and the economic cost of devolution has 'little or no significance given these overwhelming political and cultural motives'. Even in Britain where complete unification has been the starting point of the debate, political issues have consistently outflanked discussions of the relative economic merits of unification and devolution. As a result, in a short space of time the central arguments have switched from the devolution/unification controversy to arguments about the *degree* of devolution desired.

Our concern here, however, is not whether devolution is desirable nor with the optimum degree of devolution (see Tait 1975). We intend only to investigate whether devolution of macro-policy powers can contribute in any way to the alleviation of regional problems. To examine this issue, an extreme case will be postulated in which devolved macro-powers far exceed those currently envisaged for Scotland and Wales, and indeed in some cases exceed the powers desired by nationalist political parties.

Consider the polar case where full fiscal policy powers are devolved to regional authorities. Attempts by depressed regions to use their new-found tax and expenditure powers to boost demand in their regional economies would face even more problems than in a unified fiscal system which deliberately discriminates between regions. In addition to the problems of large spillovers, a regional authority which did not have the power to create money would face serious constraints on the extent to which it could use budget deficits to finance its expenditures. In the existing system, the excess of expenditures over receipts in depressed regions is balanced by transfer payments from surplus to deficit regions (see King 1973). Unemployment benefit, welfare payments and cash transfers to local authorities are the most obvious examples. Without these transfers, the depressed region would have to balance its expenditure and receipts by borrowing from other regions and from abroad. But the consequence of building up large external debts would be serious, since they would impose a heavy burden on the region's taxpayers who would have to finance the debt over the longer run. Taxpayers may choose to 'vote with their feet' and migrate to other regions, increasing the burden of the debt for those who remained.

An alternative to running a budget deficit is to balance the budget and rely upon the balanced budget multiplier to expand regional income and employment (see Oates 1972). A transfer of income from the private citizen to the government will raise total spending in the regional economy since the government's marginal propensity to consume is unity, whereas the private citizen's marginal propensity to consume is less than unity. If the taxpayer's marginal propensity to consume, for instance, is 0.7, an additional £1 of tax revenue collected by the government and spent will raise regional expenditure by £0.3. It is easy to show that in a closed economy the extra spending of £0.3 would lead to an ultimate increase of income of £1 via the closed economy multiplier. Unfortunately, the actual multiplier will be much less than the closed economy one because of the old problem of import leakages (see Shaw 1974). Furthermore, in such circumstances the balanced budget multiplier approach requires a high level of taxation if it is to be effective. Yet the consequence of high taxation may be to drive high income earners out of the region.

These are pessimistic conclusions. If there is anything to be said in favour of total fiscal independence for individual regions as a means of alleviating regional problems, it is that regional authorities are likely to be more sensitive to local needs than is a national authority (see King 1973). But the disadvantages arising from the complete devolution of fiscal powers to regional authorities would far outweigh any advantages.

Clearly, there are serious problems associated with introducing tax and expenditure policies that discriminate between regions, and this applies whether the policies are locally or nationally controlled. This does not mean, however, that all divergences from the national fiscal

pattern are ruled out. There may be sound allocative
reasons for providing different bundles of public goods in
different regions (see Musgrave 1973). This is because there
may exist substantial regional differences in tastes. Citizens
in some areas may prefer higher taxes and more public
goods to lower taxes and fewer public goods. Citizens in
other areas may prefer the reverse. In addition, different
mixes of public goods may be preferred. One method of
catering for such differences in tastes is for regional fiscal
authorities to be given powers to offer different fiscal
packages in each region. This will allow citizens to increase
their welfare by choosing a residential location which gives
them their 'best' combination of taxes and public goods.

It is the devolution of these sorts of powers that has
formed the core of most of the current UK devolution
controversy. As we might expect by now, there are some
problems even with this limited form of fiscal devolution.
Firstly, different public goods are likely to have different
catchment areas. The local park or public swimming pool
caters, in the main, for people living within and close to the
town of its location. The creation of Country Parks or
National Parks creates a much wider catchment area.
Problems arise where the boundaries of tax jurisdictions do
not coincide with the catchment area within which the
benefits of these public goods are reaped. A savage example
of this arises when commuters into urban areas use and
benefit from urban facilities financed by city dwellers whilst
they themselves live in rural areas and pay lower rural
taxes. Here the tax jurisdiction (i.e. the city) is smaller than
the benefit catchment area (i.e. the journey-to-work area).
Compensatory transfer payments from one regional
authority to another are therefore needed and this requires
the coordinated action of adjacent authorities or the intervention of central government to settle any disputes. In
addition, the proliferation of public jurisdictions will
increase the costs of providing public goods, particularly if
economies of scale are lost as a result of fragmentation.
Finally, the migration of citizens to preferred jurisdictions
(i.e. those with tax/public goods mixes resembling their
preferences) is itself a costly process.

If devolved monetary powers and controls are permitted
in addition to devolved fiscal powers, then further
possibilities emerge. Let us make some extreme
assumptions. Assume that the national economy is divided

into regions, each of which has its own currency, its own banking system with power to create money, and power over its own exchange rate vis-à-vis other regions as well as other nations. In addition, assume that each region can impose tariffs, quotas or other controls on its trade.

One immediate possibility which arises from devolving fiscal powers, monetary powers, and trade controls *simultaneously* is that fiscal deficits can now be at least partially met by an expansion of the money supply. If regional government securities, for example, find few buyers, then the central bank of the region could step in and take up the securities, thereby increasing the region's money supply. This, however, would create both inflation and balance of payments problems for the region. Alternatively, the extent of the budget deficit necessary to achieve a given expansion of output could be reduced by increasing the magnitude of the regional multiplier. One drastic way of doing this would be to restrict trade with other regions in order to reduce leakages. Unfortunately, the consequent fall in trade would cause losses all round, since trade benefits all trading partners. Hence, even adding monetary powers and controls would do little to assist a policy of running budget deficits in depressed regions.

Whilst this is almost certainly correct for the majority of the existing depressed areas of the UK, the discovery of North Sea oil has transformed the position for Scotland. If an independent Scotland did succeed in obtaining the rights to the offshore oil reserves, the royalties and licence fees could well convert Scotland from a depressed area requiring transfer payments from other regions to balance its budget, to a depressed area generating capital outflows. Over the longer run, the restructuring of the Scottish economy could be 'paid for' from oil revenues without the massive problems of financing budget deficits which other depressed regions have to face. But all this is hypothetical and many political problems stand in the way of such an event. In any case, whilst such oil-financed expansion might be highly desirable for Scotland, the spillover effects raise problems for other regions in the UK.

Devolving monetary powers in addition to fiscal powers opens up further possibilities for the use of macro-policies for regional policy purposes. The 'balkanisation' of national currency areas has rather obvious advantages *in principle* for solving regional problems. The central feature of a currency area is that all regions within it face the same external exchange rate vis-à-vis the rest of the world.

The implications of this can be seen by considering the hypothetical example in figure 8.3. Suppose that initially the

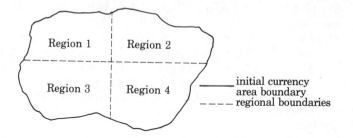

Figure 8.3 *A hypothetical currency area*

currency area is made up of four regions, all at full employment, and that the currency area as a whole operates a floating exchange rate against the rest of the world. In addition, assume that the balance of payments of the currency area is in equilibrium. This idyllic situation is now disturbed. Suppose that region 1 specialises in the production of textiles and suddenly suffers a reduction in the demand for its exports to markets outside the currency area. If wage rates are sticky downwards, region 1 will simply be forced to reduce output as export orders decline. A trade deficit opens between the currency area and the rest of the world with the result that the exchange rate of the currency area depreciates. This will eventually eliminate the deficit. It does this by partly helping the textile exports of region 1 to become more competitive, but also by stimulating the demand for the exports of regions 2, 3 and 4. Import prices will rise simultaneously as a result of the devaluation, leading to a reduction in imports to all four regions of the currency area.

The outcome, however, is that the currency area's balance of payments deficit is eliminated before the depreciation of the currency has fully restored the competitive position of region 1, which experienced the initial decline in the demand for textile exports. In the face of downwardly inflexible money wage rates, region 1 will have experienced unemployment. There is no way under the present monetary system that the unemployment can be eliminated unless labour is willing to migrate to regions 2, 3 and 4 where export demand has been stimulated. Alternatively, capital must be willing to migrate to region 1, where unemployed labour is readily available. Internal factor mobility is therefore crucial (Mundell 1961), provided of course the migration does not have the sort of long-term disequilibrating effects that were discussed in Chapter 3. It is worth noting that the smaller (in output terms) is region 1 relative to the rest of the currency area, the greater is the need for migration. A decline in textile exports will have only a tiny effect on the currency area's exchange rate if the textile region is small. Similarly, the greater the degree of specialisation by region, the greater the need for internal migration as a means of adjusting to the problem.

The problem is one of inflexibility. The region suffering a decline in its exports cannot adjust to the new position through an appropriate change in prices for two reasons: wages tend to be inflexible downwards, and the collective exchange rate will not depreciate far enough to allow it to become competitive again in world markets. The 'balkanisation' of currency areas to each of the four regions in figure 8.3 offers a possible solution. With its own currency, region 1 can depreciate against the rest of the world, *including* the other three regions of the original currency area. Conversely, regions experiencing excess demand could do the opposite.

Effectively, the introduction of regional currencies allows individual regions to adjust rapidly to changes in consumption patterns and production techniques. The effect of a decline in the demand for a region's exports would be a depreciation of its own currency and a consequent improvement in its competitive position. Export demand would recover as a direct result of the fall in the price paid by foreigners for the region's exports. The *internal* effect of the currency depreciation is quite straightforward. The rise in import prices (because of the depreciation) will reduce the real wage of workers in the region. This is the only way that the region can regain its former competitive position in the short run. By having fluctuating exchange rates, individual regions may be able to protect their competitive position, just as nations do.

All this seems to be a rosy state of affairs at first sight. But before rushing to set up a regional policy based on separate regional currency areas, it is worth pausing to reflect on some of the problems (see McKinnon 1963). To begin with, separate markets in regional currencies will have to be established for trading to take place. The costs of producing this service may be high. But more important than the costs of operating the new monetary system, however, are the costs resulting from a decline in interregional trade which fluctuating regional exchange rates could cause. Uncertainty of the value of other regional currencies may lead to a greater reluctance to trade because of the possibility of capital losses. It could be argued that uncertainty in the world's capital markets is already a major deterrent to world trade and adding to this uncertainty would be most undesirable.

There are other problems too. First, in a system in which regions are quite small and highly specialised, the burden of a depreciation is thrown on the non-trading sector of each region's economy. The openness of such small economies means that only a small section of industry does not trade and it is from this section that resources must be released either for import substitution or export expansion as the exchange rate falls. With such small non-trading sectors, there is little scope for switching resources, which means that the demand for imports and the supply of exports tend to be relatively inelastic. Consequently, changes in the exchange rate are not very effective and must be large to restore balance. Large fluctuations in real income will result.

Secondly, where the trade sector is large, exchange rate fluctuations will cause severe instability of the regional price level through its effects on the price of imports. As well as being detrimental in its own right, this has further implications. In the eyes of the typical consumer, the value of money is measured in terms of a representative 'bundle' of commodities and services. In a small, open economy these will be mainly imported goods. Yet, as we saw above, exchange rate depreciation only works if real incomes fall as import prices rise. To the extent that workers defend their real wages against increases in the price level (which rises because of the depreciation), the economy will fail to regain its competitive position and jobs will be lost as export prices fail to respond to the depreciation.

Finally, the creation of regional currency areas could interfere with the free mobility of capital. The fragmentation of the national capital market may cause wealth-owners to become more inward-looking and to seek out investment opportunities within their local region. In this case, the allocation of capital is likely to be less efficient. But provided trade is not seriously hindered between the new currency areas, such restraints on capital mobility are likely to be insignificant. Everything will depend upon the efficiency of the new monetary system.

In the light of so many problems, it is not surprising that separate regional currencies have not been seriously considered as a means of assisting depressed regions. Indeed, the whole concept of an 'optimum' currency area remains highly speculative. Moreover, in our simple example we concentrated on the problem of whether separate regional currency areas will enable a region to achieve a high level of employment, balance of payments equilibrium and price stability. The potential effect on the achievement of other goals, such as an acceptable growth rate of per capita income or greater equity, has been ignored in the above discussion (Presley and Dennis 1976, Whitman 1972).

But even if separate regional currency and exchange rate powers are not used, there still remains the possibility of devolving powers to restrict interregional trade and interregional factor movements by means of controls. Such a policy would avoid some of the problems already discussed. As we have seen, the restriction of trade would raise the regional multiplier, thus enhancing the effectiveness of regional fiscal or monetary policies. But the costs would be enormous. One of the greatest attributes of regional systems is the free movement of goods and factors of production. It is interesting to note that even the most ardent devolutionists within the UK have avoided advocating such controls. The costs of restricting interregional trade and factor movements would be so high for all concerned that this policy is a non-starter.

Conclusion

We have shown in this chapter that the potential for using macro-instruments as a means of alleviating regional problems is limited. This is so even when those instruments are designed to discriminate between regions. The macro-approach faces many as yet insurmountable problems. Not surprisingly, the main thrust of regional policy has therefore been via policy instruments designed to have micro-effects

on the location decisions of firms and households. It is to
these that we now turn.

Selected references

King (1973); Musgrave and Musgrave (1973); Oates (1972); Presley
and Dennis (1976); Tait (1975).

9
Regional Policy Options : Micro-Policy Instruments

The previous chapter concluded that the macro-approach to regional policy faces serious and as yet insurmountable problems. The present chapter is more optimistic. The micro-approach, though not without its problems, has much to offer the regional policymaker. It should therefore come as no surprise to learn that policymakers have pursued their regional policy objectives through the medium of micro-policy instruments.

The essential difference between the macro-approach and the micro-approach to regional policy is that macro-policy instruments attempt to change the geographical pattern of the demand for commodities, whereas micro-policy instruments operate more directly on the supply side of the commodity market. The aim of micro-policies is to influence the location decisions of firms and households. Capital and labour are induced to move to locations which the policymaker judges to be more desirable than the locations that would otherwise be chosen. Various 'carrot-and-stick' policies have been used in Britain to bring about a geographical reallocation of capital and labour, with most emphasis being placed on policies designed to induce the movement of capital towards the depressed areas.

The range of possible regional policy instruments is virtually infinite. Two main groups are distinguished here: (i) policy options designed to reallocate labour, and (ii) policy options designed to reallocate capital. A problem with this simplistic division of micro-policy instruments into two classes is that it ignores the fact that some instruments fall into both classes. A good example is the Key Workers' Scheme in Britain, which induces labour migration of

skilled personnel into depressed regions. The main purpose
of the scheme is not to reallocate labour but rather to make it
less costly for firms to move to the depressed areas by
meeting the financial costs of bringing key personnel with
them.

9.1 Policies to Reallocate Labour

We argued in an earlier chapter that labour does not respond
readily to regional differences in either wage rates or
unemployment rates (which happen to be only two of the
many influences acting upon the geographical movement of
workers). Indeed, labour mobility is far from perfect — either
between regions or between occupations — with the result
that distinct and quite separate geographical labour
markets exist. Policies designed to stimulate an increase in
the mobility of labour, however, have played a relatively
minor role in regional policy to date. Much greater emphasis
has been placed on policies designed to move capital into
areas of high unemployment, not just because of the
difficulties of removing the impediments to labour
migration but also because of the fear that encouraging out-
migration from depressed areas may cause regional
problems to worsen.

Ideally, manpower policies encompass all instruments
designed to induce labour to move into those economic
activities where its marginal product is highest. Policies
designed to stimulate such mobility reap an immediate
output gain in terms of increased labour productivity. They
may also assist the attainment of other objectives of
regional policy: of reduced inflation and greater income
equality, for instance. Expressed in terms of regional policy,
this suggests two basic types of policy action: transfer
policies and *in situ* mobility policies. Transfer policies are
aimed at inducing a shift in the supply of labour between
regions. *In situ* mobility policies aim at increasing the
occupational and industrial movement of labour at existing
locations.

Conceptually, three distinct groups of impediments to
labour mobility can be identified (Sjaastad 1962). First,
earnings differentials between regions, occupations and
industries may be unresponsive to corresponding
differentials in the marginal product of labour. Second, even

if such differentials *do occur*, labour may not fully perceive them. Third, even if such differentials occur *and are perceived*, impediments to labour mobility may still persist. This is because mobility is costly for the mover.

One reason for the failure of earnings differentials to reflect differences in the marginal product of labour is the existence of imperfect labour markets. Earnings differentials between regions are unlikely to reflect the efficiency of the marginal worker where collective bargaining is centralised. If occupational or industrial wages are established nationally, there is little scope for regional variations in wage rates for the same type of job (though hourly earnings may still vary between regions due to variations in bonus schemes and other incentive payments).

There are many features of labour markets which make it unlikely that geographical, occupational or industrial wages will even approximate the corresponding variations in the marginal product of labour. To the extent that these economic signals are missing, labour mobility will not occur. The inevitable consequence of such rigidity in the labour market is higher unemployment. Downwardly inflexible wages prevent workers from creating more jobs through bidding down the local wage rate. In addition, government unemployment benefit and other welfare payments play a supportive role in holding wage rates above their equilibrium level. They also discourage labour mobility.

At least as important as the failure of economic signals to appear in the form of wage rate differentials, is the failure of potential migrants to perceive the opportunities open to them. Information flows are crucial to the operation of labour markets. Most decisions to either migrate or retrain must be made on the basis of limited information. A lack of information causes uncertainty on the part of potential migrants; the latter require not only job information for themselves but also information on behalf of their family — information about housing, schools, social life, and recreational and cultural facilities. Such uncertainty may considerably reduce the migration stream. Information can, of course, be obtained but it is not costless.

Finally, there is the problem of the cost of geographical migration and the cost of changing occupations. Most obvious of these is the pecuniary cost of migration and retraining, which may be substantial. Of the numerous pecuniary barriers, the liquidity constraint is a serious one for many workers. Lack of financial resources prevents workers from moving to another location or obtaining the necessary skills even though it may well 'pay off' in the long run. The imperfections of the capital market prevent many unemployed workers from obtaining the necessary finance because they lack collateral security. Another way of looking at this financial constraint is in terms of the high risks involved in lending to potential migrants. The lack of collateral security adds a high risk premium to the interest charged on the loan.

Whilst the pecuniary costs of migration are important, the non-pecuniary costs (or 'psychic costs') of migration are likely to be of even greater significance. People are reluctant to leave the location in which they have family and other personal ties. They derive substantial consumer surplus (or more exactly, householder's surplus) from residing in a specific location, and whilst the extent of this surplus varies from individual to individual, it also seems to depend upon the length of time a person has resided in an area.

Since impediments to mobility fall into three broad groups, it is also possible to classify government policies that reduce impediments into three groups. It is interesting to note that the first group of impediments, namely the failure of 'wage signals' to appear, has not attracted the attention of government policymakers in Britain. There are several ways in which governments could bring about appropriate 'wage signals' between regions, occupations and industries. One way would be to encourage *local* plant bargaining rather than *national* bargaining. A second way would be for governments to encourage the payment of special 'bonuses' for working in certain industries or in certain regions.

The remaining two groups of impediments to geographical and occupational mobility have been the focus of government policies in Britain. The first of these, the failure of households to perceive opportunities in other areas or in other occupations, has been tackled by the creation of an extensive network of government Job Centres which are a development of the old system of Local Employment Exchanges. Whilst the policy of increasing the flow of information in labour markets is important, it is not enough. Central government has been forced to attack the financial impediments to the geographical and occupational mobility of labour in a wide variety of ways. Many private firms operate their own training, retraining and migration schemes. The government has helped to finance these programmes through the operation of bodies such as the Industrial Training Boards. In addition, the government has intervened directly to set up its own retraining centres, providing grants and allowances to trainees.

The non-pecuniary costs of mobility, and particularly the non-pecuniary costs of geographical migration, have proved to be more difficult to deal with. The relatively poor performance of schemes, such as the Employment Transfer Scheme in Britain, which meet only the pecuniary costs of migration, can be traced to the failure to subsidise the non-pecuniary costs of migration. To overcome these non-pecuniary costs, there is a need to provide the right sort of attractions in destination regions. A good example of how non-pecuniary costs can be alleviated is the British new towns policy which has provided a 'package' of job, home and urban facilities. But the construction of such 'packages' is very expensive. Furthermore, some would argue that such non-pecuniary costs can be alleviated is the British New Towns policy which has provided a 'package' of job, home utility gains from remaining where they are for the utility losses from lower incomes or unemployment, then perhaps they should be allowed to do so.

9.2 Policies to Reallocate Capital

Policies designed to increase the mobility of labour aim at improving the degree of matching between the demand and supply for labour by operating on the supply side of the labour market. The *skill* structure of labour demand, the *geographical* pattern of labour demand and the *industrial* distribution of labour demand are all taken as given. They are exogenous and it is the policymaker's job to match this 'mix' of labour demand by changing the skill structure, the geographical pattern and the industrial distribution of workers by the appropriate labour mobility policies. The complementary policy is to improve the matching between the demand and supply for labour by diverting the demand for labour to areas of high unemployment.

In addition to policies designed to transfer industrial capacity from one region to another, capital relocation policies are defined to include policy instruments the purpose of which is to induce the growth of productive capacity of indigenous activities *within* regions. One consequence of transferring industrial capacity may indeed be the inducement of some indigenous growth from within the region through the input-output linkages established between new and existing firms, or through the series of less tangible beneficial effects associated with what growth-pole theorists have called 'propulsive firms'. These include such effects as increased innovative activity and the spread of more competitive entrepreneurial attitudes.

The policy of relocating capital has traditionally formed the core of British regional economic policy, being based on the premise that many types of economic activity are relatively 'footloose' and can operate efficiently (allowing for the initial set-up costs) in a wide range of alternative locations, provided adequate basic facilities are available. A major aim of this policy is to divert job opportunities from areas where there exists an excess demand for labour into areas of excess supply. In this sense, capital mobility policies are the converse of labour mobility policies, since the aim of the latter is to shift labour in the opposite direction. Relocating industry is a typically Keynesian response to the problem of inadequate demand for labour in specific regions in that the aim of the policy is to create jobs directly where they are most needed.

Policies aimed at increasing the geographical movement of private capital take three forms: subsidies, taxes and controls. Whilst most regional inducements have been in the form of subsidies on capital and labour inputs, the competitiveness of firms in assisted areas could equally be enhanced by subsidies on other inputs, such as a reduction in transport costs through freight-rate subsidies. Alternatively, output rather than inputs could be subsidised, enabling firms to sell at lower prices. Just as inducements can be offered to firms to attract them into specific regions, firms can be discouraged from locating in other regions by imposing taxes on development or by simply forbidding firms to expand in certain locations. Since policies designed to shift capital from one region to another have been mainly either subsidies on capital inputs or subsidies on labour inputs, we shall concentrate on these two policy instruments in the following analysis.

As far as subsidies are concerned, the two main

arguments advanced in support of using subsidies as a tool of regional policy are: first, that subsidies have the same effect as would a regional devaluation, but without the disadvantages accompanying the creation of separate regional currency areas; and second, subsidies are defended on the grounds of helping 'infant' plants during their first few years of operation in depressed areas. The difference between the two arguments is simply that the first one argues for permanent subsidies whereas the latter argues for temporary subsidies until the infant industry becomes established. Temporary subsidies are usually thought of as 'carrots' designed to induce firms to set up new operations in the assisted areas. Permanent subsidies aim at raising the competitive position of depressed regional economies.

Let us consider each of these arguments in more detail. Subsidies on either output or inputs (such as the Regional Employment Premium in Britain, a per capita subsidy on the employment of labour during 1967-77) have the same effect as a currency devaluation — provided they are permanent. The opposite is true, of course, for input taxes and output taxes, which have the same effect as a currency revaluation. In so far as subsidies such as the Regional Employment Premium are used to reduce the price of commodities produced in depressed areas and are not absorbed in wage increases or in higher profits (see Brown 1967), a subsidy will stimulate regional exports and thus regional income and employment. Furthermore, whilst in a real devaluation there would be a cost to the region in terms of increased import prices, this is not the case with labour subsidies financed by the Exchequer. The cost of the 'devaluation' is borne by the tax-paying community at large and not just by the region itself.

One of the problems with this policy, as pointed out by its innovator (Kaldor 1970), is that the transfers from the Exchequer may have to be substantial if the competitive position of depressed areas is to be restored. A 6% reduction in labour costs through a labour subsidy, for example, would allow only about a 2% reduction in a region's export prices. This is because a high proportion of the total cost of regional output consists of value added by firms located in *other regions* at an earlier stage in the production process. The lower the proportion of value added to the product by the region exporting it, the smaller will be the effect of any given input subsidy on final export prices.

A further problem with permanent subsidies is that the longer-term consequences are uncertain. Like a devaluation, subsidies will improve the competitive position of the region and raise the level of its exports. But the long-run effects of this 'once-and-for-all' increase in exports are uncertain. There will be a once-and-for-all increase in output, but there is no reason to expect any permanent increase in the rate of growth of the region's output, unless the initial shift in exports generates additional investment effects via the accelerator mechanism (Dixon and Thirlwall 1976).

The infant-industries hypothesis asserts that temporary subsidies are required to induce firms to invest in underdeveloped economies so that they can overcome the initially high operating costs. As industrial development proceeds, firms will reach their optimum long-run capacity output, thus gaining any internal economies of scale which are available. External economies of scale may also be forthcoming as the economy expands and specialist subsidiary firms emerge alongside the major producers. An identical argument applies to the policy of offering incentives to firms to induce them to expand in specific regions. The purpose of capital subsidies is to help firms to overcome the initial set-up costs and to offset the higher costs that the firm may suffer during the first year or two of production. The difficulty with this line of argument is that some infants never grow up, either because locational disadvantages are never overcome or because the hoped-for external economies fail to emerge. The belief that only initial and not continuing subsidies are required is deeply rooted in both British and EEC regional policy.

Subsidies designed to induce capital to move into selected regions can vary considerably in the way they are made available to firms (see Woodward 1974b). They can take the form of capital grants, tax concessions, cheap loans, factory space at low rentals, output subsidies, labour subsidies, general subsidies on total production costs, transport subsidies and many other variations on input and output subsidies. Since the way in which subsidies are provided to firms can significantly affect the way in which firms respond to those subsidies, particularly with respect to the combination of factors of production that the firm decides to employ, it is important to give considerable thought to the nature of the subsidies. The importance of this point can be illustrated by considering the potential effects of alternative types of subsidy on firms which are assumed to employ only two factor inputs, capital and labour. Three subsidies will be considered: capital subsidies, labour subsidies and output subsidies. It should be noted that the term 'capital subsidies' refers here to the subsidisation of investment, not to the subsidisation of the use of existing capital equipment.

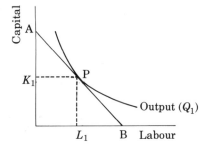

Figure 9.1 *The optimum combination of capital and labour inputs with a fixed budget*

Consider figure 9.1. This shows a manufacturing plant before the receipt of a regional subsidy. It can be regarded as either a plant already located in an assisted area or a plant currently located in a non-assisted area but which will subsequently relocate to an assisted area in order to obtain regional subsidies. With relative factor prices reflected in the slope of the isocost line AB, the firm will minimize its production costs if it employs K units of capital and L units of labour. The optimum combination of capital and labour is therefore at P. Suppose the government now decides to create more job opportunities in assisted areas and therefore introduces a new subsidy for manufacturing plants located in or relocating to such areas. It is easy to show that the effect of the subsidy on the firm's demand for labour will depend upon, first, the type of subsidy, second, the nature of the firm's production function and, third, the absolute size of the subsidy.

Consider again the three types of subsidy; capital subsidies, labour subsidies, and subsidies on total output. A subsidy on the use of capital means that more capital can be purchased with the same outlay. It is depicted diagrammatically in figure 9.2(a) as a change in the firm's budget constraint from AB to A'B, the difference AA' being the extra capital that could be employed if the whole budget

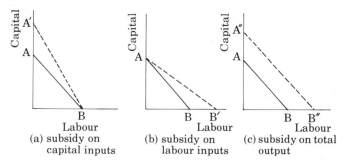

Figure 9.2 *Capital subsidies, labour subsidies and total production cost subsidies*

was spent on capital inputs and none on labour inputs. A labour subsidy changes the isocost line from AB to AB'. A subsidy on total output shifts the isocost line out to A''B'', leaving the relative price of capital and labour unchanged. It has no effect on the relative price of capital and labour since a subsidy on total output will simply leave the firm with a higher total budget (i.e. £X + subsidy).

The effects of each of these three subsidies on investment and jobs can now be shown. In each case, the effects are twofold. On the one hand, any change in the relative prices of capital and labour will cause substitution effects (unless production techniques do not allow this). On the other hand,

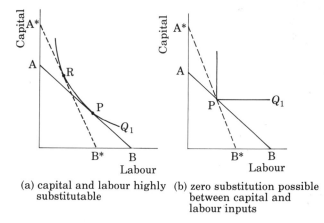

Figure 9.3 *The effect of a change in the prices of capital and labour on the optimum combination of these two inputs*

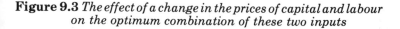

subsidies will raise the firm's budget and permit it to produce a greater output. It will be convenient to consider these two effects separately.

Let us first consider substitution effects. Intuition would lead us to expect that a capital subsidy would induce firms to employ more capital relative to labour, provided that the technical conditions of production facing firms allow them to do so. If capital and labour are highly substitutable, as shown by the shape of isoquant Q in figure 9.3(a), a fall in the price (or user cost) of capital relative to labour would lead to a substitution of capital for labour. Holding output constant, the fall in the relative price of capital from AB to A*B* will induce the firm to move from the combination of capital and labour inputs shown by P to combination R. If technical conditions of production are completely rigid, as in figure 9.3(b), the optimum combination of capital and labour remains unchanged at P. In the case of a labour subsidy, the price of labour falls relative to the price of capital. In terms of figure 9.3(a), such a case is depicted by a change in the isocost line from A*B* to AB, which shifts the optimum combination of capital and labour inputs from R to P. Once again, if factor inputs are not substitutable, the change in relative factor prices will have no effect on the optimum combination of capital and labour.

In recent years, attempts have been made to measure the empirical significance of these substitution effects (see Dixon and Thirlwall 1976, Tooze 1976 and Buck and Atkins 1976b). This involves the calculation of the price elasticity of substitution (σ) for individual industries:

$$\sigma = \frac{\triangle(K/L)}{(K/L)} \div \frac{\triangle(w/r)}{(w/r)}$$

where:
K = capital stock
L = employed labour
w = real wage rate
r = real rental price of capital
$\triangle$ = 'small change in'.

In spite of the many limitations of the data and the methodology (see McDermott 1977), the results of these various attempts to estimate the elasticity of substitution are interesting. Buck and Atkins (1976b) find that only 43% of the 77 industries considered had elasticities of substitution significantly greater than zero. Moreover, it seems possible that it is those industries in relative decline which have elasticities of substitution greater than zero. Since British regional policy is dominated by capital subsidies, the obvious conclusions would seem to be, firstly, that capital subsidies may have encouraged a certain amount of capital-intensity in the high-unemployment areas and, secondly, that labour subsidies (such as the Regional Employment Premium) would have a greater effect on employment levels than would capital subsidies. The extent of additional capital-intensity does not seem large, however, and there is little direct evidence of substantial substitution of capital for labour in depressed areas (Moore and Rhodes 1976b).

The second conclusion must also be handled with considerable care, since these estimates ignore output effects. The output effect of a subsidy enables a firm to produce more output at the same total cost. In our earlier look at the substitution effect, we deliberately held output constant, the implication being that firms will use subsidies to reduce their production costs. We now let output vary and fix the firm's budget at its initial level. The effect of this is that the firm will produce more output at the same total costs of production since its *effective* budget is raised by the existence of a subsidy.

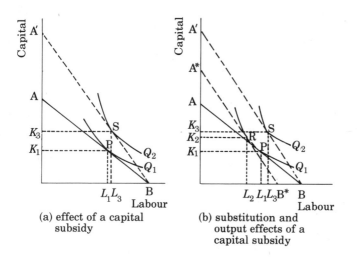

(a) effect of a capital
subsidy

(b) substitution and
output effects of a
capital subsidy

Figure 9.4 *The substitution and output effects of a capital subsidy*

Let us consider the substitution and output effects simultaneously. The introduction of a capital subsidy shifts the isocost line from AB to A'B in figure 9.4(a). The effect of this reduction in the price of capital is that the optimum combination of capital and labour changes from P to S (assuming the firm has a fixed budget, all of which is spent on capital and labour inputs). This 'price effect' can now be split into a substitution effect and an output effect.

To do this, the relative price of capital is held constant at its post-subsidy position, i.e. the price implicit in the isocost line A'B — which is then shifted downwards (to A*B*) until it is just possible to produce the initial output level of Q_1. It is clear from figure 9.4(b) that the 'new' isocost line of A*B* will be tangent to the isoquant Q_1 at a different combination of capital and labour than was the case with isocost line AB. It is exactly this difference that tells us what the substitution effect is. The move from P to R is the substitution effect, since it shows how the optimum combination of capital and labour changes when there is a change in relative prices. The output effect is indicated by the move from combination R to combination S. It tells us how the optimum combination of capital and labour changes when the firm's effective budget increases (in this case from £X to £X + the subsidy).

The substitution and output effects can now be calculated for capital and labour individually. Since the price of capital has fallen relative to the price of labour, we would expect an increase in its use — and a corresponding fall in the use of labour. The optimum input of capital increases from K_1 to K_2 as a consequence of the change in relative prices. To add to this, we also have the output effect, which in this particular case raises the input of capital from K_2 to K_3. The total effect of the capital subsidy, then, is to raise the optimum input of capital from K_1 to K_3. The case for labour is a little different. The fall in the price of capital relative to labour reduces the optimum input of labour from L_1 to L_2. The higher price of labour relative to the price of capital has induced a reduction in the input of labour, as indeed we would expect. In this particular example, however, the negative effect of the increase in the price of labour relative to capital is more than offset by a positive output effect, which induces an increase in the input of labour from L_2 to L_3, resulting in a net increase in the input of labour from L_1 to L_3.

In the example shown in figure 9.4, a capital subsidy has caused an increase in the input of both capital and labour. It should be quite obvious, however, that an example could have been devised in which the effect of a capital subsidy is to reduce the input of labour in spite of positive 'output effects' on employment. (This is easily 'achieved' by sliding the isoquant Q_2 upwards along the isocost line A'B.) A synonymous analysis could be undertaken for a labour subsidy. Without some measure of the 'output effects', however, it is impossible to say *a priori* what the effect of capital and labour subsidies on employment is likely to be. All that can be said is that the substitution effect (if any) of a capital subsidy will tend to reduce employment whilst the substitution effect of a labour subsidy will increase employment.

This kind of isoquant analysis is useful, but its limitations should be kept in mind. It is misleading to use it as a basis for arguing that subsidies on labour inputs are always preferable to capital subsidies, even where the reduction of unemployment is the prime objective of regional policy. The isoquant analysis presented above suffers from at least two potentially serious problems: it is partial and it is static. When the fuller system effects of subsidies are examined and when allowance is made for possible dynamic effects, the choices become even less clear and more controversial.

Isoquant analysis is partial in that it ignores the indirect effects of capital and labour subsidies. At first sight, one may feel that labour subsidies are likely to have greater regional multiplier effects because payments to labour enter the regional economy directly via the household sector. Second and subsequent rounds of expenditure will have a further local multiplier impact on those firms supplying the regional market since part of the extra household expenditure will remain within the region. With capital-intensive projects the immediate multiplier consequences are likely to be smaller, since much of the initial capital spending will 'leak out' of the region through the need to import the required capital goods. This leakage in the initial injection is potentially substantial and must be taken into account when calculating the multiplier effects of different types of subsidy.

But reality is more complicated. The multiplier effects of labour subsidies will depend upon the use to which these subsidies are put (see Brown 1967). They may be used to reduce commodity prices whilst wages are held constant. Or alternatively, workers may bid up the money wage through organised pressure from the unions, thus resulting in higher wages with the level of employment initially unchanged. Finally, labour subsidies may simply be absorbed into profits with the result that there is no direct effect on employment, wages and output. Any of these results is possible and may have different multiplier effects. The same qualifications hold for capital subsidies.

Even though the multiplier effects of labour subsidies are not likely to be as great as we might initially have thought, it seems reasonable to assume that the closer links of labour intensive industries with the household sector will lead to a larger multiplier effect than would the subsidisation of capital-intensive industries. But this also depends upon the inter-industry input-output linkages which are developed by the new industries. Capital-intensive firms may develop more backward and forward linkages with other firms in the region. Isoquant analysis also suffers from its static nature. It may be well worthwhile to attract capital-intensive firms rather than labour-intensive firms simply because the long term growth prospects of capital-intensive firms are more favourable. If this is so, the adverse short-term substitution effects of capital subsidies are of little consequence.

It is not simply the limitations of isoquant analysis that suggest the need for caution in deciding against capital subsidies. We have shown that whether a firm is already located in an assisted area or whether it relocates from a non-assisted area to an assisted area, capital subsidies will tend to cause an increase in the capital-intensity of production (i.e. raising the capital-labour ratio), though this may be more than offset by the output effect on employment. It is also often assumed that capital subsidies will tend to operate with a bias in terms of the types of firms induced to relocate: capital subsidies will tend to attract inherently capital-intensive firms; labour subsidies will tend to attract inherently labour-intensive firms. Although this cannot be denied, a qualifying point must be borne in mind. A capital subsidy may also induce a labour-intensive firm to move as long as the firm uses at least *some* capital with its predominant labour input. The possible substitution of capital for labour after relocation need not necessarily lead to a complete reversal of the capital/labour ratio. A labour subsidy also offers some inducement to an inherently capital-intensive firm for the same reason.

Finally, in defence of capital subsidies it should be

remembered that the capital subsidies used in regional policy are *investment* subsidies. Only marginal additions to the capital stock are subsidised. This endows capital subsidies with a further advantage over labour subsidies. Not only do they encourage the substitution of capital for labour, but in addition they encourage the substitution of newer, technologically advanced capital for older capital.

9.3 The Case for Greater Selectivity

One of the main ways in which economic policies are improved is by making them more selective and more discriminating. Regional policy is no exception. Regional instruments could be sharpened in three different ways. First, the types of region assisted could be differentiated more clearly and in more detail. Secondly, there could be greater differentiation between areas in the amount and type of assistance provided. Thirdly, there could be greater selectivity in the types of industries induced to relocate in depressed regions. Each of these will be examined in turn.

The case for greater differentiation between assisted areas
A strong case can be made for delimiting geographical areas according to the type of problem they possess and moulding a package of policy instruments more precisely suited to the needs of particular areas. At the very least, three distinct types of region can be identified for regional policy purposes: depressed industrial areas, depressed agricultural areas, and high density urban areas. In Britain, regional policy has been directed mainly towards solving the problems of depressed industrial areas. This does not mean, of course, that regional policymakers have ignored depressed agricultural areas or high density urban areas. This is far from the the truth. The setting up of the Highlands and Islands Development Board in Scotland in 1965 reflected a conscious and deliberate effort to find ways of preventing further rural depopulation of northern Scotland, and efforts have been made (admittedly on a small scale) to encourage the development of tourism in this region. In addition, grants have been made available to small firms in the fishing industry to discourage the decline of coastal communities. The Board also has substantial powers to assist industry in the rural areas of the Highlands and

Islands. Finally, policies to alleviate severe urban problems in Britain's major conurbations have been much in evidence, with the relocation of people and jobs from Greater London to surrounding New Towns in the SE, East Anglia and the East Midlands being the prime example. More recently, the attention of policymakers has turned towards the problems of inner city areas (Townsend 1977).

The diverse nature of regional problems suggests that a flexible approach is required to the delimitation of regions for the purpose of devising appropriate policy options. The type of policy package must be geared to the needs of the individual region.

The case for greater regional differentiation in the application of individual policy instruments

To a certain degree, the amount of assistance provided to regions is already tied to the region's economic circumstances in the case of British regional policy. Special Development Areas, Development Areas and Intermediate Areas show a progression from areas in most need to those in least need, with Special Development Areas having both the broadest package of policy instruments and the highest rates of assistance. A case can be made for a further sharpening of regional policy instruments. It has been argued, for example, that labour subsidies ought to be made a function of the excess supply of labour in a region. It is possible to go even further than this, however, since one of the purposes of regional policy is to reduce the excess demand for labour in regions where demand exceeds supply, thus implying the need for a tax on labour in such cases (see Hutton and Hartley 1968). If the demand for labour happens to be deficient in *all* regions, of course, a labour subsidy will be required across the board — but the rate of subsidy will have to vary between regions if regional differences in the excess supply of labour are to be eliminated at the same time as the excess supply is reduced in all regions. This takes us right back to the regionally discriminating fiscal policies discussed in the previous chapter.

To sharpen a policy instrument such as a labour subsidy, it is necesary to make it sensitive to the pressure of the demand for labour. Figure 9.5 shows two possibilities. The labour subsidy function LS, is drawn on the assumption that to be eligible for the subsidy a region must be designated as an assisted area. It is further assumed, for simplicity, that

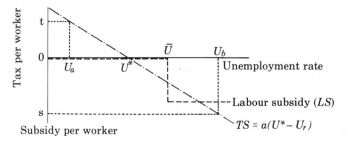

Notes
(i) U^* = equilibrium unemployment rate, i.e. demand for labour and supply of labour are equal at U^*
(ii) U_r = regional unemployment rate (e.g. U_a, U_b)
Source: Hutton and Hartley (1968).

Figure 9.5 *Labour subsidies : two possibilities*

assisted areas comprise all regions with unemployment rates greater than $\bar{U}$. An alternative is to tax the employment of labour if there is an excess demand for labour and subsidise labour if there is an excess supply. One possibility is to tax labour in direct proportion to the amount of excess demand existing in a region, and similarly pay subsidies where there exists an excess supply of labour. *TS* is such a function. Thus, region B with an unemployment rate of U_b will receive a subsidy of s per worker, whereas region A with an unemployment rate of U_a has to pay a tax of t per worker. Another alternative is to make the tax-cum-subsidy function non-linear (not shown in figure 9.5).

Note: For more details of this variable see Ashcroft and Taylor (1977).

Figure 9.6 *A measure of the intensity of the control over the location of industry in the UK (1952-73): the refusal rate for IDC applications*

Virtually any of the policy instruments could be 'sharpened' in this way. Investment subsidies certainly could. Even location controls could be sharpened. Controls can be regarded as an infinite tax on industrial development. Figure 9.6 shows the extent to which location controls have been used in Britain during the postwar period. The refusal rate for applications to expand industrial buildings was very low in the 1950s, indicating the existence of lax controls on the location of industry. The situation changed markedly during the 1960s, however, when greater efforts were made to divert industry to the Development Areas. As with labour subsidies, it has been argued frequently that the 'black and white' nature of location controls should be abandoned and replaced by a system of taxes on industrial development. The tax could be related to an indicator of aggregate demand. Alternatively, the tax could be given greater precision by levying it in areas such as Greater London according to the extent of the net social costs caused by the expansion (i.e. externalities such as congestion and pollution). This tax would be based on the difference between the social costs and the private costs of a given expansion. France operates a similar tax policy in the Paris region. It has the advantage over direct controls (such as the Industrial Development Certificate used in Britain) that it would not discourage investment by firms willing and able to pay the full social costs of expanding in these high social cost locations and who are unwilling to expand elsewhere. Its disadvantage is that it penalises both the 'footloose' firm and the firm tied to such locations, although one could presumably allow exemptions from the tax just as Industrial Development Certificates are granted to firms which have a strong case for locating in the prosperous regions. The measurement of the social costs of industrial development is, in any case, an infant science, though this should not discourage us from exploring the possibility of devising a tax system to replace controls.

The case for an industrially-selective regional strategy
The extent to which regional policy should be selective in the kind of industrial development it encourages in depressed areas is a matter of fierce controversy. The difficulty of moving towards a more industry-specific policy lies in deciding just *which* industries should be induced to expand in assisted areas. There is no general agreement as to which

types of industry should be induced to move to the assisted areas. Two distinct viewpoints, however, can be identified. First, there is the growth pole policy which calls for key industries to be attracted to specific growth point locations in depressed areas. Second, there is the policy of industrial diversification, the aim of which is to diversify the industry mix of the depressed regions.

The rationale behind the growth pole policy rests upon the supreme irony that since regional development seems to be naturally polarised — and this indeed is the reason for the emergence of regional economic disparities — then it may be possible to harness the growth potential inherent in growth poles for regional policy purposes. The growth pole approach argues that depressed regions could be induced to grow more rapidly either by creating new growth poles in such areas or by stimulating specific existing industrial centres. The intention of the strategy is to deliberately encourage growth at certain selected locations in order to reduce regional growth disparities. But in doing this, it is inevitable that growth disparities *within* the depressed region will widen, at least in the short run. Such a policy clearly carries with it the assumption that the problems of regional imbalance arise principally from *inter*regional disparities rather than from *intra*regional disparities.

At the heart of the growth-pole policy is the view that there exist 'propulsive firms', in modern economies, which are members of 'key industries'. Furthermore, these key industries are ideal candidates for providing depressed regions with the necessary stimulus to growth. They are the 'growth-inducing dynamos' of growth poles. Key industries are defined as industries that exhibit dominance in the sense of having powerful linkages, both forwards and backwards, with other firms. The linkages between firms within the growth pole result in high local multiplier effects if any change occurs in the demand for the key industry's output. In addition, firms providing inputs or purchasing the output of the key industry will be attracted to the growth pole if there are significant advantages to be gained from being located in close proximity to the key industry. The problem is how to identify a key industry. An obvious starting point is to examine input-output relations between different industries. Approaches using input-output data range from rather simple indices of industrial linkages to more sophisticated measures based on industrial-complex analysis (see Isard *et al.* 1959, Boudeville 1966, Lever 1972).

The identification of key industries is certainly a difficult obstacle for the growth-pole strategy. The selection of a key industry requires a detailed study of the comparative costs of operating at different locations and within different types of industrial complexes. Selection of a key industry also requires detailed study of internal and external economies of scale and a recognition of the dynamic aspects of Perroux's original concept. Key industries should exhibit rapid rates of growth over time and a rapid rate of innovation. They should stimulate technological advance throughout the region. Finally, key industries should be major exporting industries for the region. Whilst some of these more dynamic features are open to measurement — thus a high income elasticity of demand may indicate a higher growth potential for firms serving both the local and export markets — most are not. The development of methods to identify industries most suitable for growth-pole locations remains in its infancy.

In spite of these problems, the commitment to the growth-pole strategy is increasing, particularly in Europe (Allen and MacLennan 1970). Some countries, of which France and Italy are the best examples, already operate quite powerful growth pole strategies with a wide range of policy instruments designed to concentrate new productive capacity at designated locations. Figure 9.7 shows the Italian growth poles. In Britain, there exist elements of both the growth-pole strategy and the strategy of uniform development (which is the antithesis of the growth-pole policy). The first sign of any commitment to the growth-pole policy came in 1963 when the two White Papers on Regional Development in Scotland and the NE argued in favour of concentrating new development at certain selected growth points or within well-defined growth zones (see White Papers 1963a, 1963b). At the same time, the uniform strategy was maintained in so far as all other locations within these two regions remained eligible for development assistance should firms wish to establish new industrial plant in areas other than the designated growth poles. The intention, however, was to concentrate public investment in social overheads at the growth poles.

The role that new towns and industrial estates have played in British regional policy is an interesting one, not least because they point to two of the main deficiencies of regional economic policy in Britain. First, with the exception of new towns and industrial estates, regional economic policy has tended to be operated independently of regional and sub-regional planning. Second, regional *economic* policy has also tended to operate independently of land-use and social planning in Britain. There is a clear need, whatever the regional development strategy in operation, for a closer integration of *intra*regional planning and *inter*regional planning.

In addition there are 42 Nuclei for Industrial Development, 82 Agricultural Development and Connected Zones, and 29 Areas of Tourist Development.
Source: Pacione (1976).

Figure 9.7 *The major growth poles of Southern Italy*

In this context, it is interesting to note that France has an integrated hierarchical planning structure, with regional plans coordinated in a national plan and sub-regional plans coordinated in a regional plan (see Hansen 1968). British reticence towards the creation of a similar planning structure arises partly from the failure of the National Plan (White Paper 1965), which represented Britain's first serious attempt at indicative planning, and partly from the consequent failure of the various 'regional strategies' produced by the Regional Economic Planning Councils. Many of these early regional development strategies embodied the growth-pole concept but their influence on regional policy has been minimal. More recently, there has been a welcome revival of regional planning in the form of regional Strategic Plans set up by the Department of the Environment (NW Strategy Team 1974, Northern Region Strategy Team 1977). Unfortunately, these strategic plans have so far been 'one-off' creations, with regional planning teams existing for only two to three years and then evaporating as the grants dried up. This is a clear reflection of the general lack of interest in regional planning in Britain. There is simply no real commitment.

One of the reasons for the lack of commitment to regional planning in Britain is that there exists too much ignorance on many vital aspects of regional planning. Many crucial questions remain unanswered: What single industry or complex of industries is most suited to form the basis of a growth pole? On what basis should the locations of growth poles be selected? What are the crucial thresholds (if any) at which growth at the growth poles becomes self-perpetuating and cumulative? To what extent can the provision of social infrastructure and public services enhance the natural locational advantages of growth poles? Is it possible to identify and measure the effects of growth poles on the rate of technological progress? Our inability to answer these and other questions has meant that adherence to the growth pole policy has often more closely resembled religious belief than objective logic.

The second approach which lays heavy stress on selecting appropriate industries for depressed areas is the policy of regional industrial diversification (see Chisholm 1976). It is argued that locations which have a highly specialised industrial base may be less able to adapt to long-run structural changes. Furthermore, regional specialisation may cause regional differences in cyclical sensitivity, job opportunities and per capita incomes. If this is so, the aim of regional policy should be to diversify the industrial base of regions. Unfortunately, there is little evidence to either support or reject the argument that regional specialisation is undesirable. The specialisation of production in specific geographical areas has long been regarded as crucial for both the efficient exploitation of scale economies and to reap the benefits from trade and specialisation. If the policy of industrial diversification is to have any meaning, it is important to begin by specifying in detail the costs and benefits of such a strategy, so that the net benefits of the strategy can be quantified. It is pointless to argue that industrial diversification is desirable *per se* since it is far from clear what the term 'industrial diversification' actually means (see Taylor 1967).

Both the growth-pole policy and the industrial diversification policy are superficially attractive since they each carry a strong and simple message for the policymaker. Yet the arguments for greater selectivity ignore many complexities. The great difficulty lies in deciding *which* industries should be selected for special assistance. In any case, depressed regions are hardly in a position to pick and choose, and are more likely to snatch at any opportunities that come along. Their lot has been a desperate fight to attract any type of industry in the face of a rapidly declining indigenous sector.

Conclusion

The ferocity of the many controversies concerning the form that regional policy instruments should take remains one of the great fascinations in the study of regional economic policy. Whether capital, labour or output subsidies should be used, whether subsidies are preferable to controls, whether policy should focus on the reallocation of labour rather than capital, and whether or not policy options should be more selective, are all issues of the utmost importance. The frequent and volatile changes in British regional policy have created a climate of opinion in favour of greater stability in the future. Any future changes in policy will need to be closely argued and strongly supported by empirical research. This leads us directly to the evaluation of regional policy, which is the subject matter of the final section of this book.

Selected references

Blake (1976); Brown (1972); Hutton and Hartley (1968); Kaldor (1970); Prest (1976); Stilwell (1972); Woodward (1974b).

PART 3

The Evaluation of Regional Policy

There must be few areas of Government expenditure in which
so much is spent but so little known about the success of the
policy. The most our witnesses could say was that .... the
situation was better than it would have been without the
incentives and controls of some sort of regional policy. Yet no
one could say whether this effect was a major or a minor one.
House of Commons Papers 85, 1973-74, para. 116.

We are far from satisfied that the continuing search for a
viable regional policy has been backed by a critical economic
apparatus capable of analysing results and proposing
alternative courses. There are significant areas of obscurity
where the light has still to shine ..... Much has been spent
and much may well have been wasted. Regional policy has
been empiricism run mad, a game of hit-and-miss, played
with more enthusiasm than success. We do not doubt the
good intentions, the devotion even, of many of those who
have struggled over the years to relieve the human
consequences of regional disparities. We regret that their
efforts have not been better sustained by the proper
evaluation of the costs and benefits of policies pursued.
House of Commons Papers 85, 1973-74, para. 170.

*There can be no doubt that the evaluation of regional
policy has been neglected by economists. This is
surprising in view of the rapid growth in the magnitude
of expenditure on regional policy during the 1960s.
Between 1967 and 1972, for example, expenditure on
regional assistance to industry in Britain averaged over
£250 million per annum at 1970 prices (see figure). This
represented about 2.7% of total public expenditure.
    One of the reasons for this lack of interest in the*

207

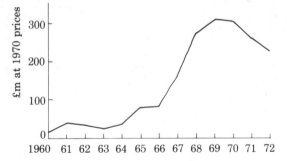

Source: **Begg** *et al.* (1975).

Annual government expenditure on regional assistance to industry in Great Britain, 1960-72

evaluation of regional policy has been the paucity and unreliability of statistical data. In spite of this, recent years have seen the emergence of several attempts to develop methods of evaluating regional policy. In this section of the book our aims are twofold. First, we will show what has been (and can be) done to evaluate regional policy within the context of available data. Second, and in more futuristic fashion, we speculate on the possibilities of developing improved methods of evaluation should more and better quality data be produced.

The following discussion of the evaluation of regional policy is divided between two chapters. This division of evaluation methods is based on the crucial distinction between two forms of policy evaluation. First there exist what we may term 'lower level' or, alternatively, 'partial' evaluation methods (Lichfield et al. 1975). The purpose of these is to estimate the effect of regional policy on variables such as employment, output and per capita income.

The second form of evaluation, which is the subject of Chapter 11, is more comprehensive than the first. It is concerned not simply with the effect of regional policy but with its effectiveness. This involves the considerably more complex task of trying to estimate which form of regional policy (if any) is the most worthwhile. The ultimate purpose of evaluation is to assist the policymaker to decide which type of policy is of most benefit to the nation. Very little headway has yet been made in this direction. *The basic analytical tools exist but the actual measurement of the advantages and the disadvantages of regional policies (i.e. the benefits and the costs) is still very much an unexplored area of applied economic research.*

It is important to be clear about just what is meant by the term 'evaluation'. To Lichfield (1975), the essence of evaluation is ' the assessment of the comparative merits of different courses of action '. We argued in Chapter 1 that it is essential to be clear about what regional policies are trying to achieve if we are to assess the merits of those policies. A policy must have objectives, and if policymakers are to be provided with estimates of the extent to which those objectives are being achieved, it is imperative that the objectives are stated as explicitly as possible. Ideally, objectives should be expressed quantitatively. Indeed, if precise estimates of the extent to which policy objectives are being achieved are to be provided, the objectives themselves will have to be quantified. One of the major objectives of regional policy, for instance, is to increase national output by creating jobs for the unemployed. Although this objective is valid per se, *it is virtually impossible to estimate the extent to which it is being achieved in the absence of (a) a numerical target specifying the number of jobs to be created, and (b) the time period within which the target is expected to be reached.*

The essential elements of the process of evaluation are illustrated in the second figure. The starting point (box 1) is the specification and quantification of the objectives of regional policy. Box 2 sets out the second prerequisite of evaluation: the investigation of a wide range of alternative courses of action. This is implicit in all evaluation exercises, since the purpose of evaluation is to help the policymaker to choose the 'best' course of action. Evaluation must address itself to questions such as: Is a growth pole strategy preferable to a strategy of uniform development? Are labour subsidies preferable to capital subsidies? Is it better to induce the movement of labour or the movement of capital?

The evaluation of government policies is often attacked for not assessing a wide range of alternative courses of action. Urban transport planning, for instance, has been heavily criticised for concentrating on the evaluation of

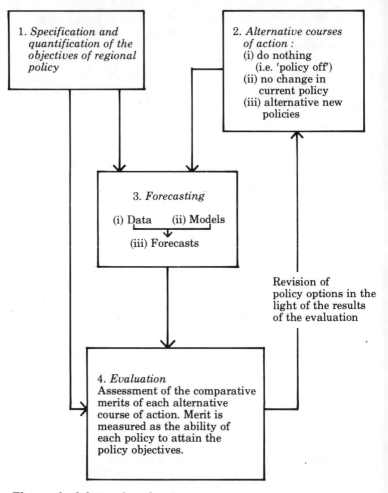

1. *Specification and quantification of the objectives of regional policy*

2. *Alternative courses of action :*
   (i) do nothing
       (i.e. 'policy off')
   (ii) no change in
        current policy
   (iii) alternative new
         policies

3. *Forecasting*

   (i) Data   (ii) Models
           (iii) Forecasts

Revision of policy options in the light of the results of the evaluation

4. *Evaluation*
Assessment of the comparative merits of each alternative course of action. Merit is measured as the ability of each policy to attain the policy objectives.

The methodology of evaluation

road investments rather than evaluating more radical public transport policies. The evaluation of regional policy must not fall into a similar trap. As the figure shows, there are three *distinct types of alternative regional policies. In addition to alternative* new *regional policy proposals, evaluation should incorporate a 'do-nothing' option (i.e. policy-off) and a 'no-change' option (i.e. continuation of existing regional policy). Attempts to evaluate regional policy have so far concentrated on either the 'do-nothing' or the 'no-change' options. There is a pressing need to develop evaluation methods which allow a wider range of possible alternative policies to be assessed (Moore and Rhodes 1977).*

If the evaluation of regional policy is to be put on to a firm footing, it is essential to investigate ways in which the possible consequences of alternative courses of action can be measured. A necessary preliminary to evaluating regional policy is an estimate of its various effects. It is therefore the purpose of Chapter 10 to discuss some of the more widely used techniques that are now available for estimating the impact of regional policy. Only if adequate tools are available for estimating the effects of regional policy will it then be possible to proceed to the even more ambitious and complex task of evaluating regional policy. The evaluation of regional policy is the subject matter of the final chapter.

10
Measuring the Effects of Regional Policy : Partial Evaluation

By far the most popular method of estimating the effect of regional policy is to observe trends in regional unemployment, employment, migration and other economic variables in order to detect any changes which can be attributed to regional policy. To take a simple example, the upward trend in the unemployment rate of the assisted areas (see figure 10.1) could be taken as evidence that regional policy in Britain has been a failure in the postwar years — in spite of the increasing expenditure during the 1960s. But the upward trend in unemployment has been universal in all parts of the British economy, and a better test would be to observe the trend in the ratio of unemployment in the

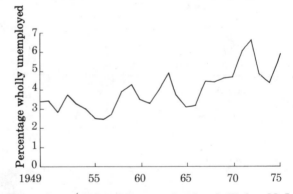

Note:
Development Areas defined here as Scotland, Wales, N. Ireland and the Northern region.
Source: British Labour Statistics Yearbook.

Figure 10.1 *Unemployment in the UK Development Areas, 1949-75*

assisted areas to unemployment in the SE, where
unemployment rates have consistently been well below the

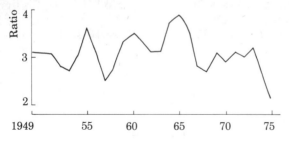

Note:
Development Areas defined here as Scotland, Wales, N. Ireland
and the Northern region.
Source: British Labour Statistics Yearbook.

Figure 10.2 *The ratio of the unemployment rate in the UK*
          Development Areas to the unemployment rate in the SE
          region, 1949-75

national average. Figure 10.2 indicates a distinct downward
trend in this ratio after the mid-1960s, which suggests that
regional policy has helped to reduce regional *disparities* in
unemployment.

The problem with this sort of casual empiricism is that
nothing can be said about the specific effect of regional
policy. It is quite possible, for instance, that regional policy
may be providing a large number of extra jobs in the assisted
areas but that this effect is being offset by a simultaneous
loss of jobs in certain declining industries. On top of this, the
creation of jobs through regional policy measures may cause
a fall in outward migration from the assisted areas, in which
case the supply of labour is responding to the increase in
demand. Furthermore, the provision of more jobs may draw
secondary workers, such as married women, into the
workforce. The result of this expansion in the supply of
labour is that the extra jobs brought in by regional policy
may have very little, if any, effect on the unemployment rate
of the assisted areas. Comparing unemployment rates in
assisted and non-assisted areas may therefore be of no help
in measuring the effect of regional policy on the problem of
regional imbalance.

Another example of casual empiricism is the suggestion
that the simultaneous increase in the strength of regional
policy and the movement of industry to the assisted areas
during the 1960s is sufficient evidence to indicate that

regional policy was having the desired effect. The average number of manufacturing establishments moving to the Development Areas during the period 1952-59, for instance, was 32 per annum. This increased to an average of 94 per annum during the 1960s (see figure 10.3). The method can

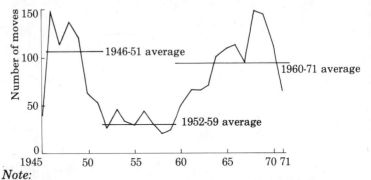

Note:
Development Areas defined here as Scotland, N. Ireland, the Northern region and the assisted areas in Wales, the SW and Merseyside.
Source: Dept. of Industry.

Figure 10.3 *The movement of manufacturing establishments to the UK Development Areas, 1945-71*

also be applied to individual assisted areas (see figure 10.4). Can we conclude that the strengthening of regional policy during the 1960s caused an increase of around 62 moves per annum? The answer is that we cannot. Industrial movement is unlikely to be explained by regional policy alone, and to measure the effect of regional policy on movement we need to know whether any other factors were responsible for any changes in movement during the 1960s.

It is clear that the search for more rigorous methods of measuring the effect of regional policy must continue. Casual empiricism is likely to lead to inaccurate estimates of the effect of regional policy. We turn first to the attempts that have been made to estimate the effect of regional policy on the creation of jobs in, and the movement of industry to, assisted areas. These methods have been specifically constructed to measure the effect of regional policy during selected time periods.

The second part of the chapter examines the methods which generally fall under the heading 'impact models'. The *general* purpose of impact models is to explain how economic

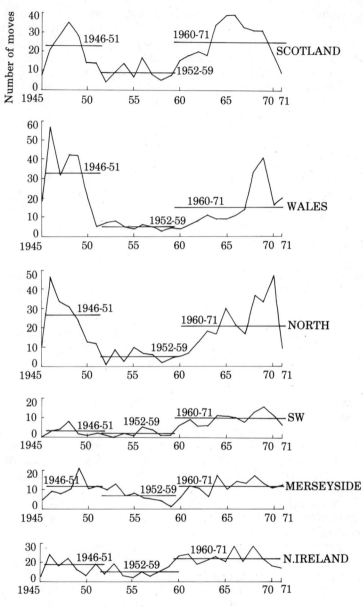

Source: Dept. of Industry.

Figure 10.4 *The movement of manufacturing industry to the UK Development Areas, 1945-71*

systems (such as a regional economy) actually operate. Their beauty lies in their 'wholeness' and in the sophistication of the economic theory underlying them. They are therefore more reliable for estimating the consequences of future changes in government policy. Data demands are severe, however, and this has restricted their use. Of course, impact models come in all shapes and sizes and in various degrees of complexity, as we shall see in the second part of this chapter.

10.1 Estimating the Effect of Regional Policy on Job Creation and on the Movement of Industry to Assisted Areas

The relocation of industry has undoubtedly dominated British regional policy during the post-war years. Considerably less emphasis has been placed either on encouraging workers to migrate from depressed regions or on stimulating indigenous industries within these regions. In view of this, it is not surprising that the attempts to measure the effect of regional policy in Britain have concentrated heavily on two major questions:

(i)   how many jobs have been created in the assisted areas as a consequence of regional policy?
(ii) how successful has regional policy been in diverting industry to assisted areas?

Measuring the effect of regional policy on employment in assisted areas
One of the most noteworthy attempts to estimate the effect of regional policy is that of Moore and Rhodes (1973a), who have adapted a technique known as shift-share analysis (see Appendix B) in order to estimate the employment creating effects of regional policy in Britain during the period 1960-71. Shift-share analysis is a fashionable, though somewhat hazardous, method of identifying the significance of a region's industry-mix in determining the growth of employment in a region. In its simplest form, the shift-share technique divides a region's growth into two component parts, a structural component and a residual. The structural component measures that part of a region's growth that is 'explained' by the region's industrial structure. The residual is attributed to 'other factors' which include locational advantages or disadvantages, as well as the effects of regional policy on the growth of the region. Put simply, the

shift-share identity is as follows:

Difference between regional and national growth in employment	=	That part *attributed* to differences in the structure of industry	+	Un-explained residual

Unfortunately, shift-share analysis has been shown to be an unreliable technique for analysing the problems facing regional economies (see MacKay 1968 and Buck 1970). In particular, lack of knowledge about the factors determining the size of the residual component considerably reduces the value of the technique. But this does not mean that shift-share analysis is of no use. Moore and Rhodes (1973a) have developed a modified version of the technique in order to estimate the effect of regional policy on the creation of jobs in the Development Areas. The procedure is quite straightforward. The object of the exercise is to estimate the effect of regional policy on the creation of jobs during a period of time when a regional policy was actively pursued. The effect of regional policy is estimated by comparing the actual level of employment in a region (or the Development Areas as a whole) to the level of employment that *would* have occurred if regional policy had not been in operation. In other words, a hypothetical 'policy-off' situation is estimated for a period of time when regional policy was actually in existence.

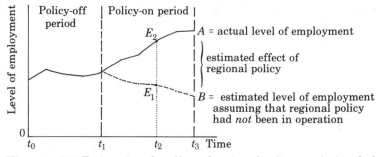

Figure 10.5 *Estimating the effect of regional policy on the level of employment in an assisted area : an illustration*

Figure 10.5 provides a picture of what this method is aiming to do. The difference between the two time series is the estimated effect of regional policy. At year t_2, for instance, the actual level of employment is at E_2 whereas E_1 is the estimated level of employment that would have occurred if regional policy had not existed between t_1 and t_2. In this illustration, regional policy has raised the level of employment by $E_2 - E_1$ over and above the level it would have reached in the absence of regional policy between t_1 and t_2.

We must now examine in detail how the effects of regional policy on employment can be estimated. The method divides into five steps.

Step 1. National growth rates per industry are applied to each industry in the region to obtain a hypothetical employment level (H_1) at time t_1:

$$H_1 = \sum_i \bar{e}_{i\,t_1} = \sum_i \left[e_{i\,t_0} \left(E_{i\,t_1} / E_{i\,t_0} \right) \right]$$

where:

$e_{i,}$ = regional employment in industry i
E_i = national employment in industry i

All this simple formula does is to estimate the regional employment level that *would* have existed at t_1 if each industry in the region had grown at the same rate between t_0 and t_1 as it did in the nation as a whole. The same procedure is carried out for every year in the study period (using the same base year for measuring the region's structure of industry, which in this example is the industry mix at t_0). The outcome is a hypothetical time series of total regional employment which can then be compared to the actual time series of total employment (see figure 10.6). This takes us to step 2.

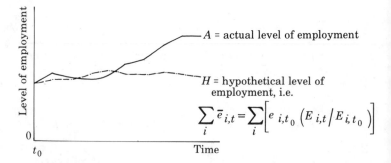

Figure 10.6 *Actual and hypothetical employment levels*

Step 2. The difference *(D)* between the actual level of employment *(A)* in the region and the hypothetical level of employment *(H)* calculated in step 1 is obtained for each year during the study period:

$$D = A - H = \sum_i e_i - \sum_i \bar{e}_i$$

This is shown in figure 10.7.

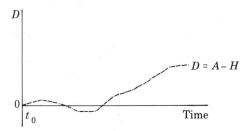

Figure 10.7 *Difference between actual and hypothetical employment levels*

Step 3. The study period is divided into a policy-off and a policy-on period (figure 10.8).

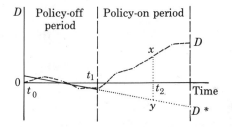

Figure 10.8 *The effect of regional policy*

Step 4. A linear trend *(D*)* is fitted to the time series of *D* for the policy-off time period and extrapolated forward into the policy-on period as shown in figure 10.8.

Step 5. Finally, the difference between the actual *D* and the extrapolated *D* (i.e. *D**) is taken as an estimate of the effect of regional policy. At time t_2, for example, the actual value of *D* exceeds *D** by the amount *xy*. This positive difference is assumed to be the beneficial consequence of regional policy on the employment level of the region in question.

The last two steps need elaborating. The assumption underlying step 4 (in which a linear trend is fitted to the *D* series for the policy-off period and extrapolated forward into the policy-on period) is absolutely crucial to the exercise. It is assumed that *in the absence of regional policy* the factors affecting the difference between the actual level of employment *(A)* and the hypothetical level of employment *(H) would continue* to affect the growth of employment in the region during the policy-on period. Moreover, we must also allow for the possibility that the effect of these diverse factors (which remain as yet unspecified) has been changing over time — hence the linear trend fitted to the *D*-series during the policy-off period and its subsequent extrapolation into the policy-on period.

On the surface, this method of estimating the effect of regional policy on employment looks to be an attractively simple device and has been used on a number of occasions (see, for instance Moore and Rhodes 1973a, 1975a; Northern Region Strategy Team 1975). Applying this method to the UK Development Areas, Moore and Rhodes estimate that about 250,000 extra jobs in the manufacturing sector resulted directly from the strengthening of regional policy during the 1960s. This estimate was obtained by applying the method described above to the period 1951-71, which was divided into two sub-periods: a policy-off period (1951-59) and a policy-on period (1960-71).

Plausible though these estimates of the effect of regional policy on the creation of jobs in the manufacturing sector may be, it is necessary to be sceptical about the method used to obtain them. The method suffers from what may turn out to be a significant weakness. It contains no explanation of why we should expect the trend in the policy-off time series of *D* to continue into the future. In particular, it is not clear why we should expect *D* to proceed along a linear time path in the absence of regional policy. If the trend in *D is* to be extrapolated, then we need a theory of what determines its slope so that we can then predict its subsequent movement rather than rely on linear extrapolation. It is possible to monitor whether or not fluctuations in *D* can be ascribed solely to regional policy by searching for evidence of other influences that might have been at work. The rise in *D* during the policy-on period may be due not to the advent of regional policy, but to an improvement in the relative economic attractiveness of the assisted areas. Obvious possibilities that come to mind are a lower rate of increase of labour costs in the assisted areas, an increase in unemployment relative to other areas, the discovery of a new raw material source, the improvement of transport links with other regions, and other factors of a similar nature that may reduce production costs in the assisted areas (see Moore and Rhodes 1976b, 1977).

Further development of this technique relies heavily upon the construction of a model to explain movements in D, which incidentally is simply the unexplained residual component in the shift-share identity. A declining D, for example, indicates that a region is growing less rapidly than we would have expected on the basis of its industry mix. This means that the region's industries have been growing more slowly than their national counterparts for one reason or another. We need to know what these reasons are if we are to construct a model capable of projecting the policy-off value of D into the policy-on period.

Measuring the effect of regional policy on the diversion of industry to the assisted areas

The dominant tactic of regional policy in Britain has been to steer industry into the less prosperous regions. Successive governments have consequently devised measures for diverting industrial capacity into designated assisted areas. We have already seen that one way of measuring the effect of this policy is to estimate the additional jobs created in assisted areas as a result of regional policy measures. An alternative way is to examine the effect of regional policy measures on the flow of industry into the assisted areas (see Moore and Rhodes 1976a and Ashcroft and Taylor 1977).

In attempting to estimate the effect of regional policy on the creation of jobs, we showed that it is necessary to construct an estimate of what *would* have happened in the absence of regional policy and then subtract this from what *actually* happened. Exactly the same procedure can be followed for estimating the effects of regional policy on the movement of industry to the assisted areas. The aim is to construct a hypothetical policy-off position, which is an estimate of what would have happened to the movement of industry to development areas if a regional policy had *not* existed during a period of time when, as a matter of fact, it *did* exist.

It is possible to obtain an estimate of the movement of industry that *would* have occurred in the absence of regional policy only if we can construct a model capable of explaining why firms move. An obvious starting point is to isolate the factors that have been observed to influence the location decisions of firms. Empirical surveys have shown that a high percentage of industrial movement is associated with an expansion of a firm's productive capacity. This is not surprising since firms may not always find it either possible or economical to expand at their existing sites and are therefore forced to search for alternative locations. This implies that the investment and the location decisions are often made simultaneously. Firms tend, by and large, to consider alternative locations for their new plant at the same time as they consider their investment plans.

The total movement of industry in the economy as a whole then, is heavily dependent on the level of aggregate investment in the economy. We would not expect to see much industrial movement when investment is at a low level. It is only at times of high demand for goods and services, relative to productive capacity, that firms will have an incentive to expand their operations. This is the time they will be looking for new locations if expansion at their present location proves uneconomic or impossible (e.g. if there are urban planning controls). We can therefore write:

$$M = f(I) \tag{1}$$

where:
M = the geographical movement of industry
I = gross investment.

There is, however, more to industrial movement than this. We need to know not only what determines the *total* movement of industry in the economy as a whole, but also what factors govern its *distribution* between the various regions of an economy. Thus an increase in total movement in Britain is of little use to assisted areas if most of it occurs between the non-assisted areas. Many factors influence the relative attractiveness of regions to mobile industry. Access to national (or even international) markets is a factor that has had a diminishing effect over time as transport and communications have improved. Possibly of more importance is the extent to which production costs vary between regions. We would therefore expect to see interregional flows of industry responding to changes in the relative economic attractiveness of regions. This relationship can be expressed as follows:

$$\frac{MDA}{M} = g(A) \qquad (2)$$

where:

MDA = the movement of industry to the Development Areas

M = the total movement of industry (as in equation 1)

A = a measure of the relative economic attractiveness of Development Area locations compared to other locations.

This two-part model of industrial movement is illustrated in figure 10.9.

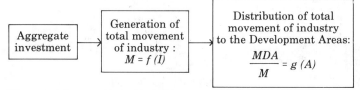

M = total movement of industry
MDA = movement of industry to the Development Areas
I = aggregate investment
A = relative economic attractiveness of Development Areas

Figure 10.9 *Investment and industrial mobility*

Up to this point, the effects of regional policy on the movement of industry have been ignored. In Britain, two principal methods have been used for diverting firms to development areas: the provision of incentives to firms willing to locate in the Development Areas and the control over the location of new industrial capacity. Both incentives and controls work on the same general principle. They are intended to make the Development Areas relatively more attractive as locations in which to invest. As figure 10.10 shows, incentives may influence industrial movement in three distinct ways. Firstly, regional incentives may boost aggregate investment. This could happen because regional incentives will raise rates of return on new projects in Development Areas *without* simultaneously reducing returns elsewhere. Some projects may be undertaken which would not otherwise have occurred. Secondly, and perhaps more importantly, investment incentives will have a direct effect on total movement even if aggregate investment remains unchanged. There will be some firms located in prosperous regions which are only just prepared to tolerate

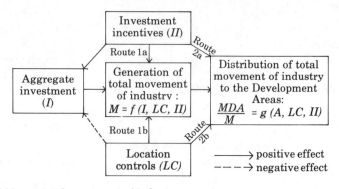

M = total movement of industry
MDA = movement of industry to the Development Areas
A = relative economic attractiveness of Development Areas

Note: See Ashcroft and Taylor (1977). See Lund (1976) for a review of alternative investment models.

Figure 10.10 *Industrial movement and regional policy*

their existing location. Investment incentives may convert the marginal net advantage of their existing location into a marginal net disadvantage and they will *transfer* their productive capacity to a new location. This is referred to as route 1a in figure 10.10. Thirdly, investment incentives may have a direct effect on the distribution of a given volume of movement by improving the relative attractiveness of Development Areas. This is shown as route 2a in figure 10.10.

Controls also affect the relative attractiveness of Development Areas, but in a much cruder way than incentives. Controls simply reduce the choice of location for firms wishing to expand or relocate. This automatically improves the relative attractiveness of Development Areas by removing some of the competition. Figure 10.10 shows that the effects of controls are threefold. On the positive side, controls will stimulate total movement *(M)* by discouraging expansion at existing locations. This is route 1b. They will also alter the distribution of moves in favour of Development Areas (route 2b). But offsetting these two positive effects is the possibility that controls will reduce aggregate investment in the economy, since firms that are refused permission to expand in a non-assisted area may decide not to expand at all, or may decide to expand abroad.

With these threefold effects of regional policy on

industrial movement in mind, a model of movement incorporating the influence of regional policies can be constructed. Total industrial movement is now determined partly by investment expenditure and partly by regional policy instruments *(RP)*:

$$M = f(I, RP)$$ (3)

The proportion of total movement going to the Development Areas is determined by the relative economic attractiveness *(A)* of the Development Areas and by regional policy instruments *(RP)*:

$$\frac{MDA}{M} = g (A, RP)$$ (4)

Once suitable equations have been estimated from empirical data, it is possible to proceed one step further and estimate the effect of regional policy on industrial movement.

The estimated effect of regional policy on industrial movement in Great Britain (1960-71) is shown in figures 10.11 and 10.12. Figure 10.11 shows the effect of regional policy

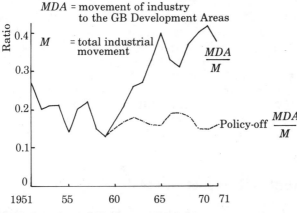

Source: Ashcroft and Taylor (1977).

Figure 10.11 *The effect of regional policy on the proportion of total industrial movement going to the GB Development Areas, 1960-71*

on the proportion of total moves going to the Development Areas. The policy-off *MDA/M* is estimated by simply 'switching-off' the regional policy instruments in the estimated *MDA/M* equation. In other words, we let *RP* = 0 in equation 4. The policy-off *MDA* of figure 10.12 is then calculated by simply multiplying the policy-off estimate of

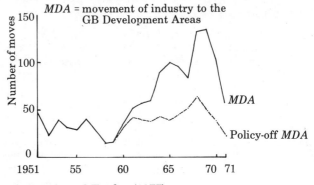

Source: Ashcroft and Taylor (1977).

Figure 10.12 *The effect of regional policy on the movement of industry to the GB Development Areas, 1960-71*

MDA/M by *M*. Hence, for 1969, the estimated policy-off *MDA/M* is 0.15, and since total movement *(M)* in 1969 was 335, this implies a policy-off *MDA* of 0.15 x 335 = 50 (as shown in figure 10.12). Subtracting this from the actual *MDA* we obtain the estimated effect of regional policy on *MDA*: 134-50 = 84 moves to the Development Areas were due to regional policy (in 1969). Similar procedures can be used to estimate the effect of regional policy on the movement of industry to individual Development Areas.

10.2 Regional Impact Analysis

Impact analysis is a method of estimating the effect on employment and income of a given change in expenditure. If the demand for a region's exports falls, for example, the effect of this on regional employment and income can be calculated by using one of the many available impact models. Similarly, impact analysis has been widely used to estimate the effect on regional employment and income of changes in government expenditure and taxation. Greig (1971), for instance, has used impact analysis to ascertain the local economic impact of a pulp and paper mill project in

Scotland, whilst Brownrigg (1971) has examined the economic impact of Stirling University. Impact analysis has also been widely used to discover the influence of such things as private tourist expenditure within regions (Archer 1973). One of the major advantages of impact analysis is its ability to give the policymaker forecasts of the effects of *future* courses of action before their implementation.

Impact analysis is not without its problems. Like the models examined earlier it suffers from the absence of clear, quantified objectives. One can use it to derive the likely effects of a policy or project on jobs and income, but there are simply no criteria for evaluating these estimates and for deciding whether the jobs or income created yield a worthwhile return on public expenditure. Furthermore, in its more sophisticated form, impact analysis is extremely demanding of data. This voracious appetite for information has prevented it from being more widely used. By necessity, therefore, there has been a rapid development of techniques enabling impact models to be constructed which have less demanding data requirements, although giving less reliable forecasts as a result.

Of crucial importance to the understanding of impact analysis is the concept of the *multiplier*. Consider three simple examples:

(i)   Suppose a new car assembly plant is constructed with government financial assistance. Impact analysis could be used to estimate the effect of the operation of the plant over time on local employment. The problem is to trace the full ramifications of the new plant on local jobs. This includes not only the *direct* employment impact (i.e. those employed at the plant itself), but also the additional multiplier effects on employment in the surrounding region. *Indirect* effects occur in industries supplying components and other inputs to the assembly plant. As demand for their products increases, they will employ more workers and purchase more intermediate inputs. As these directly employed and indirectly employed workers spend their incomes, there will be further 'rounds' of expenditure on locally produced goods and services, giving rise to further *induced* employment within the region.

(ii) Taking another example, we may wish to discover how a proposed cut in defence spending will affect localities in which military bases are located (Greenwood and Short 1973). The closure of such bases and the consequent withdrawal of military contracts held by local construction firms, catering firms and the like will have widespread *indirect* and *induced* effects on local jobs well in excess of the *direct* loss of jobs at the military base.

(iii) Finally, consider the case of a cut in labour subsidies (e.g. the abolition of the Regional Employment Premium in Britain in 1977). The consequent rise in production costs may cause employers to reduce employment. This in turn will lead to cuts in regional household consumption, the ramifications of which will affect job prospects throughout the region. Impact analysis offers a means of calculating the *indirect* and *induced* effects of such policies.

Impact analysis varies widely in the degree of detail it provides. The simplest member of the impact family is regional multiplier analysis. Regional multipliers allow estimates to be obtained of the the total employment or total income generated in a region as a result of a given change in expenditure on the region's products. The multiplier approach suffers, however, from the fact that it provides only an aggregate estimate of the effect of an expenditure change. It does not provide the kind of detailed forecasts that regional policymakers may require. A more comprehensive approach is to extend regional multiplier analysis such that it is capable of providing a detailed disaggregation of the effects of expenditure changes. By constructing an econometric model of the regional economy, it is possible to see how key economic variables other than employment and income behave in response to specific policy changes. An econometric model will show how such variables as tax revenue and transfer payments change, how output and employment in different industrial sectors change, and so on. A similarly disaggregated approach is provided by input-output analysis. Regional input-output analysis sets out in detail the economic linkages between the various sectors of a region. It may even link up different regions by tracing the input-output ties between one region and other regions, thus enabling a complete picture to be seen of the interregional chain reaction that occurs as a result of a given initial change in expenditure.

Regional multiplier analysis

There are two general approaches to regional multiplier analysis: the economic base approach and the Keynesian multiplier approach. Economic base analysis was initially pioneered by geographers and planners (see Isard 1960 for references). Not surprisingly, economists have generally favoured the Keynesian approach because of its firmer theoretical structure.

(i) Economic base approach. The economic base model was the first attempt to construct a regional multiplier. The central proposition of the economic base model is that regional employment and income relies heavily on a basic sector which sells its output to buyers who live in other regions. It follows directly that a region also possesses a non-basic sector that exists to serve the region in which it is located. This division of a region's production sector into two parts proves to be a conceptually useful device since it permits the construction of a regional multiplier.

To obtain the economic base multiplier, we begin by dividing total regional income into two component parts:

$$T = S + B \qquad (5)$$

where:

T = total regional income
S = income generated by the non-basic sector
B = income generated by the basic sector.

It is then assumed that the amount of income generated by the non-basic sector will depend upon the income level of the regional economy as a whole. The greater the level of regional income, the greater will be the need for locally produced goods and services. Assuming a simple proportional relationship,

$$S = sT \qquad (6)$$

where s is a positive fraction. Combining equations (5) and (6) we obtain

$$T = \frac{1}{1 - s} B$$

where $1/(1 - s)$ is the 'base multiplier'. The economic base multiplier can thus be derived by dividing T by B. In other words, the ratio of total regional income to the income generated by the basic sector provides us with an estimate of the regional multiplier. Thus, if the ratio of T to B is 1½, a £100 increase in basic sector income will raise total regional income by £150. To produce an employment multiplier

rather than an income multiplier, all that is necessary is to
replace the income data by the corresponding employment
data in the economic base formula.

Unfortunately, the form of the economic base multiplier
described above suffers from a number of major pitfalls, not
all of which can be overcome. Two of the more obvious
weaknesses are: first, that the non-basic sector of the
regional economy may be affected by other factors in
addition to changes in total regional income; and second,
that the basic sector may consist of a number of quite
different export sectors, each one having a different effect on
the remainder of the regional economy for any given change
in export demand.

Let us see how these two weaknesses can be at least partly
overcome. First, if the non-basic sector depends upon other
factors in addition to current regional income, the simple
proportional relationship assumed in equation (6) must be
dropped. In the short run, the relationship between the non-
basic sector and total regional income may be more
adequately described by a non-proportional relationship,
perhaps because income earners are reluctant to reduce their
demand for local services in the short run in spite of a fall in
their incomes, or perhaps because the government sector
provides jobs in the service sector which are not sensitive to
short-run changes in income. Assuming the relationship
between S and T is non-proportional, we can write

$$S = s_0 + s_1 T \qquad (7)$$

Combining equations (5) and (7), we obtain

$$T = \frac{1}{1 - s_1}(s_0 + B)$$

or

$$T = \frac{s_0}{1 - s_1} + \frac{1}{1 - s_1} B$$

from which we can see that the regional multiplier is not as
easily obtained as in the simple economic base model.
Dividing both sides by B does not provide us with an
estimate of the multiplier, as was previously the case. An
estimate can be obtained, however, if either time-series or
cross-section data of total regional income (T) and basic
sector income (B) is available. An estimate of the regional
multiplier is obtained by regressing T on B:

$$T = \alpha + \beta B$$

where $\alpha = s_0/(1 - s_1)$ and $\beta = 1/(1 - s_1)$. The latter is an estimate of the regional export base multiplier.

In the absence of regional income data, employment data can be used to estimate the corresponding employment multiplier. The method is illustrated in figure 10.13. Using

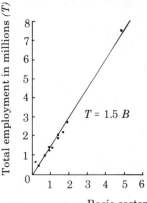

T = total employees in employment,
       all industries and services
B = total employees in employment
       minus :
       (i) gas, electricity, water
       (ii) transport and communications
       (iii) distributive trades
       (iv) miscellaneous services

Source of data: British Labour Statistics Yearbook, 1973.

Figure 10.13 *Estimating an economic base multiplier from cross section data: the UK regions (June 1973)*

cross-section data for the UK regions, the regression of total regional employment on basic sector employment (crudely defined) in each region yields an estimated employment multiplier of 1.5.

The second major problem of the economic base approach is that the basic sector may not be homogeneous. Normally, the export base of a region is made up of a number of very different exporting industries. The effect of any given change in export demand on regional income may vary considerably according to which export industry experiences the change in demand. There are a number of reasons for this, one being the different socio-occupational characteristics of workers in different industries. The expenditure pattern of workers differs according to their socio-occupational characteristics; hence a given change in the demand for the output of the basic sector will have quite a different multiplier effect on the non-basic sector depending upon which part of the basic sector receives the demand stimulus. Another reason why it is important to disaggregate the basic sector is that some industries in the basic sector may import a large proportion of their inputs whereas other industries may rely more heavily upon local inputs. The multiplier consequences of an expansion in demand will therefore vary between industries in the basic sector depending upon the source of their inputs.

If changes in export demand are expected to have a different effect on the demand for local services depending upon the basic industry experiencing the change in export demand, it is necessary to modify the economic base approach in the following way. Suppose there are three basic industries (B_1, B_2, B_3), each of which may have a different effect on the non-basic sector. This can be summarised as follows:

$$S = \alpha + b_1 B_1 + b_2 B_2 + b_3 B_3$$

Substituting this equation into the regional income identity $(T = S + B)$, we obtain:

$$T = \alpha + \left(1 + b_1\right)B_1 + \left(1 + b_2\right)B_2 + \left(1 + b_3\right)B_3$$

where   is the autonomous demand for the output of the region's non-basic sector, and $1 + b_1$, $1 + b_2$ and $1 + b_3$ are the respective regional multipliers for the three basic industries. It may therefore be more useful to calculate a *set* of multipliers for a region, one for each basic industry.

An interesting application of the economic base model is the impact study of Portsmouth (USA) by Weiss and Gooding (1968). The Portsmouth economy is first sub-divided into four sectors:

1. a non-basic sector (S)
2. a private manufacturing sector (B_1)
3. a naval shipyard employing both naval personnel and local labour (B_2)
4. an Air Force base (B_3).

Since the purpose of the exercise is to calculate employment multipliers for the three export sectors, employment data are used in the regression equations. The following estimates of the sectoral multipliers are obtained:

manufacturing sector = 1.78
naval shipyard   = 1.55
Air Force base   = 1.35

Hence, an expansion of the manufacturing sector by 100 workers would lead to a further increase in the level of employment of 78, whereas the same increase in personnel at the Air Force base would lead to a further increase in employment of only 35. The difference in the magnitude of these two effects can be explained by the fact that defence establishments have a much higher propensity to import goods and services from other regions. Government establishments tend to obtain their inputs through a central purchasing authority rather than purchasing inputs from local suppliers. In the particular case of the Portsmouth Air Force base, it was also discovered that the military personnel not living at the base tended to commute from outside the region, thus raising the import leakages from income earned within the region.

Two potentially serious drawbacks of the economic base approach have thus been overcome. Other serious problems, however, still remain, one of the most intractable being the difficulty of distinguishing between basic and non-basic industries. Firm X, for example, may sell the whole of its output to firm Y within the region, and could thus be regarded as part of the non-basic sector. But if firm Y sells all of its output outside of the region, a financial merger of the two firms would mean an arbitrary transfer of firm X from the non-basic to the basic sector. The merger has effectively 'internalised' a non-basic activity into the basic sector. Furthermore, some firms simultaneously produce both for the local market and for markets in other regions.

One way out of this dilemma is to regard activities as non-basic provided they are not over-represented in a region compared to their relative importance in the national economy. If a particular activity is over-represented, then part of this activity is included in the basic sector. A location quotient (LQ) is used to sub-divide the activity into basic and non-basic components:

$$LQ_i = \frac{y_i \div \sum_i y_i}{Y_i \div \sum_i Y_i}$$

where:

y_i = regional output (or income or employment) of the ith industry

Y_i = national output (or income or employment) of the ith industry.

If the location quotient exceeds unity, this implies that the industry in question is over-represented, and any output in excess of the region's 'fair share' of output is assumed to be exported and is added to the basic sector. Thus the method aims at separating the output produced for local consumption by households and the output produced for markets outside the region.

A serious limitation of the location quotient method of dividing each individual industry's output into a basic and a non-basic component is that an industry may have a location quotient of unity or less and still export some (or even all) of its output. The location quotient method fails to recognise the fact that regions are importers as well as exporters, and thus that goods and services may be purchased from outside the region at the same time that similar goods and services are being sold to other regions. This is particularly true where very broad industry groups are used in the analysis and where there may be significantly different *types* of products produced by firms within the industry. Exactly which industries form part of the export base and which do not also depends upon where the boundary of the region is drawn. Goods and services sold across this line are classed as exports. Those sold within the boundary are not. Delimiting regions, as we have seen in Chapter 7, can be an extremely arbitrary procedure.

Finally, the economic base approach fails to take into account the possibility that a given increase in output by the basic sector can be achieved in a number of different ways, each one giving rise to a different multiplier effect on output (see Pratt 1967). The same criticism applies, of course, to all types of impact analysis since they all ignore the supply side of the market. The supply response to an increase in the demand for the output of an exporting industry can differ substantially according to the availability of spare capacity in a region. The increased output may be produced by employing the existing labour force more intensively or by taking on workers who are currently unemployed. The multiplier effects within the region of a given increase in output may be smaller, for instance, if the extra output is produced by extending overtime working for workers who already have jobs rather than by using currently unemployed workers. This would happen if either the marginal propensity to save or the marginal propensity to import tended to rise with the level of personal disposable income. Furthermore, the progressive nature of income tax will guarantee a greater leakage from the regional economy if the extra output is obtained through overtime working rather than by employing currently unemployed workers.

(ii) The Keynesian approach. An alternative method of constructing a regional multiplier is to utilise the simplest version of Keynesian theory (see Archibald 1967). Indeed, this alternative method is almost identical to the simplest open economy version of the Keynesian model, the only difference being that imports and exports refer to the region instead of to the nation. Since this model is well known, only a brief summary of it is required here.

We begin in traditional style by defining regional income as the sum of consumption spending, investment spending, government spending and exports minus imports. Both consumption spending and imports of consumption goods are assumed to be a function of disposable income, which is defined as total income less direct taxes. The model is summarised as follows:

$$Y = C + \overline{I} + \overline{G} + \overline{X} - M \tag{8}$$
$$C = \overline{C} + cY^d \tag{9}$$
$$M = \overline{M} + mY^d \tag{10}$$
$$Y^d = Y - tY \tag{11}$$

where:

Y = regional income

C = regional consumption; $\overline{C}$ = autonomous consumption; c = marginal propensity to consume

$\overline{I}$ = autonomous regional investment spending

$\overline{G}$ = autonomous government expenditure within the region

$\overline{X}$ = autonomous regional exports

M = regional imports of consumption goods; $\overline{M}$ = autonomous imports of consumption goods; m = marginal propensity to import consumption goods

Y^d = disposable income in region

t = rate of income tax.

(Note: Strictly, imports should be expressed as a function of consumption, not disposable income — see Kennedy and Thirlwall (1977). We adopt the conventional formulation above, however, to keep the multiplier simple.)

On substituting equations (9), (10) and (11) into (8), we

obtain
$$Y = k \, (\overline{C} + \overline{I} + \overline{G} + \overline{X} - \overline{M})$$
where
$$k = \frac{1}{1 - (1 - t)(c - m)} \qquad (12)$$

Equation (12) is the regional multiplier. More complex multipliers can be constructed by using a more realistic model of the regional economy. Government transfers, such as unemployment benefit or other welfare payments, could be built into the model by simply expanding the definition of disposable income. In addition, the assumption that exports are autonomous can be dropped and replaced by the more realistic assumption that they are a function of income in other regions. This modification leads us towards the *interregional* trade multiplier, the elements of which can be understood by considering two regions A and B which trade with each other. Suppose region B increases its imports from region A. This increase in exports from A represents an injection into A's circular flow of income which will have multiplier effects in A. The resultant increase in A's income, including these multiplier effects, will raise A's demand for B's exports and B will now experience an increase in its own income. The initial increase in the demand for A's output by B thus has a feedback effect which raises the demand for B's output, and the subsequent increase in B's income will cause it to import even more from A, and the cycle of feedback effects begins again. It is a simple task to modify the multiplier formula to take such interregional repercussions into account in a two-region economy. As more regions become involved, the construction of the multiplier formula becomes increasingly complex.

Table 10.1 *Values of the regional multiplier for various combinations of t and c−m*

Marginal propensity to consume locally produced goods (c− m)	Tax rate (t)		
	0.10	0.20	0.30
0.1	1.10	1.09	1.08
0.2	1.22	1.19	1.16
0.3	1.37	1.32	1.27
0.4	1.56	1.47	1.39

PARTIAL EVALUATION

237

The crucial variable in the regional multiplier formula is the marginal propensity to consume locally produced goods (i.e. $c-m$). The numerical importance of $c-m$ can be seen from table 10.1 which shows the effect on the regional multiplier of varying the tax rate (t) and $c-m$. A low marginal propensity to consume locally produced goods results in a multiplier that only just exceeds unity, and this is true even with a tax rate as low as 10%. Marked differences in the tax rate, in fact, have very little impact on the magnitude of the regional multiplier when $c-m$ is low. As we would expect, the multiplier is very sensitive to variations in $c-m$, rising quite rapidly as $c-m$ increases.

The marginal propensity to consume locally produced goods has been shown to have a crucial impact upon the magnitude of the regional multiplier. Proceeding one step further, we can show that the regional multiplier is likely to increase in size as a region becomes larger. This follows from the fact that the marginal propensity to consume locally produced goods is likely to be positively related to the size of a region. Larger regions are likely to have a more diversified production base and will consequently import less in relation to total expenditure. A small town, for example, will have a much larger marginal propensity to import than a large city (holding all other determinants of the marginal propensity to import constant). Consequently, the small town's multiplier will be smaller than the large city's multiplier. The remoteness of a region may also have an effect on the regional multiplier, raising it in relatively

Table 10.2 *Regional multipliers in Great Britain*

Region	Multiplier
SE	1.57
E Anglia	1.33
SW	1.42
W Midlands	1.33
E Midlands	1.45
Yorks & Humberside	1.26
NW	1.39
North	1.42
Wales	1.38
Scotland	1.77

Source: Steele (1969).
Note: Includes interregional feedback effects.

isolated regions because of their lower import leakages.
Table 10.2 suggests that both a region's size and its
remoteness may have a significant effect on the magnitude
of the regional multiplier. The multiplier is probably high in
the SE because of its large, diversified industrial base,
whereas the high multiplier in Scotland is due partly to its
relative remoteness from the other British regions.

Attention has so far been concentrated on the
construction of the multiplier. Nothing has yet been said
about the multiplicand (i.e the injection), even though the
latter may have a considerable part to play in determining
the impact of a change in exogenous spending on a region's
income and employment (see Brownrigg 1971, Kennedy and
Thirlwall 1977). The multiplicand must be modified to allow
for two distinct items. Firstly, there may be substantial
import leakages from the initial injection, thus reducing the
magnitude of the multiplicand. Secondly, the initial
injection may have an accelerator effect within the region.

Consider the effect of an increase in autonomous
investment spending in a region, such as the investment in
coal mining in the East Midlands. This investment
spending would normally constitute the multiplicand. But
some of the investment inputs, such as capital equipment,
will have to be purchased from other regions and will
therefore never get the chance to generate multiplier effects
locally (ignoring interregional feedback effects). The
multiplicand must be modified to allow for this possibility:

$$\Delta Y = kI_1(1 - m_i)$$

where:

ΔY = change in regional income
I_1 = initial investment injection in new coal-mines
m_i = proportion of initial investment injection spent
        directly on imports from other regions, where
        $M_i = m_i I_1$
k = regional multiplier.

The increase in investment expenditure in the region may
also have an accelerator effect, as would occur if capital
goods industries within the region responded to the
expansion of the coal industry by expanding their own
capacity to meet the extra demand. Another possible
accelerator effect is that industries supplying goods and
services for local consumption will expand their capacity to
meet the increased demand coming from the inflow of new
workers into the area. Thus, we have:

$$\Delta Y = k[I_1(1-m_i)] + k[I_2(1-m'_i)]$$

where:

ΔY, I, k and m_i are as before, and

I_2 = additional investment induced by the accelerator effects of the initial injection

m'_i = proportion of investment inputs (of the induced investment) imported into the region.

Similarly, if the multiplier effects of changes in exports are being estimated, it is necessary to allow for the import leakages from the initial injection and modify the multiplicand accordingly:

$$\Delta Y = k\Delta X(1-m_x)$$

where:

ΔX = change in regional exports

m_x = import propensity of export expenditure.

The need to allow for initial leakages applies, of course, to all the autonomous demand elements.

Finally, the multiplier is essentially a dynamic concept and its usefulness increases if the multiplier effects of autonomous injections can be estimated through time. The time path of a given injection of autonomous spending will vary according to the type of injection and the characteristics of the region. The construction of a branch plant in a Development Area, for example, may be a once-and-for-all occurrence with little further expansion, whereas the transfer of the main plant to a Development Area may lead to an expansion of capacity over a long period of time. To calculate the time path of the multiplier effects on income it is necessary to obtain detailed projections of intended investment spending in the region.

(iii) Two applications of regional multiplier analysis. Regional multiplier analysis is a potentially useful device for estimating the aggregate effects of any changes in autonomous spending in a region, no matter where this change in spending originates. Two policy applications of the regional multiplier are considered below. The first examines the effect of an increase in investment spending in a regional economy. The second examines the effect of out-migration from a depressed region on the level of unemployment in that region.

(a) Measuring the economic impact of public investment expenditure in the Scottish fishing industry. The Highlands and Islands Development Board (HIDB) was set up with the

intention of discovering ways in which the economic decline
of the Highlands and Islands of Scotland could be arrested.
Out-migration from the Highlands and Islands (because of a
lack of employment opportunities) is a continuing problem,
and alternative ways of developing the region are being
investigated by the HIDB. Consequently, investment grants
have been made available for numerous economic ventures
in the Highlands and Islands, including industrial
development, tourism and fishing. Since one of the purposes
of the investment grants is to stimulate output and
employment in the remoter parts of the Highlands and
Islands, multiplier analysis would appear to provide useful
information in evaluating such projects. With this in mind,
Greig (1972) has estimated the impact on regional income
and employment of the grants made available to the fishing
industry in this part of Scotland.

The reason for undertaking a multiplier analysis of the
HIDB investment in the fishing industry is that it is
important to know whether the grants have had the desired
impact on income and employment in the region. It is also
useful to undertake a multiplier analysis in order to compare
the impact of different types of development grants, such as
grants to the tourist and manufacturing sectors.

Estimating the impact of public expenditure in the fishing
industry of the Scottish Highlands and Islands divides
neatly into two parts: the construction of the multiplicand
and the construction of the multiplier. To construct the
multiplicand, the direct effects of the investment grants on
the region had to be estimated. The direct impact of the
grants was to create additional jobs in the fishing industry,
including those firms supplying services to the fishing fleet
such as repair yards, processing and transportation. An
increase in the size of the fishing fleet could therefore be
expected to cause an increase in the earnings at each of the
ports receiving investment grants. But not all the increase in
earnings will necessarily be spent at these ports, or even
within the Highlands and Islands region. The extra services
needed to transport the increase in the amount of fish caught
and landed may be provided, for instance, by hauliers from
other regions. The more remote the port, the smaller will the
immediate leakage from the multiplicand become, since
more of the subsidiary services will have to be provided
locally.

The estimation of the multiplier does not present any
formidable problems, and only two minor modifications

need be made to the multiplier formula given above (equation 12). Government expenditure *(G)* is divided into two components: an autonomous component *(G̅)* and an induced component *(gY)*. The induced part of government expenditure allows for the effect of the increase in employment on the provision of local government services in the areas affected. This can be expressed as follows:

$$G = \overline{G} + gY \qquad (13)$$

An additional effect is that local unemployment in the area will fall if the number of jobs increases. The reduced flow of unemployment benefit into the region will therefore have to be taken into account. This is easily done by modifying the definition of disposable income (i.e. equation 11):

$$Y^d = Y + T_p$$

where

$$T_p = T_0 - tY - uY$$

therefore

$$Y^d = Y + T_0 - tY - uY \qquad (14)$$

where: T_p = net transfer payments flowing into the region, T_0 = autonomous transfer payments (i.e independent of Y), uY = inflow of unemployment benefit and other welfare payments into the region (see Greig 1972 for a detailed discussion).

Note that the transfer of unemployment benefit and other social security payments into the region is negatively related to the income level, as indeed we would expect, since regional unemployment and regional income will be negatively related in the short run. This will result in a reduction in the amount of unemployment benefit flowing into the region. Equations (13) and (14) can now be substituted into the regional income identity (together with the regional import function given by equation 10) to obtain a slightly enlarged regional multiplier:

$$k = \frac{1}{1 - g - (1 - t - u)(c - m)}$$

An interesting feature of Greig's study is that he calculated both an income multiplier and an employment multiplier for each sub-region within the study area. The Highlands and Islands region is divided into four separate sub-regions (i.e. Argyll, Orkney plus rest of mainland, Outer Isles and Shetland) so that the impact of the investment grants can be estimated for different types of area. Estimating the income multiplier for each sub-region in the way described above indicated that the income-generating effects of the investment grants were very similar in all sub-regions (see table 10.3). For every £1,000's worth of income generated in the fishing industry, the four sub-regions experienced a total increase in income of between £1,400 and £1,500. The income-generating effects of the investment grants were apparently quite considerable.

The employment multipliers were calculated on a different basis. The total employment generated by the HIDB investment grants to the fishing industry was expressed as a ratio of the men actually gaining employment on the fishing boats. It is not surprising, then, to find that the employment multipliers are considerably higher than the conventionally estimated income multipliers (see table 10.3). In addition, we can see that the employment

Table 10.3 *Estimates of the regional multiplier for the HIDB investment in the fishing industry, by sub-region*

Sub-region	Income multipliers	Modified employment multipliers
Argyll	1.42	1.68
Orkney and rest of Mainland	1.44	2.17
Shetland	1.48	3.30
Outer Isles	1.50	1.86

Source: Greig (1972).

multipliers vary considerably between sub-regions. The marked difference in the magnitude of the employment multipliers for the sub-regions of the Highlands and Islands can be partly explained by differences in remoteness. Shetland's employment multiplier, for example, was twice the size of Argyll's. The reason for this is simply that a much greater proportion of the fish landed in Shetland was processed within the sub-region than was the case for Argyll. The effect on employment in other industries directly related to fishing was therefore much greater in Shetland. This suggests that the input-output structure of the sub-regional economy plays a major part in determining the total impact of a change in the demand for a region's output. The indirect effects on other industries in Argyll were apparently small because interindustry linkages were with firms outside of the Argyll sub-region. We shall have more to say about interindustry and interregional linkages later when we consider input-output analysis.

We ought finally to examine whether multiplier analysis has proved a useful device for evaluating the impact of HIDB investment grants to the region's fishing industry. The impact of the investment grants was substantial in terms of the effect on regional income and regional employment. Yet this does not necessarily imply that more resources ought to be devoted to this particular activity. Before any long-run decisions are made to develop the fishing industry of the Highlands and Islands further, it will be necessary to explore the alternatives — such as investment in the tourist industry or in small scale manufacturing plants. With the recent appearance of North Sea oil, of course, the Highlands and Islands has now to face up to a new dilemma. If the development of large-scale petrochemical complexes at coastal growth points is encouraged, this will cause further rural depopulation as people migrate towards the rapidly growing areas. Efforts to expand employment opportunities in the Highlands and Islands (apart from the areas receiving a stimulus from the exploitation of North Sea oil and its derivatives) may therefore have to be intensified if many parts of the region are to remain economically viable.

(b) Effect of out-migration from a depressed region on the level of employment in that region. Another useful role for multiplier analysis is the estimation of the impact of out-migration from depressed regions on the level of employment in those regions (see Archibald 1967). The effects of out-migration on employment may be quite complex. Thus, on the one hand, the out-migration will tend to reduce the amount of unemployment in the region, either because of the out-migration of unemployed workers or because the out-migration of employed workers leaves job vacancies that are subsequently filled by the unemployed. Yet on the other hand, the loss of migrants will have an adverse effect on regional employment because of the fall in the demand for locally produced goods and services.

A question that regional multiplier analysis can help to answer is: 'how many out-migrants will it take to cause the loss of one further job in the region?' To answer this question we need to know the magnitude of the regional multiplier (k) and the marginal propensity to consume locally produced goods $(c-m)$. Consider a realistic case where $k = 1\frac{1}{2}$ and $c - m = \frac{1}{3}$. Let unemployment benefit be £35 per week and average

weekly earnings for men be £70 per week. The loss of *one*
male migrant causes the regional payroll to fall by £35. Out
of this, only £35 x ⅓ would have been spent on locally
produced goods. The multiplicand is therefore £35 x ⅓ .This
fall in local consumption will have further negative
multiplier effects on regional income as follows:

£35 x ⅓ x 1½ = £17.50

where 1½ is the regional multiplier. The loss of one migrant
will therefore reduce regional income by £17.50. With
average earnings at £70 per week, this is equivalent to ¼ of a
job lost to the region (i.e. £17.50/£70). Thus, for every four
male workers leaving the region, one further job will be lost.
We should note that as the regional multiplier increases, it
will take a smaller number of out-migrants to cause the loss
of a job to the region. The same applies to the marginal
propensity to consume locally produced goods and services.

In an extension to Archibald's work on the multiplier
effects of out-migration, Vanderkamp (1972) has estimated
the impact of out-migration on unemployment in the
Canadian Maritime Provinces during the decade 1951-61.
The basis of Vanderkamp's argument is that regional
employment (N) depends upon two factors, employment in
the basic sector (N_x) and the magnitude of out-migration
from the region (M). A fall in the demand for the region's
exports will cause a decline in basic sector employment and
an even greater decline in total regional employment
through the operation of the regional multiplier. Out-
migration will have a similar effect. But there is more to the
model than this. Out-migration will itself be determined, at
least in part, by the availability of jobs which means that a
fall in regional employment will lead to an increase in out-
migration. This two-part model can be summarised as
follows:

$$N = f(N_x, M)$$
$$M = g(N)$$

Thus, we see that the model is simultaneous. A fall in the
demand for the region's exports, for example, will cause a
fall in regional employment, which in turn causes an
increase in out-migration. The increase in out-migration
causes a further multiplied reduction in regional
employment, which again has feedback effects on out-
migration. These interactions are shown schematically in
figure 10.14.

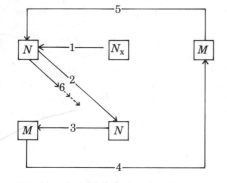

N = regional employment
N_x = employment in the basic sector
M = out-migration from region

Figure 10.14 *Interaction between regional employment and out-migration: the effect of a fall in the demand for the region's exports*

Using this model, Vanderkamp estimated that for every 50 emigrant workers leaving the Canadian Maritime Provinces, an extra 12 jobs were lost to the region. In this particular case, out-migration had a stabilising effect on the region in the short run since the out-migration of 50 workers would reduce regional employment by only 12 jobs, thus causing a *net* fall in unemployment of 38.

Extending regional multiplier analysis: regional econometric models
There can be little doubt that the evaluation of regional policies would benefit greatly from a more sophisticated econometric modelling of economic relationships within and between regions. A major weakness of regional multiplier analysis is that it provides us with estimates of only the aggregate effects of expenditure changes. Econometric models have the distinct advantage that they provide more detail of the structure of the regional economy, the linkages between the various sectors of the regional economy, and the links between the region and the outside world. The principal constraint on the construction of such models has already been noted: lack of adequate data. Indeed, data availability dictates the structure of regional econometric models since measurements of economic variables are often

available only at national level. This is the case, for
example, with the econometric model of the Mississippi
economy constructed by Adams, Brooking and Glickman
(1975). Whilst a Keynesian-type macroeconomic model
would have been preferred, the Mississippi model is forced
by data limitations to use a simpler economic base approach.

The basic structure of the Mississippi model can be
appreciated by considering a simplified version. The model
is represented as a series of equations and sub-divides into
four main sections:

1. the determination of output
2. the determination of employment
3. the determination of wages and unemployment
4. the determination of income and tax revenue.

Table 10.4 summarises the main elements of the model.
Lower case letters refer to regional variables and upper case
letters refer to national variables. All national variables are
assumed to be predetermined, with the exception of tax
revenue (T^R), and are thus taken as *given* (e.g. national
output, wage rates, prices and tax rates). Some of the
regional variables are determined within the model (e.g.
output and employment) and some are predetermined (e.g.
regional tax rates and regional government expenditure). It
should immediately be obvious that for such a model to be
realistic and useful for policymaking the region for which it
is constructed must be small in relation to the national
economy. If changes in the regional economy have
significant effects on the national economy, it would be
wrong to treat national variables as *given*. A more complex
interregional model would be required in this case.

Consider first the output section, which divides into three
parts: a manufacturing sector, a construction sector and a
service sector. A simple definition of the region's export base
is used, with the manufacturing sector being assumed to
produce goods entirely for export from the region whereas
the construction and service sectors produce only for
markets within the region. Manufacturing output is
assumed to be determined partly by the competitiveness of
the region, as measured by the ratio of regional to national
wage rates, and by the growth of the manufacturing sector
at national level. Construction depends upon two
'exogenous' variables: manufacturing investment and
government investment. Service sector output is determined
by the level of disposable income.

Table 10.4 *An extended economic base model*

1. *Output determination*	*Description of variables*	

$$x^m = f(\frac{w}{W}, X^M)$$

$x^m, X^M =$ real output in manufacturing

$w, W =$ wage rate

$$x^c = f(\frac{i^m}{P}, \frac{i^g}{P})$$

$x^c =$ real output in construction

$i^m =$ manufacturing investment

$$x^s = f(\frac{y^d}{P})$$

$i^g =$ government investment

$P =$ price level

$x^s =$ real output in services

$y^d =$ disposable income

2. *Employment determination*

$$n^m = f(x^m, \frac{w}{P})$$

$n^m =$ employment in manufacturing

$$n^c = f(x^c, \frac{w}{P})$$

$n^c =$ employment in construction

$$n^s = f(x^s, \frac{w}{P})$$

$n^s =$ employment in services

$$n = n^m + n^c + n^s$$

3. *The wage rate and the unemployment rate*

$$w = f(u, W)$$

$u =$ unemployment rate

$$u \equiv u_{-1} + \Delta u$$

$\Delta u, \Delta U =$ change in unemployment

$\Delta n =$ change in total employment

$$\Delta u = f(\Delta U, \frac{\Delta n}{n_{-1}}, \frac{\Delta pop}{pop_{-1}})$$

$\Delta pop =$ change in population

4. *Income and tax revenue*

$$y^d \equiv y - t^r - T^R$$

$t^r, T^R =$ tax revenue (net of transfer payments)

$y =$ gross income

$$y \equiv (w \times n) + y^{nw}$$

$y^{nw} =$ non-wage income

$t, T =$ tax rate

$$t^r \equiv t(y - t^p)$$

$t^p, T^p =$ transfer payments

$$T^R \equiv T(y - T^p)$$

Note:
Lower case letters refer to regional variables and upper case letters to national variables.

The employment section of the model divides into the same three sectors as the output section, with output playing a major role in determining the employment level in each of the three sectors. In addition, the demand for labour in each sector is postulated to depend upon the real wage, which is itself determined in part by the level of unemployment in the region. This takes us through into the third section of the model, the purpose of which is to determine the regional wage rate and regional unemployment. The latter depends, in the main, on the relationship between the growth in employment and the growth in the population, though the short-run fluctuations in regional unemployment are likely to be strongly related to national business fluctuations, hence the inclusion of the change in the national unemployment rate.

Finally, the fourth section consists of four identities. Disposable income is defined as the difference between gross income and the amount taken in taxes (net of transfer payments) by the regional and national governments. Gross income is defined as wages and salaries plus non-wage income (i.e. rent, profits, dividends and transfer payments), and tax revenue (net of transfer payments) is defined as the difference between taxes and transfer payments such as welfare benefits.

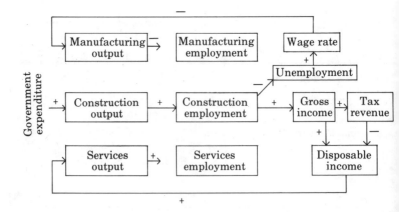

Figure 10.15 *Flow chart of the first-round effects of an increase in construction expenditure*

The potential usefulness of modelling the regional economy in detail can be demonstrated by showing how the impact of a given change in government expenditure (or indeed any other change in one of the exogenous variables of the model) would affect the region. The initial effects of an increase in government expenditure on, for instance, highway construction is shown diagrammatically in figure 10.15. The injection of government spending into the construction industry raises output and consequently employment in the construction sector. The increased pressure of demand for labour will then force up the regional wage rate. Higher wage rates and the higher level of employment will combine to raise gross income, which will have the effect of raising disposable income, though this will be partly offset by the increase in tax revenue resulting from the increase in gross income. It is at this point that the first major feedback effect occurs: the increase in disposable income raises the demand for goods produced for local consumption (i.e. services) and this subsequently has a positive effect on output and employment in the service sector. On the negative side, the increase in the wage rate will reduce the competitiveness of the region's export sector (assuming national wages remain unchanged) and will also have a negative effect on employment in the construction and service sectors. Subsequent effects on the system will gradually diminish until a new equilibrium is reached.

The government can, of course, influence regional employment and output in ways other than through direct expenditure changes or by changing tax rates. Capital subsidies to private industry, for example, may cause an increase in manufacturing investment, and regional labour subsidies will reduce relative labour costs, thereby improving the competitiveness of the region. The advantages of econometric models for estimating the impact of regional policies are obvious. Unfortunately, adequate data are not yet available to enable the construction of such models, except for one or two isolated cases.

10.3 Regional Input-Output Analysis

During the past three decades, regional multiplier analysis has grown in complexity and has consequently become a more powerful tool of regional planning. The development of econometric models is a particularly exciting and potentially valuable approach to estimating the consequences of alternative regional policy strategies. Exactly the same is true of regional input-output analysis, which has also made significant strides during recent years. This section examines the application of the input-output technique (pioneered by Leontief) to regional problems and regional policymaking.

The great attraction of the input-output approach is that it concentrates on the links that tie together all the various economic activities operating within the economy. Thus, in the case of a regional input-output model the aim is to identify and measure the linkages between the various economic activities within the region. In the case of firms, there exist both backward and forward linkages. The backward linkages take the form of inputs and components purchased either from other firms, or from households which own the basic factors of production — land, labour and capital. The firm itself may in turn sell intermediate output forward to other firms, or may sell final output directly to consumers. Similarly, households are linked 'backwards' to firms through their purchases of goods and services, and 'forwards' to firms via the factor services which they provide.

Having identified and measured the linkages between the various sectors of the regional economy, input-output analysis can then be used to predict the effect of any given change in one part of the regional economic system on the rest of that system. A change in the demand for the output of one industry, for example, may have diverse effects on a wide range of other industries in the region because of the production linkages that tie industries together.

Basic elements of the input-output method
Before turning to actual applications of input-output analysis in a regional context, it is necessary to briefly demonstrate how the building blocks of input-output analysis are assembled (see Miernyk 1965, Yan 1969, Isard and Langford 1971).

Transactions table. The production function is the basis of input-output analysis: industries purchase inputs in order to produce output. They purchase their inputs from other industries, from households and from the government, and they sell their output either to other industries or to 'final demanders' such as households. If an industry's output is sold to another industry, the output becomes an input. Hence we have an input-output system. This system can be neatly and simply summarised in a *transactions table*, which records all the production flows occurring within an economy. The transactions table is therefore one way of constructing a region's economic accounts. It is essentially an exercise in book-keeping.

The main features of the transactions table can be seen by considering the input-output linkages in the simplest of regional economies: a two-industry economy producing only cars and steel. Table 10.5 describes the linkages between various sectors of this two-industry economy, including the links between the processing sector (cars and steel) and the payments sector (which supplies essential inputs to the processing sector such as labour sevices, government services and imports). The numbers in table 10.5 show

Table 10.5 *An input-output transactions table for a hypothetical two-industry economy*

Output produced by:	Inputs purchased by:		Final demand:			Gross output
	Car industry	Steel industry	House-holds	Govern-ment	Exports	
Car industry	0	20	90	30	60	200
Steel industry	100	0	20	50	50	220
Payments sector:						
Households	50	150	0	0	0	200
Government	10	20	10	0	0	40
Imports	40	30	20	0	0	90
Gross outlay	200	220	140	80	110	750

output and input flows, which are normally measured in terms of their money value (otherwise the columns and the rows cannot be added) but physical units can be used if necessary (see Isard and Langford 1971). By reading along the first row of table 10.5, we can see that the car industry produces a gross output of £200, £20 of which is sold to the steel industry. The remaining £180 worth is sold to the final demand sector: households, the government and buyers in other regions. This is the output side of the car industry's activity as a producer. By reading down the first column, we can see exactly what inputs are required by the car industry to produce its gross output of £200. The car industry purchases £100 worth of steel, £50 worth of labour services, £10 worth of government services and £40 worth of imports. Notice that the value of the gross output of the car industry is exactly equal to the value of its inputs (i.e. its gross outlay). The same is true for the steel industry. This must be the case, since the transactions matrix is constructed on the principle of double-entry book-keeping, which means that the entire output of each industry must be accounted for by the inputs used up during production — including the return to the entrepreneur. This latter item is the residual left over when all other factor inputs have been paid for and is included in the household row of the payments sector.

The transactions table therefore tells us exactly where the inputs of an industry come *from*, and where the output of an industry goes *to*. The interdependencies prevailing in the economic system are clearly visible from this table. Indeed, the purpose of the transactions table is to quantify these interdependencies so that the effects of expected changes in demand can be estimated. The use of input-output analysis as a forecasting device is discussed in the next section.

Technical coefficients matrix. Industry production flows are the heart of input-output analysis. It is these interindustry linkages that we must now investigate in some detail. We begin by constructing a *technical coefficients matrix*. To do this we express the inputs of each industry as a ratio of the gross output of that industry. Taking an example from table 10.5, we can see that the steel industry buys inputs worth £20 from the car industry in order to produce £220 worth of steel. In this case, the technical coefficient would be £20/£220 = 0.09. Thus, on the assumption that the relationship between inputs and output is proportional, we can write:

$$x_{ij} = a_{ij} X_j$$

where:

x_{ij} = flow of output from industry i to industry j, reading i as a row and j as a column, e.g. x_{12} = £20.

X_j = gross output of industry j, e.g. X_2 = £220

a_{ij} = the technical coefficient relating x_{ij} to X_j (i.e. a_{ij} = x_{ij}/X_j)

e.g. $a_{12} = x_{12}/X_2$ = 20/220 = 0.09

A technical coefficients matrix can therefore be constructed from the information provided in the transactions matrix. Using the information given in table 10.5 we obtain:

$$\begin{bmatrix} a_{11} & a_{12} \\ a_{21} & a_{22} \end{bmatrix} = \begin{bmatrix} \dfrac{0}{200} & \dfrac{20}{220} \\ \dfrac{100}{200} & \dfrac{0}{220} \end{bmatrix} = \begin{bmatrix} 0 & 0.09 \\ 0.50 & 0 \end{bmatrix}$$

Estimating the impact of changes in final demand

Once the technical coefficients matrix has been calculated, it can then be used to estimate the effects of any change in the final demand for an industry's output. These coefficients show, for example, that in order to raise its exports from £60 to £260, the car industry has to purchase an extra £100 worth of steel (i.e. 0.50 x £200). This indicates that we can obtain the required change in inputs by multiplying the change in final demand by the relevant technical coefficient. But this only provides us with the *direct* effect of a given change in final demand. We must also take into account the fact that the industry supplying the extra input may require more inputs itself if it is to increase its own output. A chain reaction of indirect effects is therefore set in motion because of the interindustry linkages that exist within the system. A hypothetical example will help make this clear.

Consider again the increase in the final demand for cars, which causes the car industry to double its output from £200 to £400. To produce more cars, the car industry requires more steel. An extra £200 worth of cars could be produced only if the car industry purchased an extra £100 worth of steel. The steel industry has therefore to increase its own output by £100 in order to meet the extra demand for steel by the car industry. But if the steel industry is to produce an additional £100 worth of steel, it will itself have to purchase an extra £9 worth of cars (i.e. 0.09 x £100 = £9). This in turn means that the car industry will have to produce more cars than it had initially foreseen, since not only has final demand increased by £200 but intermediate demand has increased as well — by £9. Since the car industry has to produce an extra £9 worth of cars, however, it will require an extra £4.50 worth of steel (i.e. 0.50 x £9 = £4.50) over and above the initial increase in the demand for steel. And so the interindustry interactions continue to chase each other in ever diminishing circles around the system. Figure 10.16 demonstrates the interaction between the car industry and the steel industry and shows the total effect on output of the two industries when the final expenditure on cars increases by £200. The initial increase in the final demand for cars of

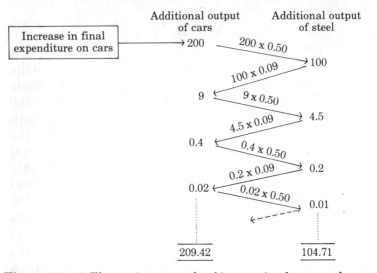

Figure 10.16 *Illustrative example of interaction between the car industry and the steel industry*

£200 eventually leads to an increase of approximately £209.4 in the total production of cars and an increase of approximately £104.7 in the total production of steel.

These figures can be usefully expressed in another way. A £1 increase in the final demand for cars will raise *gross* output in the car industry by £1.047 (i.e. £209.4/£200), and will raise *gross* output in the steel industry by £0.524 (i.e. £104.7/£200). If these two coefficients are added together, we can see that a £1 increase in the final demand for cars will raise total output in *all* industries by £1.571. The coefficients for the steel industry can be calculated in the same way, giving us the following matrix of 'direct plus indirect coefficients':

	Car industry	*Steel industry*
Car production	1.047	0.094
Steel production	0.524	1.047
	1.571	1.141

The sums of these two columns are the sectoral output multipliers for the car industry and the steel industry respectively. They show the total increase in output that will result from a £1 increase in the output of each industry. A problem with the calculation of the sectoral output multipliers, however, is that where there are a large number

of industries in the input-output table, the interindustry
linkages are extremely complex with the result that
advanced mathematical techniques have to be used to
calculate the necessary coefficients (see Hadley 1961).
Fortunately, the computer is ideally suited to carrying out
the necessary arithmetic.

A further problem with the sectoral output multipliers is
that they tell us nothing about the effect of changes in final
demand on household income or on employment. It is
therefore useful to modify the transactions table such that the
household sector is treated in the same way as an industry.
Householders own all the land, labour and capital inputs of
the economy. The services of these factors of production are
purchased by the industries of the processing sector and in
order to produce these services, the household 'industry'
itself must consume inputs from other industries within the
region. By bringing the household sector into the processing
sector we are making it endogenous, which means that
households can no longer be treated as if their demands were
independent of changes in household income. An increase in
the output of cars, for example, can only be achieved if the
car industry uses more labour. But if households supply more
labour to the car industry, household income and thus
consumption will rise as well. In a regional context,
households are likely to increase their demand for local
services, which will in turn cause a further round of income
and expenditure increases. Since such a feedback effect will
occur, it is obviously necessary to treat the household sector
as if it were part of the processing sector. Households thus
become a kind of additional processing industry, their
output being factor services and their inputs being goods
and services — some of which are supplied by firms located
in the same region.

The conversion of the household sector into an industry
requires a little elaboration. The logic of making households
endogenous rests on the interaction between households and
the industries of the processing sector. A feedback effect
from the household sector becomes more plausible when the
processing sector is defined to include service industries as
well as manufacturing industries. In the example of table
10.5, the household sector consumes 45% and 10% of the
output of the car industry and the steel industry respectively.
In a more realistic model there would also be a service sector
producing services for the direct benefit of the households.

Thus, any increases in the demand for manufactured goods would cause household income to increase as more labour is employed by manufacturing industries. Some of the extra income would be spent, in turn, on services which would add a further boost to the household sector, especially since services are highly labour-intensive.

Once the household sector is incorporated into the processing sector, the consequences of a given increase in expenditure on the region's output can be seen to be greater than the case where households are not included in the processing sector. The table of coefficients showing the effect of a £1 increase in the demand for both cars and steel for the case where households are *not* part of the processing sector is repeated below together with a table of coefficients for the case where households *are* included in the processing sector:

Sector	Households not included in the processing sector		Households included in the processing sector	
	Car industry	Steel industry	Car industry	Steel industry
Car industry	1.047	0.094	1.507	0.643
Steel industry	0.524	1.047	0.849	1.435
Households	—	—	0.669	0.797

Hence, if the final expenditure on cars increases by £1 the effect of this is to raise *gross* output by £1.507 in the car industry and by £0.849 in the steel industry when households are included in the processing sector. Note the increase in these two coefficients (over the corresponding coefficients in the first column) when household feedback effects are taken into account. *Gross* output in the region has therefore increased by £2.356 due to the £1 increase in the expenditure on cars. Perhaps more interestingly, however, we see that household income has risen by £0.669 as the result of this £1 increase in the final demand for cars. Similarly, an increase of £1 in the final demand for steel will raise household income by £0.797.

Regional applications of input-output analysis
The potential value of input-output analysis to regional policymaking can best be seen by examining some actual applications of the technique. The first regional input-output model we shall consider is one constructed by the Northern

Region Strategy Team for the Northern region of the UK (1976a). It will be useful to discuss the Northern region model since it is small (consisting of only seven production sectors) and is therefore easy to handle. The second model we shall examine is the Welsh model constructed by Nevin, Roe and Round (1966). This is more ambitious than the Northern region model in that it contains more production sectors. An additional feature of the Welsh model is that it specifies interregional production flows as well as interindustry production flows within the Welsh economy. The purpose of both models, however, is similar. The Northern region model was developed mainly for experimental purposes and was not intended to be used as an aid to forecasting. Many of the estimated input-output flows are simply informed guesses. The Welsh model was also experimental in so far as the aim was to assess the forecasting performance of a regional input-output model constructed by non-survey methods. (See Hewings 1971 for a review of non-survey methods and an application to the Midlands region.) Finally, we shall examine the urban input-output model constructed for Peterborough by Morrison (1971). It differs from the previous two models in that it uses primary data collected by a direct survey of firms in the Peterborough sub-region. Similar attempts are currently being made to construct a Scottish input-output model from primary data (see the *Economist*, 16 July, 1977) and efforts are also being made to construct a large scale interregional model for the UK (Gordon 1977).

(i) Northern region model. The seven-sector Northern region model concentrates on the interindustry flows within the region, the purpose of the exercise being to gain a better understanding of the linkages between the region's industries rather than to use the model for forecasting purposes. Indeed, the fact that the model was not constructed from a detailed survey of firms in the region means that the input-output relationships described by the model must be treated with great caution. Nevertheless, the Northern region model is of interest in so far as it illustrates the potential value of input-output analysis in regional planning.

Table 10.6 shows the estimated input-output flows between the various industrial sectors of the Northern region. The chemical industry, for example, sells £6m of its

Table 10.6 *The transactions matrix for the Northern region, 1971 (£m at 1970 prices)*

Output	Inputs							Household spending	Other final demand	Exports from region	Total output
	Primary	Chemicals	Metals	Engineering	Other mfg.	Construction	Services				
Primary	11	18	15	5	10	5	20	94	16	120	314
Chemicals	6	25	8	3	12	2	18	18	18	486	596
Metals	7	1	30	30	2	5	5	1	2	211	294
Engineering	3	3	5	13	5	5	8	8	59	498	607
Other mfg.	8	5	2	6	10	10	20	73	14	538	686
Construction	10	5	5	5	5	35	24	40	215	34	378
Services	35	30	8	23	93	28	180	460	521	19	1397
Imports into region	56	334	132	241	311	104	158	583	396	—	2315
Household income	151	110	83	239	173	142	854	—	—	—	1752
Other income	27	65	6	42	65	42	110	408	60	79	904
Total input	314	596	294	607	686	378	1397	1685	1301	1985	9243

Source: **Northern Region Strategy Team,** *Technical Report No. 4,* p. H7.

output to the primary sector, £25m to itself (i.e. to other firms in the same industry), £8m to the metal industry, and so on. In addition, the table shows how much each industry sells to final demand sectors (such as households) within the region and how much is sold to buyers outside the region. For instance, the chemical industry sells £18m of its output to households within the region and £486m to buyers outside the region, including households, firms and the government. Finally, the table tells us how much each industry buys from other industries within the region, from households within the region and from suppliers in other regions.

Informative though table 10.6 may be, in that it is an excellent device for describing the structure of industry within a region, of even greater usefulness is the matrix of coefficients that can be obtained from the transactions table. Just as the transactions table in our car and steel industry example was transformed into a matrix of coefficients, so too can the transactions matrix for the Northern region. Once these coefficients have been calculated, they can be used for forecasting the effect of a given change in final demand on the output of each regional industry. Table 10.7 contains these coefficients, each of which indicates the effect of a change in expenditure of £1 on the output of the industry in question. An increase of £1 in the expenditure on the region's chemicals, for example, will cause an increase in the gross output of the chemical industry itself of £1.053. Similarly, the increased expenditure on chemicals of £1 will cause an increase in the

Table 10.7 *Sectoral output multipliers for the Northern region, 1971*

Sectors	Primary	Chemicals	Metals	Engineering	Other mfg.	Construction	Services
Primary	1.098	0.057	0.097	0.054	0.053	0.064	0.084
Chemicals	0.040	1.053	0.044	0.020	0.032	0.022	0.036
Metals	0.032	0.006	1.120	0.060	0.008	0.022	0.012
Engineering	0.021	0.010	0.026	1.029	0.014	0.023	0.020
Other mfg.	0.076	0.029	0.040	0.045	1.046	0.069	0.070
Construction	0.071	0.025	0.044	0.035	0.031	1.131	0.059
Services	0.438	0.188	0.233	0.265	0.339	0.337	1.495
Sectoral output multipliers	1.776	1.368	1.604	1.508	1.523	1.668	1.776

The sectoral output multipliers are the sums of the respective columns. Each number is a coefficient which measures the direct, indirect and induced effects of a £1 change in expenditure in the output of the sector in question.
Source: Northern Region Strategy Team, *Technical Report No. 4*, p. H10.

expenditure on primary products of £0.057, and so on for the output of the other industries (reading down the chemical industry column). Adding up these coefficients, we obtain the 'sectoral output multiplier' for the chemical industry, which is 1.368.

Comparing the sectoral output multipliers of the chemical and construction industries, we see that the latter is considerably higher (1.668 compared to 1.368). The reason for this is clear from the two columns in table 10.7 headed 'chemicals' and 'construction' respectively. An increase of expenditure on construction has a larger impact on the remaining industrial sectors of the region than does the chemical industry. This is particularly the case for the effect on the service sector, the reason being that construction is more labour-intensive than chemicals. An increase in output in the construction industry quickly feeds through into local services since labour costs constitute a much larger proportion of total input costs in the construction industry than in chemicals.

For some purposes, it is useful to convert the output coefficients given in table 10.7 into employment coefficients, which is easily done provided we know the output/labour ratio in each sector. The employment coefficients are useful since they enable the regional planner to forecast the effects on *all* sectors of any given change in employment in *one* of the sectors. Again taking the chemical industry as an example, an *initial* increase of 1,000 jobs in this industry will lead to an ultimate increase of 1,053 jobs in chemicals, 936 in services, 208 in the primary sector, and 175 jobs in the remaining four industries (see column 2 of table 10.8). The total effect of an initial increase of 1,000 jobs in the chemical industry is therefore 2,372 (as indicated by summing the column of table 10.8 labelled Chemicals).

Table 10.8 *Sectoral employment multipliers for the Northern region, 1971*

Sectors	Primary	Chem-icals	Metals	Engin-eering	Other mfg.	Cons-truction	Services
Primary	1.098	0.208	0.200	0.063	0.084	0.090	0.061
Chemicals	0.011	1.053	0.025	0.006	0.014	0.008	0.007
Metals	0.016	0.011	1.120	0.034	0.006	0.015	0.004
Engineering	0.018	0.032	0.046	1.029	0.019	0.028	0.013
Other mfg.	0.048	0.067	0.052	0.033	1.046	0.061	0.072
Construction	0.051	0.065	0.065	0.029	0.035	1.131	0.031
Services	0.599	0.936	0.656	0.420	0.732	0.644	1.495
Sectoral employment multipliers	1.841	2.372	2.164	1.614	1.936	1.977	1.643

The sectoral employment multipliers are the sums of the respective columns. Each number is a coefficient which measures the direct, indirect and induced employment effects of a unit change in employment in the sector in question.
Source: Northern Region Strategy Team, *Technical Report, No. 4*, p. H11.

(ii) Welsh input-output model. The Northern region input-output model described above is a truly 'regional' model in the sense that all other regions are deliberately ignored — except in so far as the Northern region trades with the outside world. Interregional models represent a significant advance on purely regional models. The basic outline of a two-region model is shown schematically in table 10.9 from which it can be seen that the processing sector is split into four separate components. Components I and IV show interindustry linkages *within* regions 1 and 2 respectively

Table 10.9 *An interregional input-output model : an illustration*

Output produced by:		Inputs purchased by: Region 1		Region 2		Final demand: consumers, government, foreigners	Gross output
		Industry 1	Industry 2	Industry 1	Industry 2		
Region 1	Industry 1	x_{11}	x_{12}	x_{13}	x_{14}	Output sold to final demand by industry 1	Gross output of region 1
		I		III			
	Industry 2	x_{21}	x_{22}	x_{23}	x_{24}	Output sold to final demand by industry 2	
Region 2	Industry 1	x_{31}	x_{32}	x_{33}	x_{34}	Output sold to final demand by industry 1	Gross output of region 2
		II		IV			
	Industry 2	x_{41}	x_{42}	x_{43}	x_{44}	Output sold to final demand by industry 2	
Payments sector: e.g. labour, imports, government services		Region 1's inputs of labour, imported goods and government services		Region 2's inputs of labour, imported goods and government services			

Explanatory note:
Boxes I and IV contain all the *intra*regional production flows and boxes II and III contain all the *inter*regional production flows. Consider cell x_{32}. The entry in this cell is the flow of output *from* industry 1 in region 2 *to* industry 2 in region 1.

whilst components II and III show the trading links between the two regions. The great advantage of interregional models is obvious. The effects of a given change in expenditure may be extremely wide-ranging in terms of the industries and the regions affected, and interregional models provide an excellent framework for identifying these effects.

The Welsh input-output model constructed by Nevin, Roe and Round is an example of the simplest type of interregional model, consisting as it does of only two regions — Wales and the Rest of the UK. It also has another interesting feature: it was constructed primarily by non-survey methods. In view of the high costs involved in collecting primary data for the transactions matrix, it will be useful to examine the Welsh model since it offers the possibility of developing cheaper non-survey methods of constructing regional and interregional models (see also Hewings 1971).

The non-survey approach to constructing the transactions table typically involves the assumption that input-output relationships between industries are the same in the region as they are in the nation. Two further assumptions were added in the construction of the Welsh model in order to estimate interregional flows of output (i.e. the output flows in boxes II and III of table 10.9):

(a)   Welsh industries were assumed to buy all their intermediate inputs from other Welsh industries if at all possible — provided Welsh industries produced sufficient output to satisfy these demands.

(b)   Industries in the rest of the United Kingdom (viz. RUK) were assumed to buy all their intermediate inputs from other RUK industries if at all possible — again provided RUK industries produced sufficient output.

It follows from these two assumptions that Welsh industries would export to RUK any output that could not be sold within Wales. A simple example will make this clear. If the Welsh steel industry produces 100 units of output, 50 of which are sold to the final demand sector, the remaining 50 units will be purchased by other industries as intermediate inputs. But if the demand for steel in Wales is such that only 40 units of steel are required as intermediate inputs into other Welsh industries, it is assumed that 40 units of steel output are sold to other Welsh industries and that 10 units are sold to industries in RUK (or are exported abroad if RUK demand is not adequate). The essence of the transactions table estimated for the Welsh model is described in table 10.10.

Whether or not Welsh industries buy their intermediate inputs from other Welsh industries will be heavily dependent on transport costs (and other costs associated with distance between buyers and sellers). Unfortunately, in

Table 10.10 *The construction of the Welsh-RUK interregional model*

Output produced by:	Inputs purchased by:		Final demand	Gross output
	Welsh industries 1 2 3 31	RUK industries 1 2 3 31		
Welsh industries 1 2 3 ⋮ ⋮ ⋮ ⋮ ⋮ ⋮ 31	[Wales to Wales] National technical coefficients are used for each industry in the processing sector. Add the assumption that Welsh industries purchase from other Welsh industries if adequate supplies are available in Wales. Any 'excess' output is exported to RUK or abroad. Corresponding assumptions are used for RUK industries.	[Wales to RUK]	Estimated as follows: $$F_j^W = \frac{X_j^W}{X_j^{UK}} \times F_j^{UK}$$ where X_j^W = gross output of Welsh industry j X_j^{UK} = gross output of UK industry j F_j = final demand for j's output	X_1^W X_2^W ⋮ ⋮ ⋮ X_{31}^W
RUK industries 1 2 3 ⋮ ⋮ ⋮ ⋮ ⋮ ⋮ 31	[RUK to Wales]	[RUK to RUK]	Estimated as follows: $$F_j^{RUK} = \frac{X_j^{RUK}}{X_j^{UK}} \times F_{,j}^{UK}$$ where X_j^{RUK} = gross output of RUK industry j X_j^{UK} = gross output of UK industry j F_j = final demand for j's output	X_1^{RUK} X_2^{RUK} ⋮ ⋮ ⋮ X_{31}^{RUK}

the case of Wales the geographical distribution of industry is such that this assumption is unlikely to be correct in many instances. The industries of North Wales are likely to have much firmer input-output links with Merseyside and the Midlands than with South Wales; and the industries of South Wales are likely to have much firmer input-output links with Bristol and the Midlands than with North Wales.

The assumption 'that Welsh industries buy from other Welsh industries' also implies that individual industries at the regional level are capable of supplying the full range of output produced by the national industry. Yet it is highly probable that a regional industry will specialise in a much narrower range of products than the national industry, in which case we may find the regional industry selling only a very small proportion of its output to other industries in the same region whilst other industries import intermediate inputs from firms in the same industry group but which are located in other regions. Hence, the assumption 'that Welsh industries buy from other Welsh industries' is almost certainly a serious weakness of the Welsh model, with the effect that the interregional trade flows generated by this assumption are likely to be inaccurate.

In spite of the limitations of using non-survey techniques to produce the transactions matrix for the Welsh model, it was found that the model predicted more accurately on the whole than simple extrapolation based on time series data. But it is clear that more attention will have to be devoted to estimating interregional trade flows if models based on non-survey methods are to become useful instruments for forecasting. More recent developments of the non-survey technique indicate that further progress has been made since the construction of the Welsh model, and it is now looking increasingly likely that input-output analysis will serve a useful role in regional policymaking and planning in the years ahead.

(iii) Peterborough model. Finally, we briefly consider an urban input-output model. The Peterborough model differs from the previous two input-output models in that it was constructed by the time consuming, but more accurate, method of collecting data on input-output relationships from individual firms in the Peterborough sub-region. The aim of the exercise was to estimate the consequences on each industry of an expansion of Peterborough's population from 80,000 in 1968 to a planned figure of 190,000 in 1983.

In spite of the fact that the Peterborough sub-region is reasonably well isolated from other urban areas, there was still some difficulty in defining the input-output system. Some industries with close input-output linkages with plants located in Peterborough, for example, were located outside the administrative boundary of the area. The Peterborough input-output system was thus defined to include any industries located outside of the administrative boundaries which were an essential part of the Peterborough economic system (e.g. brickmaking).

In constructing the transactions table, emphasis was placed upon disaggregating the service sector as far as was practicable since it is within the service sector of towns that most of the local input-output interaction takes place. The smaller the region, the more likely are manufacturing industries to trade with manufacturing industries located in other regions of the economy. Linkages between the manufacturing sector and the service sector do exist, of course, but mostly via the linkage between the household and service sectors. An increase in output in the manufacturing sector, for example, will be accompanied by an increase in the amount of labour inputs purchased from the household sector. The additional income accruing to the household sector will then have feedback effects on services, as we explained earlier in this section.

Once an input-output model has been constructed for an urban economy, it can be used for a number of different, though related, planning purposes. We have already seen that the main purpose of the Peterborough model was to forecast the structure of the economy through until 1983 (i.e. forecast the transactions table for 1983). But this is not the only reason for constructing an urban input-output model. As we saw earlier, separate sectoral multipliers can be calculated for each industry. The brick industry, for example, was found to have an output multiplier of 1.7, which means that an increase in the final demand for bricks of £100 would cause an increase in gross output of £170. As expected, the highest output multipliers were found to exist in the service sector, where intraregional output flows were most extensive.

The main usefulness of small area input-output models is that they provide the planner with a 'first estimate' of the likely impact of a specific type of development on the structure of the local economy. By providing the planner with estimates of the impact of alternative development plans, a range of schemes can be more easily appraised. In addition, possible bottlenecks to expansion will be highlighted by the projections. Recent research has been directed towards using the input-output approach to provide a more comprehensive framework for development planning by the metropolitan authorities in Britain (Broadbent and Morrison 1977).

Some limitations of input-output analysis
Potentially valuable though input-output analysis may be, it is essential to realise that this technique is not free from problems. The most serious limitation is the high cost of

collecting the necessary primary data, especially for highly
dis-aggregated input-output models such as the
Philadelphia model constructed by Isard and associates (see
Isard and Langford 1971 for details). It is not difficult to
imagine the burden of work involved in collecting input-
output data for the Philadelphia model given that it covered
496 producing sectors. With 496 producing sectors, the
processing sector consists of a possible 246,016 interindustry
production flows. Most of these possible transactions will
not, of course, occur (i.e. the processing sector includes a vast
number of zero elements), but the task of collecting data on
such a highly dis-aggregated basis is nonetheless a highly
time-consuming and expensive one.

It is because of the high costs involved in collecting
primary data that many transactions tables have been
constructed by non-survey methods. Instead of constructing
the technical coefficients matrix from primary data, many
investigators, as in the Welsh model examined earlier, have
used national coefficients in regional input-output models.
The use of national technical coefficients in regional models
is fraught with difficulties, however, since the production
techniques of industries are likely to vary between regions.
The reliability of forecasts will therefore depend upon the
errors introduced into the model by the assumptions used to
by-pass the expensive task of collecting data by direct
enumeration of input-output flows.

The great advantage of input-output models, provided the
transactions matrix is a sufficiently accurate representation
of actual production flows between sectors, is their internal
consistency. All the effects of any given change in final
demand can be taken into account and since all
interindustry linkages are stated explicitly, the indirect as
well as the direct effects resulting from a given change in
final demand are accounted for. Yet this supreme advantage
of input-output models is quickly eroded if the technical
coefficients are unstable and likely to change rapidly over
time. The need to assume stability of the relationships
embodied in the table (and therefore in the derived technical
coefficients matrix) represents a second problem of major
dimensions for input-output analysis.

The transactions table is constructed for a specific period
of time, usually a calendar (or financial) year. If production
technologies are changing rapidly through time, input-
output linkages are also likely to change. Estimating the

potential impact of a change in final demand on the output level of each industry will consequently be subject to considerable error, the amount of error depending upon the extent to which the technical coefficients matrix changes over time. A change in production techniques is not the only factor affecting the pattern of input-output linkages. The relative prices of inputs may change, causing one input to be substituted for another. One of the clearest examples of this in Britain was the large-scale substitution of oil for coal during the 1950s and 1960s. Indeed, it is conceivable that the very change in final demand being examined may be of such a high magnitude that input prices are forced up and therefore cause substitution effects to occur, which will lead to changes in the technical coefficients matrix.

One way of improving the predictive performance of input-output models is to construct a technical coefficients matrix from specially selected samples of firms. If input-output analysis is being used, for example, to estimate the impact of the growth in final demand for an industry's output, the accuracy of the forecasts will probably be improved by using the technical coefficients of the most efficient (or 'best practice') firms in the economy under investigation. Such forecasts are likely to be more accurate because the technical coefficients matrix will be changing (if at all) in the direction of the most efficient firms. In other words, the technical coefficients matrix of the economy in a few years time is likely to be more accurately approximated by the current technical coefficients of the most efficient firms than by the average technical coefficients of all firms. Alternatively, the technical coefficients can be projected into the future by obtaining estimates of the likely changes in input-output relationships from engineers and technologists. The opposite procedure can be undertaken if the purpose is to estimate the impact of a *decline* in final demand, in which case the technical coefficients of the least efficient (or 'worst practice') firms would be used since it is these firms which are likely to close first. Thus, the technical coefficients matrix can be modified depending upon the problem being studied.

An additional drawback of the input-output approach is that the technical coefficients matrix assumes that all industries exhibit constant returns to scale. A doubling of output will require a doubling of inputs. This should be clear from the proportional relationship we assumed to exist between output and inputs in our earlier discussion of the technical coefficients. This assumption is restrictive, but it is one that it is necessary to make in the absence of information on returns to scale in individual industries.

Finally, when the input-output method is being used for predicting the impact (on a region) of changes in final demand, it is important that supply constraints are built into the model. A rapid output expansion may not be possible in the short run because of a shortage of a necessary input, such as labour. Inward migration into the region may remove this particular constraint over a period of time, but labour availability is certainly likely to operate as a constraint on expansion in the short run. Similar constraints may exist for other inputs, such as intermediate inputs, and producers may have to switch to 'outside' suppliers in the short run if output is to be increased. In view of such problems, capacity constraints — with a time dimension — have to be incorporated into input-output models.

Conclusion

The range of techniques discussed in this chapter is not exhaustive, and we have highlighted only some of the principal ways in which economic analysis can be used to measure the *effects* of regional policy. It is important to recall, however, that these methods enable only a partial evaluation of regional policies. They can tell us, for instance, how much income or employment is generated by regional policy measures, but they cannot tell us whether the generated income or employment is in any sense 'adequate'. This is because they ignore so many other important effects of regional policies — effects on the distribution of income, on the type and range of job opportunities created, on the efficiency of business enterprises, and on the long-term growth prospects of regions. These partial evaluation methods are simply incapable of saying whether a particular policy is the optimum one, or even whether it is worthwhile. The answers to these more fundamental questions must be sought with more comprehensive evaluation methods. It it to these that we turn in the next chapter.

Selected References

Adams, Brooking and Glickman (1975); Archibald (1967); Ashcroft
and Taylor (1978); Greig (1972); Hewings (1971); Miernyk (1965);
Moore and Rhodes (1973a); Nevin, Roe and Round (1966);
Vanderkamp (1972); Weiss and Gooding (1968).

11
The Comprehensive Evaluation of Regional Policy

The purpose of the previous chapter was to demonstrate the wide range of methods that are available for estimating the effect of regional policies on employment and income levels. In spite of the great attraction of some of these techniques, it must be realised that they represent only the first step towards a full evaluation of the effectiveness of regional policy. To be comprehensive, the evaluation of a policy must weigh all the costs of the policy against all the benefits, so that its net social worth may be ascertained. This chapter explores the possibility of evaluating regional policy comprehensively.

The comprehensive evaluation of the full range of costs and benefits of regional policy is undoubtedly a formidable and daunting task. The difficulties are magnified by the absence of clear policy objectives, since without a clear idea of what regional policy is designed to achieve it is impossible to specify the costs and benefits stemming from the policy. Another problem of major dimensions is one that is common to all attempts to evaluate government policies: many of the costs and benefits are of such an intangible nature that quantification is at best extremely hazardous — and at worst quite impossible. Furthermore, the impact of regional policy is often so diverse and far-reaching that all the costs and benefits are unlikely to be identifiable.

But this lack of accuracy in predicting the consequences of government action should not be regarded as fatal. If the evaluation of government policy is to be improved, it is necessary to move in the direction of comprehensive evaluation despite the existence of apparently intractable problems. This chapter examines the potential value of social cost-benefit analysis as a means of evaluating regional policy.

11.1 Cost-Benefit Analysis

Surprisingly little use has been made of the cost-benefit technique in the evaluation of regional policy despite its obvious attraction as a method of appraising alternative ways of achieving policy objectives. None the less, enough work has been done to suggest that cost-benefit analysis is a potentially valuable approach provided its many limitations are clearly understood.

As far as the evaluation of regional policy is concerned, it is useful to divide the discussion of the cost-benefit approach into two parts: the appraisal of the *private* costs and benefits of regional policy and the appraisal of the *social* costs and benefits. Private appraisal involves calculating the costs and benefits of regional policy for specific groups within society, whereas social appraisal attempts to calculate the effects of regional policy on all members of society. This distinction between private costs and benefits and social costs and benefits focuses attention on the comprehensive and all-embracing nature of the cost-benefit approach. We begin by examining the private costs and benefits of regional policy.

Private appraisal of regional policy
The private appraisal of regional policy involves measuring the costs and benefits for two specific groups. Firstly, there are the direct *recipients* of regional policy incentives: firms benefit from capital grants, labour subsidies, tax relief and other incentives; workers benefit from relocation and retraining grants. Secondly, the costs and benefits of regional policy can be computed for the Exchequer — the *donor* of regional policy expenditure.

Recipients of regional policy incentives. Private manufacturing firms in the UK (and more recently firms in the service sector) are the recipients of a wide variety of regional financial incentives, the intention of which is to stimulate industrial development in depressed regions. By raising the rate of return on capital in depressed regions relative to other regions in the economy, it is hoped to induce

more industry to expand in the depressed areas than would
otherwise have been the case. Expressing the value of
financial incentives in present value terms, investment
incentives for manufacturing firms in Britain can be seen to
have been biased in favour of the Development Areas during
the 1960s and early 1970s (see figure 11.1). The effect of

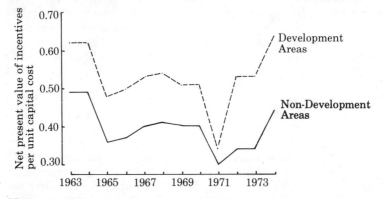

Notes:
1. The net present value is calculated per unit of capital cost.
2. A fixed rate of discount of 10% has been used throughout.
3. Firms are assumed to be sufficiently profitable to claim full tax
   allowances.
4. Maximum percentage grants are assumed to be paid.
Source: Melliss and Richardson (1976), table 5.

Figure 11.1 *Estimated net present value of incentive schemes for
plant and machinery in Development Areas and Non-
Development Areas in GB (1963-74)*

regional financial incentives on the rate of return on
hypothetical capital investment projects can also be
calculated for assisted and non-assisted areas, as shown in
table 11.1. If we also knew how firms were likely to react to
regional differences in rates of return it would be possible to
estimate the consequences of regional policy incentives on
industrial investment in depressed regions. This would be a
significant step forward in estimating the potential effects
of regional policy.

Attempts to estimate the effect of regional incentives on
the rate of return on capital, however, face a number of
severe problems. The estimates provided in table 11.1, for
example, are based on the internal rate of return method of
evaluating investment projects. Yet many firms use only the

Table 11.1 *Estimated real rates of return in non-assisted areas, Development Areas and Special Development Areas, 1960-74*

Year	Capital-intensive project			Labour-intensive project		
	Non-Assisted areas	DAs	SDAs	Non-Assisted areas	DAs	SDAs
1960	6.1	7.7	—	6.5	7.3	—
1963	9.6	15.2	—	8.3	11.8	—
1966	6.6	9.7	—	6.5	9.2	—
1968	6.8	10.2	12.6	6.7	10.0	11.7
1970	6.5	10.4	11.6	6.7	10.2	12.3
1972	7.5	12.7	13.0	7.5	11.5	11.7
1974	9.1	14.3	14.5	9.0	13.2	13.4

Notes:
1. Allowances are assumed to be claimed against profit immediately.
2. The internal rate of return method was used to estimate the real rates of return *(i)* given above. This method calculates the value of *i* such that:

$$\sum_t \frac{R_t}{(1 + i)^t} = \sum_t \frac{C_t}{(1 + i)^t}$$

where R_t is the financial return on the project in year t and C_t is the financial cost. Regional financial incentives raise rates of return by either reducing C_t (e.g. capital grants, labour subsidies) or increasing R_t (e.g. price subsidies).
3. A hypothetical 'labour-intensive' and a hypothetical 'capital-intensive' project are used as the basis of the calculations.
4. A project life of 10 years is assumed, with no replacement.
Source: Northern Region Strategy Team, *Evaluation of the Impact of Regional Policy on Manufacturing Industry in the Northern Region,* Technical Report No. 2, 1975, table C1.

crudest of appraisal techniques and may be swayed in their location decisions far more by factors such as the effect of inducements on their immediate liquidity position or the speed at which an investment outlay is recovered. A further problem is the uncertainty which often surrounds regional incentives. There was a good deal of uncertainty, for example, in how long regional labour subsidies would continue to be provided to firms located in the UK Development Areas. Uncertainty also arises if the grants or subsidies are at the discretion of the government or, as with many tax allowances, if a company must be earning sufficient profits before it can fully exploit tax allowances.

The estimation of the effect of regional incentives on rates of return is made more difficult by the fact that regional policies may have a different effect on different types of project. As far as British regional policy is concerned, table 11.1 shows that incentives have displayed a distinct bias towards capital-intensive projects. The same has been the case for Canada (Woodward 1974a). Ideally, a range of estimates is required, one for each type of project. The capital bias of regional policy raises a further problem. Since the price of capital is effectively reduced relative to the price of labour in assisted areas, projects may be designed with a greater capital-intensity compared to their counterparts in non-assisted areas. In producing comparative rates of return such as those in table 11.1, it is therefore important to compare *identical* projects in assisted and non-assisted areas.

In spite of these difficulties, estimating the effects of regional policies on the rate of return on investment projects can provide useful information on the private benefits of regional policy to individual firms. In 1974, the regional policy incentives available in Britain gave a fillip of between 4% and 5% to the internal rate of return on projects located in assisted areas. Advantageous though regional policy incentives may appear to have been to individual firms, however, the benefits to society as a whole depend crucially upon how firms react to these incentives. If the incentives are ignored and have no effect on the location of industrial investment, the social benefits will be nil. If firms react positively to the incentives, the social benefits are likely to far outweigh the direct advantages to individual firms, as we shall see later.

Migration and retraining policies have traditionally played a smaller role in British regional policy than incentives to firms. In principle, however, there is nothing to prevent a private appraisal of migration and retraining schemes. Government expenditure on retraining, for example, reduces the costs incurred by the individual and by doing so raises the rate of return on the individual's investment in his own human capital (Hughes 1970). The same applies to government migration incentives. Migration policies such as the Employment Transfer Scheme in Britain are designed to increase the rate of return from migration by meeting some of the financial costs incurred by migrants. Unfortunately, the predominance of the non-pecuniary costs of migration means that estimating the effects of government incentives on the financial rate of return to migration is of little practical value.

Donor of regional policy expenditure. Just as it is possible to undertake a financial appraisal of regional policy from the point of view of the firms and individuals receiving incentives, it is also possible to financially appraise regional policy from the point of view of the donor — the Exchequer. In the case of firms and private individuals, the effect of regional policy is to raise the rate of return on capital expenditure, retraining and migration. From the point of view of the Exchequer, however, regional policy *itself* becomes the project being appraised. Appraisal involves calculating the time-stream of financial outlays and financial returns accruing to the Exchequer as a direct consequence of regional policy. These cash flows can then be discounted (to obtain the present value) and the result expressed as the net present value or rate of return on regional policy to the Exchequer.

In a study of the Exchequer implications of British regional policy in the early 1960s, the discounted financial returns to the Exchequer were estimated to exceed the outlays by £900 per employed worker (Needleman and Scott 1964). It may seem strange that regional policy could actually yield a *positive* net return to the Exchequer. The reasons for this can be seen in table 11.2, which sets out the results of an Exchequer appraisal of British regional policy from 1963 to 1970 estimated by Moore and Rhodes (1975b). The cash transfers are expressed as annual averages and discounted values are not calculated. Item 1 constitutes what is frequently and misleadingly referred to as the 'cost of regional policy', namely the financial outlays on subsidies, grants and other incentives. Item 2 shows that various financial clawback effects may eventually more than match these direct outlays. These clawback effects result from the reduction in unemployment due to regional policy. For each person employed as a result of regional policy, the Exchequer reaps a twofold gain. Firstly, unemployment benefits and other welfare payments are lower. Secondly, increased tax payments will accrue to the Exchequer. Item 3 is also a type of clawback by the Exchequer. Regional policy leads to a reduction of net out-migration from assisted areas and this in turn reduces government expenditure on public services and infrastructure in the regions to which the migrants would otherwise have moved.

Finally, item 4 reflects "... the seemingly paradoxical proposition that regional policy although requiring initially increased Exchequer expenditures leads to all regions

Table 11.2 *Exchequer implications of British regional policy, 1963-1970*

	Cash flows		*Annual average (1963-1970)* *£ million (at current prices)*
1.	Exchequer outlays on regional policy net of directly recoverable items (e.g. loans)		−125
2.	Exchequer 'clawbacks' from regional policy , comprising:		
	(a)	Higher employee and employer national insurance contributions	(20 to 23)
	(b)	Higher corporation tax yields	(25 to 28)
	(c)	Higher distributed profits tax yields	(5 to 6)
	(d)	Higher income tax yields	(29 to 34)
	(e)	Higher indirect tax yields	(35 to 40)
	(f)	Reduced unemployment benefits, national assistance and supplementary benefits payments	(18 to 26)
			+ 133 to + 156
3.	Net reduction in infrastructure and public service expenditure as a result of reduced net migration		+ 20 to + 6
4.	Reduction of tax yields required to restore pressure of demand in fully employed areas		− 122 to −133
	Net increase (−) or decrease (+) in Exchequer budgetary deficit as a result of regional policy		−94 to −96

Notes:
1. Clawback estimates refer to the position after restoring the pressure of demand in fully employed areas.
2. Where a *range* of estimates is given this reflects the choice of either a 'low net migration' or a 'high net migration' assumption. With the former it is assumed that regional policies reduced the net migration losses of the Development Areas by 100,000 people. With the latter it is assumed that net migration fell by 300,000 people during 1963-70 as the result of regional policy.
Source: Moore and Rhodes (1975b), table 2.

realising an increase in income through a general reduction in tax rates and no sacrifices of output or employment in any region" (Moore and Rhodes 1975b). Over the period 1960-71, regional policy is estimated to have led to the creation of 300,000 new jobs in the Development Areas of the UK (Moore and Rhodes 1976b). Many of these jobs represent employment opportunities diverted away from the non-Development Areas; that is, regional policy has diverted demand away from regions which had a labour shortage during the 1960s and towards regions with high unemployment. In so far as it is fully employed regions which act as 'inflation leaders' and therefore constrain the government's efforts to expand the national economy, this diversion of demand will have enabled the government to operate a more expansionary demand management policy. This assumes, of course, that inflation is the major constraint facing governments wishing to operate a more expansionary demand management policy. But governments have to face other constraints in addition to inflation, and it can be argued that in some periods (e.g. high unemployment in all regions) constraints such as the balance of payments or the public sector borrowing requirement may predominate.

Moore and Rhodes estimate that regional policy would enable the Exchequer to cut taxes (or raise government expenditure) by around £130m per annum in order to restore demand in the fully employed areas to the level it would have reached in the absence of regional policy between 1963 and 1970. But whether the government has the power to regulate demand such that it can discriminate between regions is quite another matter. Macro-policy instruments are clearly not sufficiently sensitive to operate a regionally discriminating fiscal policy (House of Commons 1973b). The size of item 4 thus remains a matter of controversy, but the fact that it is controversial does not remove the necessity of explicitly allowing for the implications of regional policy on government fiscal and monetary policy. Restoring the pressure of demand in fully employed areas represents the *tax cost* of regional policy. In this case, the tax cost is negative — a tax cut is appropriate. This is just as much a financial cost to the Exchequer as the item 'gross Exchequer outlay' in table 11.2.

It should also be borne in mind that whilst there is a financial drain on the Exchequer resulting from an expansionary fiscal policy of the type needed to restore demand in non-assisted areas, such policies actually yield benefits to society in the form of higher output and more jobs. The Exchequer costs are thus illusory. Whether or not regional policy results in private Exchequer costs is of little relevance. What is needed, of course, is a full evaluation of the social costs and benefits of regional policy.

Social appraisal of regional policy
In social cost-benefit analysis, the evaluation is extended from the firm, the private individual or the Exchequer to society as a whole. Expressed in net present value (NPV) terms, we have:

$$\text{NPV} = \sum_t \frac{R_t}{(1 + r)^t} - \sum_t \frac{C_t}{(1 + r)^t}$$

where R_t is the time-stream of social benefits of regional policy and C_t is the time-stream of social costs, and r is the social discount rate. Considerable controversy exists over the choice of an appropriate social discount rate, the two main alternatives being a measure of the time preference of society or a measure of the social opportunity cost of capital employed (see Layard 1972).

Cost-benefit analysis has its roots set firmly in welfare economic theory. The sophistication and theoretical wholeness which this gives to cost-benefit analysis should not, however, blind us to its many weaknesses. The cost-benefit approach is not the pinnacle of perfection. On the contrary, its operational and theoretical problems are considerable and have provided fuel to one of the fiercest controversies in modern economics. Almost every single aspect of the welfare theory underlying cost-benefit analysis has aroused passionate debate. Of greater importance here, however, are the more specific problems raised in applying the technique to the evaluation of regional policy.

The problem of multiple objectives. Cost-benefit analysis is concerned with measuring the effects of regional policy on the welfare of all individuals within society. The fundamental concept is that of a 'Pareto improvement': a policy is judged to be worthwhile if it leads to an increase in the welfare of at least one individual in society without making anyone else worse off. One of the major objectives of regional policy is to improve the *efficiency* with which society uses its resources to produce goods and services. Regional policy, for example, by bringing unemployed labour and other resources into productive use increases the production of goods and services, the consumption of which increases economic welfare.

In practice, cost-benefit analysis is effectively constrained to measuring these 'efficiency' implications of regional policy and ignores the equity implications. If regional policy improves the efficiency with which a nation uses its resources it is deemed to be worthwhile; if it does not increase this efficiency it will be deemed not to be worthwhile. This concentration on the economic efficiency aspects is a serious limitation, especially in the case of evaluating regional policy, since regional policy can only improve the welfare of society by simultaneously making some people better off whilst at the same time making others worse off. The strict criterion for a 'Pareto improvement' is not met. Recourse is therefore needed to the compensation principle; that is, a Pareto improvement is said to occur if those who gain could compensate those who lose and still be better off. This amounts to a side-stepping of the equity objectives of regional policy. To many people, the essence of the case for regional policy is the redistribution of income from prosperous to depressed regions. Hence, even if those gaining (in depressed regions) could *not* compensate those losing (in prosperous regions) and still remain better off, there may still be a positive social gain from regional policy arising from the desire to redistribute income.

In principle, it is a relatively simple task to take equity goals explicitly into account in cost-benefit analysis. The costs and benefits falling on lower income groups (i.e. those predominating in depressed regions), can be given a larger weight in the final cost-benefit calculation than those falling on higher income groups. The problem is not how to incorporate equity objectives, but rather to determine what weights to use. Attempts to determine these weights have varied from extracting the equity bias implicit in past government decisions to a simple explicit statement of the equity aims of the policymaker. Most cost-benefit studies either ignore the problem, or at best simply set out the redistributive implications of the policy. The policymaker is then left to weigh the importance of the redistributive effects himself.

The concentration of policy evaluation on the economic

efficiency aspects of regional policy has led to the neglect of other objectives in addition to that of income redistribution. Though the objectives of regional policy are often vague, there is no doubt that its aims range far beyond those of economic efficiency. Important political, strategic and other non-economic objectives of regional policy are ignored. Once again, it is left to the policymaker to subjectively weigh any efficiency costs of regional policy against its non-economic benefits.

The extension of cost-benefit analysis towards multi-objective evaluation, and in particular towards the measurement of the redistributive effects, will greatly increase the information requirements of the evaluation exercise. In addition to requiring equity weights, the effects of regional policies on all income groups in all regions will need to be estimated. The problems are clearly immense.

The problem of defining the accounting unit. Cost-benefit analysis attempts to measure the costs and benefits of regional policy to society as a whole and not to any particular group within society. The standard convention is to define society as the present generation of individuals. There are two problems in defining society in this way.

First, a decision has to be made whether or not to estimate the costs and benefits of regional policy to the nation as a whole or simply to the assisted areas. Since the economic justification for regional policy lies in its ability to assist governments in attaining *national* policy objectives, such as full employment, stable prices and the equitable distribution of income, it is clearly appropriate to use the entire nation and not just the assisted areas as the accounting unit.

The second problem is more severe. By its very nature, regional policy is likely to generate its full rewards only over a very long period of time. Apart from the difficulty of quantifying these long-term effects, there is the problem that many of the benefits of regional policy are likely to accrue to future generations whilst the costs will fall on the present generation. How to incorporate the benefits accruing to future generations into the analysis is a problem of great complexity. It is not simply a question of extending the accounting unit beyond the present generation, since the present generation itself may take account of the welfare of future generations in the form of a weaker time preference (i.e. a lower discount rate) for the benefits of government policies.

Measuring the social costs and benefits of regional policy. The most intractable problems of cost-benefit analysis concern the identification and measurement of the individual costs and benefits. The need to value all the costs and benefits in money terms means that costs and benefits are often difficult, and sometimes quite impossible, to measure. Three distinct problems stand out. First, *shadow prices* must be computed for costs and benefits for which no market price is available, or for which a market price exists but is not an adequate measure. Many recreational amenities, such as the services provided by national parks, are simply not sold on the open market. In the absence of a market price for this amenity, the willingness of consumers to pay the cost of travelling to the amenity is often used as a shadow price. Secondly government policies invariably involve *transfers* of income from one group within society to another, which means that the resulting distributional effects must be taken explicitly into account. Thirdly, dangers of *double-counting* arise when social costs and benefits are transmitted from one person to another. To see how severe these problems can be, we will consider some of the main costs and benefits of regional policy in detail.

(a) Costs and benefits of reducing regional unemployment. We have previously argued that the cornerstone of the case for regional policy is the reduction of the high levels of unemployment that persist in some regions. It should be noted that regional policy may also bring other resources, such as capital, into employment. It is, however, the employment of labour that would otherwise have been unemployed which is arguably the most significant of the benefits stemming from regional policy. Attempts to place a monetary value on this social benefit have proved to be more difficult than might be expected. Indeed, it is a classic example of the need for shadow pricing in cost-benefit analysis.

Estimating the employment effects of regional policy is not a simple task. Figure 11.2 shows three separate avenues through which regional policy may increase the *demand* for labour in assisted areas. Extra jobs may be created in assisted areas either by diverting the demand for labour from non-assisted areas to assisted areas, or by inducing foreign firms to settle in the assisted areas, or by creating

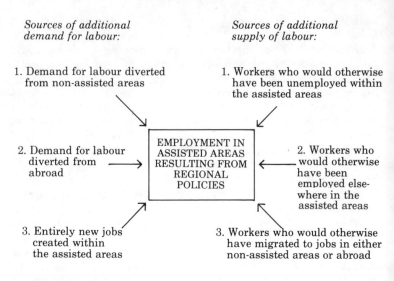

Figure 11.2 *Regional policy and the employment of labour*

entirely new jobs in the assisted areas. Not all the extra jobs created in the assisted areas are therefore necessarily at the expense of jobs lost by the non-assisted areas.

Even if the number of jobs directly created in the assisted areas through these three avenues can be accurately estimated, there remains the problem of estimating the additional jobs created through subsequent multiplier and accelerator effects. The openness of regional economies means that these multiplier effects will not be confined to their region of origin, but will rapidly be passed on to other parts of the economy. The techniques of impact analysis discussed in the previous chapter can, in principle, be harnessed to trace through these multiplier effects. Interregional input-output models in particular have proved to be useful in estimating the effects of specific government expenditures, since they can be used to pinpoint the individual occupations, industries, and regions experiencing the increase in labour demand (Haveman and Krutilla 1968). Even detailed interregional impact models, however, have their limitations. Their application is curtailed by the absence of suitable and sufficient data — in particular of the linkages between regions through which multiplier effects are transmitted. Estimating the likelihood that increases in demand in assisted areas will be met by local firms rather than by firms in other regions — i.e. the 'regional preference function' (Blake 1973) — is an almost impossible task. Furthermore, impact models are essentially static and fail to measure the longer-term induced investment which hopefully follows in the wake of successful regional policies (Haveman 1976). Many countries, for example, have used regional policies to encourage large 'propulsive' industries to locate in assisted areas in the hope that their presence will attract, over time, a range of other linked industries.

Returning to figure 11.2, we can see that the additional demand for labour in assisted areas can be met by an increase in the labour *supply* from three sources. Firstly, the additional job opportunities may be filled by workers who would otherwise have remained unemployed within the assisted areas. It is important to realise that this need not necessarily lead to a fall in *registered* unemployment. Additional workers may also be drawn from the ranks of the *unregistered* unemployed and especially from the pool of unregistered unemployed females. Moore and Rhodes (1977), for example, estimate that between 1960 and 1974 the industrial and regional policies of Eire had reduced registered unemployment by 25,000 and had simultaneously increased activity rates such that a further 25,000 previously unregistered unemployed workers had found jobs. Secondly, the additional demand for labour may result not in an increase in employment but rather in the diversion of workers from other jobs within the region. This is more likely to occur if unemployed workers lack the skills required by expanding industries. Thirdly, the additional demand for labour may reduce the out-migration of workers who would otherwise have migrated to take up jobs in either non-assisted areas or abroad. In Eire, for instance, the combined effect of industrial and regional policies before 1974 may have reduced national emigration by about 100,000 workers.

Estimating the net benefits of creating jobs in the assisted areas requires the estimation of the opportunity cost of employing the extra workers. What must be forgone elsewhere by employing more workers in assisted areas depends both on the origin of the *supply* of extra workers employed and on the origin of the additional *demand* for their labour (see figure 11.2). Let us consider supply first.

The social cost of employing workers who would otherwise have been unemployed is zero, whereas the social cost of employing workers who would otherwise have been employed is the output in their alternative occupations. The shadow wage of workers who would otherwise have been unemployed may therefore be taken to be zero, whilst the shadow wage of workers who would otherwise have been employed is measured by the earnings they would have obtained in their alternative jobs. Determining the social cost of employing workers who would otherwise have migrated is more difficult. Since we have defined the accounting unit of the cost-benefit analysis as the nation as a whole, the social cost of employing workers who would otherwise have migrated to jobs in non-assisted regions is their earnings. The output in non-assisted areas will be lower than it otherwise would have been. However, in the case of employing workers who would otherwise have migrated abroad, the social cost involved is zero as far as the nation is concerned. The reduction of output overseas is of no relevance.

Determining the extent to which regional policy will create jobs for workers who would otherwise have been unemployed rather than workers who would otherwise have been employed is therefore of crucial importance to the evaluation. A factor of major significance in determining

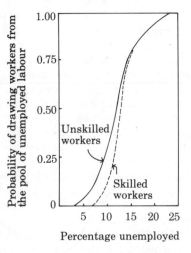

Figure 11.3 *Hypothetical response functions*

the probability of drawing workers from the unemployment pool is the level of unemployment itself. Detailed work in the USA (Haveman 1970) has shown that the probability of drawing workers from the pool of unemployed rises very quickly as the unemployment rate increases beyond a certain minimum level. Figure 11.3 provides two hypothetical examples of this effect. The probability of drawing workers from the unemployment pool rather than from other employers is likely to be higher, at each rate of unemployment, for unskilled than for skilled workers, as indicated in the diagram. Ideally, response functions of the type depicted in figure 11.3 would be calculated for each type of labour and for each region. These could then be used, in conjunction with the employment estimates generated by an interregional impact model, to determine the number of workers drawn from the unemployment pool in each region.

Attractive though this approach may be, the high cost of data collection involved has forced researchers to use a more aggregative approach. Moore and Rhodes (1976b), for example, have estimated the total employment effect of regional policy in the UK from 1960 to 1971 by subtracting the level of employment they estimate *would* have occurred in the Development Areas in the absence of regional policy from the actual employment level (see the previous chapter). In this way, they obtain an estimate of the total number of *additional* jobs in the assisted areas resulting from regional policy. They found that, allowing for multiplier effects, employment in the assisted areas increased by 300,000 from 1960 to 1971. As we have seen, however, not all of this extra employment represents a reduction of unemployment in the assisted areas. Net migration from assisted areas also fell by between 35,000 and 100,000 workers between 1963 and 1971 as the result of the success of regional policy.

The social cost of employment in assisted areas resulting from regional policy clearly depends on where the newly employed workers originate. Only those who would otherwise have remained unemployed can be regarded as having a zero social cost. Unfortunately, the social cost of labour also depends on the source of the additional demand for labour as well as on the origin of the workers who eventually fill the jobs. Moore and Rhodes estimate that in order to expand employment in the Development Areas of the UK by 300,000 between 1960 and 1971, 150,000 jobs were lost in the non-assisted areas. Even if all the new jobs created in assisted areas are filled by workers who would otherwise have remained unemployed, there is still a social cost involved in employing them. Employment has fallen elsewhere in the economy. To the extent that employment falls in the non-assisted areas, there is a loss of output which must be weighed against the gains in employment and output in the assisted areas. Each new job created in an assisted area which has been diverted from a non-assisted area means that a job 'gained' is also a job 'lost' to the nation.

Plausible though this view may seem, it does not stand up to scrutiny once it is realised that the jobs 'lost' in the non-assisted areas (as a result of the diversion of jobs to the assisted areas) can be replaced, at least in principle, by appropriate fiscal and monetary action by the government. If jobs in non-assisted areas have been 'lost' to assisted areas, the government can presumably replace those lost jobs by expanding demand in the non-assisted areas. The obvious way to restore the lost jobs in the non-assisted areas would be to expand *aggregate* demand. If the government can restore the jobs 'lost' in the non-assisted areas then clearly these will no longer represent a social cost of regional policy. The beauty of regional policy is that not only does it create the need to replace jobs lost in non-assisted areas, but it also provides the government with the means to replace them.

Governments are normally constrained from increasing the pressure of demand in the economy in two ways. There may be adverse effects on the rate of inflation and there may be adverse effects on the balance of payments. If it is accepted that inflationary pressures tend to be generated in low unemployment regions rather than high unemployment regions (as argued in Chapter 6), it follows that the diversion of jobs to assisted areas will reduce inflationary pressures in the economy. This is the essence of the inflation case for a regional policy. This reduction in inflationary pressures will make it possible to expand aggregate demand up to the point where the inflationary pressures are restored to their initial level. Whether the extra jobs created by the expansion of aggregate demand (in both the assisted and non-assisted areas) will be sufficient to wipe out the loss of jobs in the non-assisted areas (due to regional policy) is an empirical matter. As we pointed out in our discussion of the regional aspects of inflation in Chapter 6, the extent to which regional policy can alleviate inflationary pressures and thereby allow the economy to be operated at a higher level of demand is still unknown.

The effect of regional policy on the balance of payments position is equally difficult to estimate. The higher overall level of employment in the economy resulting from regional policy will increase the demand for imports, thus worsening the balance of payments position. But this ignores the possibility that part of the expansion will be in the export industries or industries producing import substitutes. It also ignores the inflow of foreign investment attracted by regional incentives. It is impossible to say *a priori* what the net effect on the balance of payments will be. Empirical research is required to resolve this problem. More fundamentally, nothing has been said about the exchange rate. If regional policies do lead to a balance of payments deficit, the appropriate response may be to allow the currency to depreciate, in which case the real cost to the economy would be a deterioration in the terms of trade. The balance of payments cost of regional policy will therefore depend on its effect on the balance of payments position and on the government's response. If the government responds by restraining demand in order to prevent a balance of payments deficit, the diversion of jobs from non-assisted to assisted areas will result in a loss of jobs in the non-assisted areas. If the response is to permit the exchange rate to depreciate, the effect will be a fall in the terms of trade: each unit of domestic output will purchase a smaller quantity of imports. In both cases, there will be social costs to bear — assuming, of course, that such policies adversely affect the balance of payments.

(b) *The problem of externalities.* In spite of the many problems involved in estimating the social costs and benefits of labour resources brought into use by regional policy, at least there is a market price (i.e. the wage rate) which can be taken as the starting point of the analysis. There is a second group of social costs and benefits arising from regional policy, however, that also requires the construction of shadow prices. These are the costs and benefits for which there is simply no market price available. Foremost amongst these are the external costs and the external benefits which by definition fall outside the market mechanism. Shadow prices have to be constructed if these externalities are to be valued.

Most of the externality effects of regional policy arise from its effect on the pattern of urbanisation. If it can be shown that regional policy prevents an over-rapid expansion of large urban centres in the non-assisted regions, the reduced social costs resulting from less congestion and pollution will constitute a gain to society. On the other hand, it can be argued that the diversion of industrial activity from non-assisted to assisted areas may result in the failure to exploit the external economies that exist at the firm's original location. Shifting firms away from these low cost locations could injure the long-term growth prospects of the whole nation.

Apart from the few experiments in estimating shadow prices for certain types of urban pollution, such as noise, very little progress has yet been made on constructing shadow prices for such external costs and benefits. Most experimental approaches have relied on the market price of some other commodity as a surrogate for the shadow price of the externality under scrutiny. The effect of noise levels on house prices around airports, for example, has been used as an index of the social costs of aircraft noise. We are clearly a long way from being able to quantify the external costs and benefits of regional policy.

The final major social benefit of regional policy requiring some form of shadow pricing is the extra benefit experienced by individuals who would otherwise have remained unemployed or who have been forced to emigrate from the assisted areas. Earlier, we noted that the social benefit of employing workers who would otherwise be idle is simply the value of the output that they produce. Added to this, however, are the reduced costs of unemployment that stem from the social stigma attached to being unemployed, though this particular cost will be partly offset by the loss of leisure. Such utility gains and losses fall entirely outside the labour market mechanism but may nevertheless affect social costs and benefits substantially.

The reduction in net out-migration from regions with high unemployment results in similar social benefits. Some of the social benefits of reduced out-migration can be valued fairly accurately. This is the case for any reduction in resource outlay required to provide public services for incoming migrants in non-assisted areas. It may be cheaper, for instance, to provide such services at the existing locations of would-be migrants. Similarly, a reduction in the flow of migrants involves readily measurable savings in transport and other migration costs. But perhaps the major part of the social benefits arising from reduced out-migration accrues as a utility gain to the individuals concerned. The non-pecuniary costs of migrating from familiar surroundings may be immense. In economic terms, these non-pecuniary costs can be regarded as the consumer's surplus lost when migrants leave their homes.

(c) *Transfer payments and the problem of double-counting.* One of the greatest problems in using cost-benefit analysis to assess the net social worth of government policies occurs because the benefits do not necessarily accrue to those who bear the cost. The redistributive effects of regional policy should ideally be taken into account in the cost-benefit analysis. Unfortunately, of course, it has proved impossible to devise weights for the costs and benefits falling on different groups within society. The best that can be hoped for is that the redistributive effects of regional policies can be identified and spelled out as clearly as possible.

Much of the redistributive effect of regional policies occurs through transfer payments. As we saw when we discussed the Exchequer implications of regional policy, the effect of regional policy on taxes and on fiscal transfers is both complex and controversial. If a regional policy necessitates an increase in taxation, there is a transfer of income from tax payers in general to the recipients of the government expenditure on regional policy. On the other hand, it can be argued that an effective regional policy may actually lead to a reduction in the burden on taxpayers in general by generating 'clawback' effects such as reduced payments of unemployment benefit and by enabling the government to reduce general taxation as a means of restoring jobs 'lost' in the non-assisted areas (Moore and Rhodes 1975b). In this case even residents in non-assisted areas reap some of the benefits of regional policy. Their higher after-tax incomes enable them to obtain some of the additional output resulting directly from regional policy.

Care must also be taken not to double count. Consider the case of a worker who would otherwise have been unemployed were it not for regional policy. If his gross earnings are being used to measure the social benefit of his employment, then that part of the extra earnings passed on to the Exchequer in the form of increased income and other taxes is not an additional social benefit.

Evaluating alternative policies

An easily neglected problem in the application of cost-benefit analysis is the failure to consider an adequate range of alternative methods of achieving the same policy objectives. This is no less true in the evaluation of regional policy. Ideally, the evaluation of regional policy should include the investigation of a policy-off situation, a no-change situation and a reasonable range of alternative policy options.

To simply compare existing regional policy with a policy-off situation is useful, and indeed necessary, but it may produce misleading policy recommendations unless *other* policy alternatives are considered as well. When there is general unemployment in all regions, for example, 'almost any project is better for the country than no project' (Prest and Turvey 1965). It is not difficult to justify any public expenditure under such circumstances by comparing it with a policy-off situation, hence Keynes's recommendation that burying pound notes down disused mine shafts in areas of high unemployment is better than no policy at all. Even when full employment exists in some regions and unemployment is localised in depressed regions, it is extremely likely that a regional policy which utilises resources that would otherwise be idle will be socially preferable to having no regional policy. The social worth of existing regional policy must be assessed by comparing it not just with a policy-off situation but with a range of alternative policy strategies. Using a policy-off situation as the benchmark for evaluating existing regional policy may be a useful starting point, but it ignores the fundamental rule of cost-benefit analysis that a project (or policy) must be evaluated by comparing it with feasible alternatives. The road ahead is a difficult one for at present 'hypothetical alternative strategies have not been clearly spelt out by their proponents, and any impact attributable to them must be highly speculative' (Moore and Rhodes 1977). It is essential to proceed along this more tortuous path, however, if regional policy is to be comprehensively evaluated.

11.2 The Planning Balance Sheet: An Extension

The planning balance sheet is a near-relative of cost-benefit analysis (Lichfield 1975). Indeed, it is essentially an extension of the cost-benefit approach in so far as it forces the decision-maker to consider social costs and benefits that cannot be reduced to money values.

The planning balance sheet is probably best regarded as a superior form of *presentation* of cost-benefit analysis. No costs and benefits are ignored and where possible they are valued in monetary units, thus allowing the theoretical consistency of cost-benefit analysis to be retained. The planning balance sheet, however, includes much information normally excluded in cost-benefit studies, a special feature of this approach being that the costs and benefits are shown for specific groups — such as the Exchequer, firms and private individuals. Disaggregating the costs and benefits of regional policy has the distinct advantage that it may help policymakers to see the redistributive effects of the policy more clearly.

The great attraction of the planning balance sheet is that monetary values of the costs and benefits do not *have* to be available before they can be included in the analysis. If quantification in monetary units is not possible, the costs and benefits may be measured in any alternative units that are available. Thus, if regional policy reduces the net outflow of workers from a region, this benefit can be expressed in terms of the number who were induced to remain in the region. Indeed, even those costs and benefits that cannot be quantified can still be included in the planning balance sheet provided they can be identified and described.

The planning balance sheet therefore preserves all the advantages of cost-benefit analysis but at the same time it ensures that no spurious accuracy is attached to the results in so far as nothing that is known is omitted from the final statement of costs and benefits. By the same token, the planning balance sheet also possesses all the disadvantages of cost-benefit analysis. In the end, it is the policymaker who must bear the responsibility for weighing the quantifiable costs and benefits against those that are unquantifiable.

Conclusion

The main point that we have tried to make in this chapter is that the proper evaluation of regional policy is a complex and difficult task. It does not simply involve an estimation of the effects of regional policy on variables such as income and employment, though there can be little doubt that such effects are of considerable importance in determining whether or not a particular policy is worthwhile. To evaluate regional policy correctly, a comprehensive approach must be undertaken. We take the view that there is no viable alternative, in the long-run, to a full-scale cost-benefit analysis if evaluation is to be comprehensive.

The use of comprehensive evaluation methods such as social cost-benefit analysis, planning balance sheet methods, or even goals achievement matrix approaches (see Lichfield 1975) will necessarily take us to entirely new ground. This will involve careful and painstaking research into finding ways of defining regional policy objectives more precisely — and this includes social, political and cultural, as well as economic objectives. Even more difficult problems face the researcher in his efforts to find ways of measuring the extent to which different types of regional policy can be expected to contribute to the attainment of the policy objectives. But such problems must be confronted if progress is to be made in evaluating regional policy. An enormous void remains between what has been achieved so far and what must be done to estimate the 'full economic and social welfare effects on all regions and citizens, the counsel of perfection' (Haveman 1976).

Selected references

Blake (1973); Dasgupta and Pearce (1972); Haveman (1976); Lichfield, Kettle and Whitbread (1975); Moore and Rhodes (1975b); Moore and Rhodes (1977).

Appendix A

Some Additional Notes on the Neoclassical Growth Model

1 Deriving the growth equation from the production function

Given the production function $Q = F(K,L)$ and assuming constant returns to scale, we can express the rate of change of Q as a linear combination of K and L using α (capital's share of national income) and $1-\alpha$ (labour's share) as the respective weights.

Begin by differentiating the production function with respect to time:

$$\frac{dQ}{dt} = \frac{\delta Q}{\delta K}\frac{dK}{dt} + \frac{\delta Q}{\delta L}\frac{dL}{dt}$$

Dividing through by Q, multiplying the first and second expressions on the right by K/K and L/L respectively, we obtain:

$$\frac{dQ}{dt}\frac{1}{Q} = \frac{\delta Q}{\delta K}\frac{K}{Q}\left(\frac{dK}{dt}\frac{1}{K}\right) + \frac{\delta Q}{\delta L}\frac{L}{Q}\left(\frac{dL}{dt}\frac{1}{L}\right) \quad (1)$$

Assuming that factors are paid their marginal products, we can write:

$$\frac{\delta Q}{\delta K} = r \quad \text{or} \frac{\delta Q}{\delta K}\frac{K}{Q} = r\frac{K}{Q} \quad (2)$$

and

$$\frac{\delta Q}{\delta L} = w \quad \text{or} \frac{\delta Q}{\delta L}\frac{L}{Q} = w\frac{L}{Q} \quad (3)$$

where r is the real rental on capital and w is the real wage.

Since $Q = rK + wL$, the shares of total output accruing to capital and labour respectively can be obtained by adding (2) and (3):

$$r\,\frac{K}{Q} + w\,\frac{L}{Q} \;=\; \alpha + (1-\alpha)$$

where α and $1-\alpha$ are the respective shares of capital and labour.

Equation (1) can now be expressed more simply:

$$\dot{Q} = \alpha\,\dot{K} + (1-\alpha)\dot{L}$$

where:

$\dot{Q} = \dfrac{dQ}{dt}\,\dfrac{1}{Q}$ = rate of change of output with respect to time

$\dot{K} = \dfrac{dK}{dt}\,\dfrac{1}{K}$ = rate of change of capital with respect to time

$\dot{L} = \dfrac{dL}{dt}\,\dfrac{1}{L}$ = rate of change of labour force with respect to time.

Similarly, $\dot{Q} = \dot{A} + \dot{K} + (1-\alpha)\dot{L}$ can be derived from the more complex function $Q = A(t)\,F\,(K,L)$, where A is technical progress and $\dot{A}$ is the rate of technical progress.

2 Long-run equilibrium growth in a simple neo-classical model

We start with an aggregate production function (which is again assumed to exhibit constant returns to scale):

$$Q = F(K,L)$$

Letting k be the capital/labour ratio (K/L) and q be output per worker (Q/L), we can write:

$$q = \frac{Q}{L} \;=\; \frac{F(K,L)}{L} \;=\; F\!\left(\frac{K}{L},1\right) \;=\; f(k)$$

This functional relationship between output per worker and capital per worker is shown in figure A1. The assumption of diminishing marginal productivity explains why the slope of $q = f(k)$ diminishes as the capital/labour ratio increases.

Assume that aggregate savings (per period) are proportional to aggregate output. As a result, savings *per worker* will increase in proportion to output *per worker*.

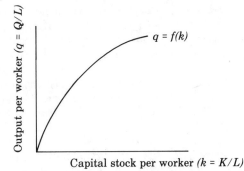

Figure A1 *The production function: output per worker expressed as a function of capital per worker*

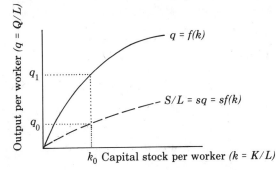

Note that savings per worker is equal to investment per worker, assuming full employment equilibrium.

Figure A2 *Output per worker, savings per worker and investment per worker*

Thus, in figure A2, when output per worker is at q_1, savings per worker is at q_0, the difference between the two being consumption per worker $(q_1 - q_0)$. If we now assume that savings are always invested (i.e. we assume a situation of long-run equilibrium), the savings function of figure A2 gives us the actual level of investment per worker at each level of the capital/labour ratio. In other words, as the capital/labour ratio increases, investment per worker will also increase, each level of investment per worker being indicated by the savings function (since we have assumed a situation of long-run equilibrium).

Having established what the actual level of investment per worker will be at each level of the capital/labour ratio, we now ask the question 'what level of investment spending *is required* in order to maintain the capital/labour ratio at any given level?' With a labour force that is growing at a constant rate, a given amount of investment will be required each year to equip each additional member of the workforce with the required capital in order to maintain the capital/labour ratio at its existing level. Moreover, the higher the initial level of the capital/labour ratio, the higher will be the investment per worker required to maintain the capital/labour ratio at its initial level. Similarly, the higher is the rate of growth of the labour force, the higher is the required investment per worker. An additional allowance must be made for the depreciation of capital equipment, since a greater amount of investment per worker will be required each period to replace worn out equipment the higher the initial capital/labour ratio. Figure A3 shows the

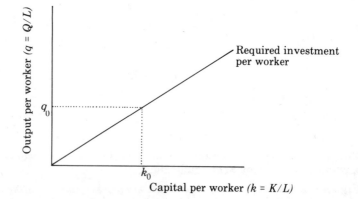

Figure A3 *Investment per worker required to maintain the capital/ labour ratio at any given level*

amount of investment per worker which is required just to maintain the capital/labour ratio at each given initial level of the capital/labour ratio. A simple proportional relationship is assumed to hold. Thus, if the capital/labour ratio is initially at k_0, the investment per worker required to keep the capital/labour ratio at this level is q_0. If investment per worker were at q_0 whilst the capital/labour ratio exceeded k_0, the capital/labour ratio would decline over time since investment per worker would not be adequate to keep up with the growth of the workforce and to replace worn out equipment.

Since we know (i) how much investment per worker *actually occurs* at each level of the capital/labour ratio, and (ii) how much investment per worker *is required* at each level of the capital/labour ratio to maintain the capital/labour ratio at its initial level, we can now proceed to determine the equilibrium level of the capital/labour ratio (and thus output per worker). Two facts are important: if actual investment per worker exceeds the investment per worker required to maintain the capital/labour ratio at its initial level (e.g. at k_0 in figure A4), the capital/labour ratio will increase; if actual investment per worker falls short of the investment per worker required to maintain the capital/labour ratio at its

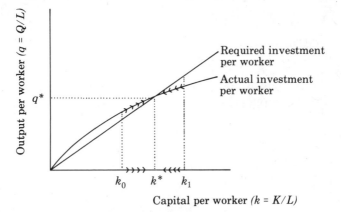

Figure A4 *The equilibrium capital/labour ratio*

initial level (e.g. at k_1 in figure A4), the capital/labour ratio will fall. Figure A4 shows that equilibrium is attained at k^*, which is the steady state capital/labour ratio (assuming a constant rate of growth in the labour force, a depreciation rate which is proportional to the capital stock, a constant propensity to save, an economy which is in full employment equilibrium, and no change in the parameters of the production function).

The same result can be obtained more formally by expressing the functional relationships algebraically. Assume that savings *(S)* are proportional to output and that all savings are invested *(I)*:

$$I = S = sQ, \qquad 0 < s < 1 \qquad\qquad (4)$$

where s is the propensity to save. We define the rate of change of the capital/labour ratio as follows:

$$\dot{k} = \dot{K} - \dot{L} = \frac{dK/dt}{K} - \dot{L} \tag{5}$$

where

$$dK/dt = I - D \tag{6}$$

I = gross investment
D = replacement investment = K

Substituting (4) and (6) into (5), we obtain:

$$\dot{k} = \frac{sQ}{K} - \theta - \dot{L} = s\frac{Q/L}{K/L} - \theta - \dot{L} \tag{7}$$

which can be written:

$$\dot{k} = \frac{sq}{k} - \theta - \dot{L} \tag{8}$$

For the capital/labour ratio to be in equilibrium, there must be no tendency for this ratio to change, which means that $\dot{k} = 0$, or:

$$\frac{sq}{k} = \theta + \dot{L}$$

which can be written:

$$sq = (\theta + \dot{L})k$$

or

$$sf(k) = (\theta + \dot{L})k$$

where $sf(k)$ is the actual investment per worker at each level of the capital/labour ratio (see figure A2) and where $(\theta + \dot{L})k$ is the investment per worker required to maintain capital per worker at its initial level (see figure A3).

3 The approximation of the growth of capital per worker

Several methods exist for approximating the difference between the growth of capital and the growth of the labour supply (i.e. $\dot{K} - \dot{L}$). One method is as follows:

$$\dot{K} - \dot{L} = \frac{\Delta(K/L)}{K/L} \quad \text{(approximately)}$$

which is the numerator of the elasticity of substitution (σ).

The latter is defined as the proportionate change in the capital/labour ratio divided by the proportionate change in factor prices. It measures the responsiveness of the capital/labour ratio to a change in relative factor prices, and is defined as follows:

$$\sigma = \frac{\Delta (K/L)/(K/L)}{\Delta (w/r)/(w/r)} = \frac{\dot{K}-\dot{L}}{\dot{w}-\dot{r}} \qquad \text{(approximately)}$$

where w and r are the real wage and the rate of return on capital respectively. With constant returns to scale, σ equals unity (see Chiang 1974, p. 416) which means that $\dot{K}-\dot{L}=\dot{w}-\dot{r}$. If the rate of return on capital is similar between regions, as seems likely given that capital is mobile, it follows that *regional variations* in $\dot{w}$ will be closely associated with regional variations in $\dot{K}-\dot{L}$.

Selected references

Branson (1972); Eltis (1973).

Appendix B

Measuring the Impact of a Region's Industry-Mix on its Employment Growth: Shift-Share Analysis

The technique known as 'shift-share analysis' has been widely used to assess the influence of a region's industry-mix on its employment growth. A numerical estimate of the effect of the industrial structure on the growth of employment in a region can be obtained by the application of a simple standardisation procedure. This is done by applying national growth rates per industry to the region's industry-mix (at some specified base date) so that a hypothetical growth rate is obtained for the region. We may find, for example, that the region's employment level *would* have increased by 10% if each industry in the region had grown at national rates of growth per industry. If we also know that national employment increased by 5%, we can conclude that the initial industrial structure of the region was favourable (in terms of its potential ability to generate employment growth). The difference between this hypothetical growth rate for the region and the national growth rate is therefore an estimate of whether the industrial structure was initially favourable or otherwise: the greater the positive difference, the more favourable the industrial structure, and conversely for negative differences.

As far as we are aware, the shift-share technique was first used by J.H. Jones in 1940 (in an appendix to the Barlow Report on the Distribution of the Industrial Population). A 'shift' was defined as the amount by which the expansion of an industry in a particular region exceeded or fell short of the region's 'fair share' of the expansion of that industry. Using data on the insured population for a selection of GB regions (1923-37), the GB growth rate per industry was applied to each of 45 industries in selected regions to provide a

hypothetical growth rate for each region. Similar work was
undertaken by Creamer (1943) in the USA. The aim was to
calculate how much of the regional variation in employment
growth could be accounted for by regional differences in the
structure of industry.

Shift-share analysis is therefore a method of calculating
the extent to which the difference between a region's growth
and the nation's growth can be explained by the region's
industry-mix. The method is easily explained. We start with
three definitions.

1. Regional growth rate (g_r)

$$g_r = \frac{\sum_i r_i^t - \sum_i r_i^0}{\sum_i r_i^0}$$

where:

r_i = regional employment in industry i

$\sum_i r_i$ = sum of employment across all industries in the region

t = final year of study period

0 = initial year of study period

2. National growth rate (g_n)

$$g_n = \frac{\sum_i n_i^t - \sum_i n_i^0}{\sum_i n_i^0}$$

where:

n_i = national employment in industry i

$\sum_i n_i$ = sum of employment across all industries in the national economy.

3. Regional growth at national growth rates per industry (g_{rn})

$$g_{r\bar{\bar{n}}} = \frac{\sum_i \left[r_i^0 \left(n_i^t / n_i^0 \right) \right] - \sum_i r_i^0}{\sum_i r_i^0}$$

This is the crucial calculation. It is the growth rate that
would have occurred in the region if each industry had grown

at the same rate as the corresponding national industry during the study period. In other words, national growth rates are applied to the region's industry mix as it existed at the beginning of the study period.

With the help of these three definitions, the regional growth rate can be divided into three separate elements:

$$g_r \equiv (g_r - g_{rn}) + (g_{rn} - g_n) + g_n$$

Taking the elements in reverse order, the third element (g_n) is the region's 'share' of national growth. The faster the national growth in employment, the faster we expect the region to grow. The second element $(g_{rn} - g_n)$ is the structural component. It is the difference between:

(i) the rate at which we expected the region to grow (given its industry mix and given national growth rates for each industry),

(ii) the national growth rate.

Thus, if the region possesses a 'favourable' industry mix we would expect this element to be positive since g_{rn} would exceed g_n in that case. If the region is endowed with an 'unfavourable' industry mix we would expect this element to be negative since g_n would exceed g_{rn}. Finally, the first element $(g_r - g_{rn})$ is simply that part of the region's growth that remains unexplained. It is a residual, or a 'rag-bag' which can be given a wide variety of interpretations (MacKay 1968). A positive residual $(g_r > g_{rn})$ means that the region's growth rate has exceeded the growth rate that would have occurred if each industry in the region had grown at the same rate as its national counterpart. A negative residual $(g_r < g_{rn})$ means the reverse.

Though shift-share analysis suffers from many serious problems, as we shall see later, it nevertheless provides us with a starting point for measuring the effect of a region's industry-mix on its employment growth. During the inter-war years, for example, the industrial structure apparently had a considerable effect upon interregional growth differences in the UK. The results presented in table B1 (taken from the Barlow Report, White Paper 1940) indicate that those regions with a relatively favourable industry mix in 1923 experienced the fastest growth in employment during the subsequent 14 years.

Possibly the most useful aspect of the shift-share

Table B1 *A shift-share analysis of selected GB regions (1923-37)*

Region	Percentage change in insured workers (1923-37)		Components of the shift-share identity (see text)		
	Actual	Hypo-thetical			
	g_r	g_{rn}	$g_r\text{-}g_n$	$g_r\text{-}g_{rn}$	$g_{rn}\text{-}g_n$
SE	42.7	40.2	+20.4	+2.5	+17.9
W Midlands	28.2	29.2	+5.9	-1.0	+6.9
E Midlands	15.0	8.9	-7.3	+6.1	-13.4
NW	7.6	11.0	-14.7	-3.4	-11.3
N	4.7	3.6	-17.6	+1.1	-18.7
Wales	-4.3	0.5	-18.0	-4.8	-13.2
Scotland	9.5	18.1	-12.8	-8.6	-4.2

Definition of regions
SE = London, Home Counties
W Midlands = Midland Counties
E Midlands = W Riding, Notts, Derbyshire
NW = Lancashire
N = Northumberland, Durham
Wales = Glamorgan, Monmouth
Scotland = Mid-Scotland

Definition of shift-share components
$$g_r - g_n = (g_r - g_{rn}) + (g_{rn} - g_n)$$
where:

$g_r - g_n$ = regional growth rate minus national growth rate
$g_r - g_{rn}$ = residual component
$g_{rn} - g_n$ = structural component

Source: Royal Commission on the Distribution of the Industrial Population (1940), Cmnd 6153 (reprint), HMSO.

technique is that it provides us with a method of measuring the *changing* influence of the industrial structure of a region over time. Table B2 summarises the results of several analyses of employment growth in the UK regions during four post-war periods. These results exhibit three distinct features. First, it is immediately clear that some regions have suffered from a permanently unfavourable industry mix (such as the E Midlands, Yorkshire and Humberside, and Wales) whilst other regions have enjoyed a permanently favourable industry mix (such as the SE). But an unfavourable industry mix does not necessarily mean that a region will grow slowly compared to other regions. The E Midlands, for example, was able to overcome its poor industry mix during the 1960s and grow more quickly than the national average. Apparently, individual industries in

Table B2 *A shift-share analysis of the GB regions (1948-71)*

Region	Component	1948-54	1954-58	1959-67	1965-71
SE	structural	3.0	2.3	3.2	2.6
	residual	4.3	0.0	-0.3	-3.9
E Anglia	structural	3.0	2.2	—	0.2
	residual	7.5	8.4	—	7.3
SW	structural	2.9	2.2	0.2	0.9
	residual	0.0	1.0	3.4	5.5
W Mids	structural	-0.3	0.9	1.4	-0.3
	residual	-1.8	-0.2	0.9	0.6
E Mids	structural	-1.5	-2.8	-4.7	-4.1
	residual	1.5	1.7	9.1	5.4
Yorks	structural	-2.5	-2.6	-3.2	-3.0
Humberside	residual	-3.1	0.0	0.6	0.5
NW	structural	0.2	-2.4	-0.8	-0.7
	residual	-2.0	-2.7	-4.2	-2.0
N	structural	-2.7	1.8	-5.0	-2.7
	residual	-1.7	-7.2	0.3	3.5
Wales	structural	-5.5	-1.0	-3.5	-1.7
	residual	6.3	0.2	0.6	6.1
Scotland	structural	-0.1	0.1	-1.9	-0.7
	residual	-4.3	-4.1	-2.7	0.2

Notes:
a Structural component = $g_{rn} - g_n$ (see text).
b Residual component = $g_r - g_{rn}$ (see text).
c E Anglia included in SE in 1959-67 period.
Sources:
1948-54 and 1954-58 analyses are for the manufacturing sector only
    and were obtained from Watson (1971).
1959-67 analysis obtained from Stilwell (1968).
1965-71 analysis computed by the authors.

the E Midlands were growing more quickly than their
national counterparts so that the unfavourable effects of a
poor industry mix were more than compensated by a better
than average growth performance of individual industries.

Secondly, the fact that individual industries have grown
more slowly (on average) in the SE during 1965-71 than their
national counterparts suggests that the policy of diverting
industrial growth away from the SE and towards the
Development Areas may have had the expected effect on
employment growth in the SE. Yet the faster than average
growth of individual industries in E Anglia, the SW and E
Midlands during the same period suggests that one of the
effects of the location of industry controls may have been to
divert industry to adjacent regions.

Thirdly, comparing the two sub-periods 1959-67 and 1965-
71, there was a distinct improvement in the growth

performance of individual industries in the assisted areas
(i.e. Wales, Scotland, N, NW and SW) and a corresponding
deterioration in the growth performance of individual
industries in the non-assisted areas, particularly the SE and
E Midlands. This suggests that regional policy may have
had an effect on employment growth, encouraging growth in
the assisted areas and discouraging it in the non-assisted
areas.

The shift-share technique thus appears to have a useful
part to play in 'explaining' regional growth differences in
that it measures the effect of a region's industry mix on its
growth performance. Admittedly, we are then left with an
'unexplained residual', but this is all we can expect of such a
simple standardisation procedure. Shift-share is not a
theory; it is an identity. It is thus unreasonable to expect it to
be capable of providing a comprehensive explanation of why
some regions grow quickly whilst others grow slowly. But by
extracting the specific effect of the industry mix on a region's
growth, it does at least eliminate one possible influence from
the wide array of possible causal factors. To the extent that it
does this, shift-share can be regarded as a useful starting
point in the analysis of regional growth differences.
Unfortunately, the technique suffers from a number of
problems which throw some doubt on its ability to achieve
even this rather limited objective.

One of the most serious drawbacks of the shift-share
technique is that it treats individual industries as though
they existed quite independently of other industries within
the region. Yet interindustry linkages may have an important part to play in determining the growth rate of an
industry. An industry in region A, for example, may grow
more rapidly than the same industry in region B because of
the presence of a related industry in region A. The growth of
the industry in region A may be due entirely to the fast
growth of the related industry. This is likely to be the case for
local service industries — both personal services and industrial services — since the growth prospects of these trades will
depend heavily upon industries serving markets outside the
region. In a shift-share analysis of regional growth, the
faster growth of region A's industry (relative to the same
industry in region B) would be reflected in the unexplained
residual component, yet it could be argued that region A had
a more favourable industry mix than region B.

The implication to be drawn from this example is that the

structural component in the shift share identity may seriously underestimate the effect of the region's industry mix on its growth performance. The industry mix may therefore contribute more to a region's growth than is reflected by the structural component. In short, part of the industry mix effect may be inextricably intermingled with all the non-structural influences included in the residual component (MacKay 1968).

A second drawback of shift-share analysis is that the results are partly dependent upon the actual definition of the industrial structure adopted. To undertake a shift-share analysis, it is necessary to begin by selecting a suitable industrial classification. Different levels of disaggregation are possible, ranging from the simple division of employment into primary, secondary and tertiary industry groups to the division into a large number of product-based industrial categories (as specified by the *Standard Industrial Classification,* HMSO 1968). This freedom of choice in deciding what level of disaggregation to adopt may appear to give the shift-share technique some flexibility. But it has the serious disadvantage that the level of disaggregation can affect the results. Finer levels of disaggregation have the advantage of ensuring that the industries selected are more homogeneous. We may find, for example, that a region may experience faster-than-average growth in its chemicals industry simply because it specialises in, say, fast-growing pharmaceutical products (Buck 1970). As the level of disaggregation is increased, however, the magnitude of the structural component tends to increase and the unexplained residual decreases. The reason for this is obvious. In the extreme case, each establishment would be defined as an industry in its own right. Clearly, in this case no single industry can be located in more than one region. The individual establishment becomes the national industry and the growth rates of the regional and national industry are identical by definition. It follows directly that regional growth at national growth rates per industry (g_{rn}) must be identically equal to actual regional growth (g_r), which means that the unexplained residual $(g_r - g_{rn})$ is equal to zero — by definition. It thus appears that the relative importance of a region's industry mix in 'explaining' the overall growth of employment in the region will be affected by the level of industrial disaggregation adopted in the first instance.

Finally, it is important to realise that the shift-share

technique is an identity, not a theoretical model. Shift-share analysis divides a region's growth rate into component parts, using a simple accounting formula. The object of the exercise is to measure how much of the difference between regional and national growth can be accounted for by the region's industry mix. The portion of the growth rate that cannot be accounted for by the region's industry mix is then 'attributed' to other factors, such as locational advantages and disadvantages, or the effect of regional policy, or regional differences in the efficiency of management or workers. It is therefore difficult to take shift-share too seriously as it stands since it makes no attempt to *explain* why regional growth differences occur. It simply attributes a portion of the regional-national growth difference to 'structural factors' and leaves us with a residual.

The most that shift-share analysis is capable of doing is to indicate, very broadly, the effect that the region's industry mix has had on its growth performance. The unexplained residual also tells us something in so far as it is a measure of the extent to which individual industries have grown either more or less rapidly than their national counterparts. But this is as far as the technique is capable of taking us in the absence of further information. It is certainly not possible to infer, as some early users of shift-share analysis have done, that the division of a region's growth performance into a structural and a residual component can be used to indicate the type of policy required to improve the region's growth performance. It has been suggested, for instance, that if a region is growing slowly because of a predominance of slow growing industries, the appropriate policy would be to inject new growth industries into the region; and if a region is growing slowly because individual industries are growing less rapidly in that region than in other regions, it is argued that the region must be suffering from either locational disadvantages or inefficient production methods. In the case of locational disadvantages, new infrastructure would be required to improve the locational efficiency of the region.

In the absence of other information to support such assertions, however, it would be extremely dangerous to rely upon shift-share analysis to determine the type of policy instruments required in particular instances. If shift-share analysis is to prove useful as a guide to the formulation of regional policy (in its role as a method of identifying and measuring the nature of a region's problems), effort must be directed towards explaining the determinants of the unexplained residual component: why might it vary between regions or over time within a region?

Selected references

Buck (1970); Houston (1967); MacKay (1968).

Appendix C

A Chronology of British Regional Policy, 1928-77

Major policy measures are in italics

Date	*Policy Measure*	*Main Provisions*
1928	Industrial Transference Scheme and Juvenile Transfer Scheme	Minor grant and loan assistance for unemployed migrants. Retraining centres established.
1934	*Special Areas (Development and Improvement) Act*	Four Special Areas designated in South Wales, Scotland, the North-East and West Cumberland, with two Special Area Commissioners appointed to administer the limited loan and aid powers. Establishment of first Trading Estates. Loan powers strengthened by the Special Areas Reconstruction (Agreement) Act of 1936.
1937	Special Areas (Amendment) Act	Extension of loan powers in Special Areas. Tax, rent and rates subsidies for firms in Special Areas. Extension of Trading Estates. Initial sum of £2 million provided.
1940	General Transfer Scheme	Wartime, much-strengthened migration assistance for displaced workers. Replaced Industrial Transference Scheme.
1940	*Royal Commission on the Distribution of the*	Strong, influential report. Has had a major effect on postwar

	Industrial Population (Barlow Report)	regional policy. Urban congestion and regional problems seen as interrelated. Redistribution of population and industry recommended.
1944	White Paper on Employment Policy	Commitment to full employment.
1945	*Distribution of Industry Act*	Assisted areas enlarged and designated as Development Areas. Basic responsibility for regional policy given to the Board of Trade, which acquired (from the Special Area Commissioners) powers of factory building and leasing, finance for Trading Estates, land reclamation, and grants and loans for firms on the advice of the Development Areas Treasury Advisory Committee (DATAC). The system of building licences was retained as a disincentive to expansion in the prosperous regions. The Distribution of Industry Act marks the beginning of the first 'active' phase of British regional policy.
1946	Resettlement Scheme	Gradual replacement of wartime General Transfer Scheme. Unemployed migrants from *all* regions eligible. Wide range of migration costs met. Incorporated a facility to assist temporary migrants (the Voluntary Temporary Transfer Scheme), as well as provision to assist key workers required by their firms to move to assisted areas. Extended in 1946 to workers sent by new firms in assisted areas for retraining in other regions (subsequently known as the Nucleus Labour Force Scheme).

1947	*Town and Country Planning Act*	Extension of wartime building controls into the full Industrial Development Certificate (IDC) system. All new manufacturing establishments or extensions of over 5000 sq.ft required an IDC. This exemption limit has been altered frequently since 1947.
1950	Distribution of Industry Act	A further, but small, extension of Board of Trade loan and grant powers for firms moving to Development Areas. Regional policy throughout the 1950s was only weakly applied.
1951	Key Workers Scheme	Assistance to migrating key workers of firms moving to Development Areas separated out from the Resettlement Scheme, becoming a scheme in its own right. As with the industrial location policies, the resettlement policies were also less actively pursued in the 1950s. Assistance to temporary migrants discontinued from 1950-1957.
1958	Distribution of Industry (Industry Finance) Act	Extension of loan and grant assistance to a number of development 'places' (high unemployment locations outside the Development Areas). Marks a gradual renewal of the vigour of regional policy, with a tightening up of IDC restrictions and increased policy expenditure.
1960	*Local Employment Act*	Repeal of Distribution of Industry Acts. Broad Development Areas replaced by fragmented patchwork of Development Districts delimited on the basis of unemployment rates exceeding 4½%. Retention and strengthening of earlier Board of Trade powers. Introduction of new building grants. Reform of

		Industrial (formerly Trading) Estate policy. IDC policy retained.
1962	Resettlement Transfer Scheme	Resettlement Scheme replaced by a strengthened Resettlement Transfer Scheme, along with the retained Key Workers Scheme and Nucleus Labour Force Scheme. Marks a more active resettlement policy.
1963	*Local Employment Act*	Introduction of standard investment and building grants.
1963	*Budget*	'Free' depreciation introduced for firms in assisted areas. This allows firms to write off investment in plant and machinery against Corporation Tax at any rate they wish. Allows Corporation Tax to be avoided in the initial years of new projects. Marks the beginning of the second major 'active' phase of regional policy.
1963	White Papers on Central Scotland and North East England (Hailsham Report)	Critical of Local Employment Acts and their emphasis on localised unemployment. Growth pole strategies emphasised, together with the need for public infrastructure investment in depressed areas.
1964	Regional Planning	Regional Economic Planning Councils and Boards set up by the Department of Economic Affairs.
1964	*Industrial Training Act*	Industrial Training Boards (ITBs) established for (an eventual) twenty-four industries, with a levy on firms. The programme of Government Training Centres slowly expanded. Training schemes, as with resettlement schemes, are controlled by the Department of Employment.

1965	Control of Office and Industrial Development Act.	Controls on office development in London and Birmingham. Office Development Permits. Rapidly extended to other areas in prosperous regions.
1965	*Highlands and Islands Development (Scotland) Act*	Highlands and Islands Development Board established with extensive powers of grants, loans, equity participation and new factory building for a wide range of economic activities within the area of the Board.
1966	*Industrial Development Act*	The 165 Development Districts replaced by 5 broad Development Areas covering almost half of the land area of Britain. Replacement of 'free' depreciation by a system of 40% investment grants in Development Areas (20% elsewhere). Retention of remainder of policies — IDC's, building grants (25-35%) etc. Land reclamation grants of 85% (50% elsewhere).
1967	*Finance Act*	A labour subsidy, the Regional Employment Premium (REP), introduced. Administered through the Selective Employment Tax (SET) system, with manufacturing firms in Development Areas reclaiming not only their SET, but also a Selective Employment Premium (37½p per man per week), and a Regional Employment Premium (£1.50 per man per week — lower rates for women and juveniles). SET and SEP subsequently withdrawn after 1970, but REP continued in existence until 1977.
1967	*Special Development Areas*	Special Development Areas established in Scotland, the North East, West Cumberland and Wales, with additional incentives of rent-free premises, 35% building

		grants and some operating cost grants, compared with their Development Area counterparts.
1969	Commission on the Intermediate Areas (Hunt Report)	Examination of the problem of Intermediate (or 'Grey') Areas. The recommended strong incentives for these areas were not fully accepted.
1969-	Strategic Plans	Series of *ad hoc* regional strategy teams set up — beginning with South East region. Preparation of regional economic and land-use plans as framework for structure plans of local government and as a framework for central government policymaking.
1970	*Local Employment Act*	Seven Intermediate Areas established. Government-built factories, building grants and derelict land clearance grants. Financed by withdrawal of SEP from Development Areas.
1970	*October Mini-Budget*	Investment grants replaced by 'accelerated' depreciation in the Development Areas. Other existing powers retained and strengthened.
1972	*Industry Act*	A major strengthening of regional policy, involving: (i) extension of 'accelerated' depreciation to whole country; (ii) return to investment grants (Regional Development Grants) for plant and machinery, and for building; (iii) proposed phasing out of REP by 1974; (iv) IDCs ended in Development Areas and Special Development Areas; (v) increase of other forms of existing assistance; (vi) selective assistance (Section 7) for industry; grants and low-interest loans for services; (vii) post of Minister of Industrial Development.

1972	*Training Opportun-ities Scheme (TOPS)*	Major extension of government training centre programme. Financial allowances for trainees.
1972	Employment Transfer Scheme	Strengthening of Resettlement Scheme and re-named Employ-ment Transfer Scheme. Key Worker and Nucleus Labour Force Schemes retained.
1973	*European Economic Community*	Britain entered the EEC and became eligible for loans, grants and other assistance from Community financial instru-ments — the European Coal and Steel Community (ECSC), European Investment Bank (EIB), European Social Fund (ESF), European Agricultural Guidance and Guarantee Fund (EAGGF). Britain also required to adhere to Competition Policy of EEC. This sets limits on investment subsidies on 'central' regions of the EEC (including Intermediate Areas), and disapproves of contin-uing subsidies such as REP. Regional subsidies must also be 'transparent' (i.e.easily assessed).
1973	*Employment and Training Act*	Manpower Services Commission set up to oversee the Employment Services Agency (which controls the extended and reformed Jobcentre and local employment office functions of the Department of Employment), and the Training Services Agency (which operates the expanded TOPS retraining programme and the Industrial Training Boards). Rapid expan-sion of government training schemes.
1973	Royal Commission on the Constitution (Kilbrandon)	Qualified support for elected Scottish and Welsh assemblies and English Regional Advisory Councils. Devolution of limited economic powers proposed.

1973	Hardman Report	Proposals to disperse 31,000 London-based civil service jobs.
1974	Reform of Local Government	New system of County and District Councils established.
1974	Regional Employment Premium	REP rate doubled.
1974	White Paper on Devolution	Scottish and Welsh elected assemblies proposed.
1975	*Industry Act*	National Enterprise Board (NEB) established with an initial £1,000 million available for wide-ranging intervention. Planning Agreements with firms proposed. Designed to assist depressed areas in particular. Some relaxation of rules of selective assistance of 1972 Industry Act.
1975	*European Regional Development Fund*	An EEC Fund established to offer investment grants, and interest rebates on European Investment Bank loans in depressed regions. A Regional Policy Committee also established to coordinate member state and EEC regional policies and to stimulate regional research and planning.
1975/ 1976	*Development Agencies*	Scottish and Welsh Development Agencies established. Scottish Development Agency in particular has substantial powers to invest in industry, create new companies, provide finance and advice for industry, to build and manage Industrial Estates, to lease or sell advance and custom-built factories, to reclaim derelict land and rehabilitate the environment.
1976	'Fire-fighting' Employment Policies	Series of *ad hoc* policies designed to alleviate temporary unemployment problems. Includes: Job Creation Programme; Training

		Award Scheme; Youth Employment Subsidy; Temporary Employment Subsidy; Community, Industry and Work Experience Scheme, etc. Employment Subsidy for small manufacturing firms.
1976	Service and office location subsidies	Strengthening of grants and rent relief for service and office firms locating in assisted areas. Preferential loans.
1977	*Regional Employment Premium*	REP abolished in Britain. Selective Employment Premium continues in Ulster.
1977	*Development Board for Rural Wales*	Development Board for Rural Wales established with powers to build houses for incoming key workers, control over advance factories, and financial assistance for infrastructure and social projects within the Board's area.
1977	*EEC Regional Policy*	Proposals for a major extension of scope and powers of the European Regional Development Fund.

Sources: Randall P., 'The History of British Regional Policy', in Hallet *et al.* (1973); Department of Industry, *Incentives for Industry;* McCrone (1968); *British Economic Survey;* Department of Employment, London; Commission of the European Communities (1973b, 1975a, 1976, 1977a, 1977b).

Bibliography

Books and articles

Adams F.G., Brooking C.G. and Glickman N.J. (1975), 'On the specification and simulation of a regional econometric model: a model of Mississippi', *Review of Economics and Statistics.*

Allen K. and MacLennan M.C. (1970), *Regional Problems and Policies in Italy and France,* Allen and Unwin.

Alonso W. (1971), 'The economics of urban size', *Papers and Proceedings of the Regional Science Association.*

Archer B. (1973), *The Impact of Domestic Tourism,* Bangor Occasional Paper in Economics No. 2, Wales University Press.

Archibald G.C. (1967), 'Regional multiplier effects in the UK', *Oxford Economic Papers.*

Archibald G.C. (1969), 'The Phillips curve and the distribution of unemployment', *Papers and Proceedings of the American Economic Association.*

Archibald G.C., Kemmis R. and Perkins J.W. (1974), 'Excess demand for labour, unemployment and the Phillips curve: a theoretical and empirical study', in Laidler D. and Purdy D.L. (eds), *Inflation and Labour Markets,* Manchester University Press.

Armstrong H.W. (1978), 'Community regional policy: a survey and critique', *Regional Studies* (forthcoming).

Ashcroft B. and Taylor J. (1977), 'The movement of manufacturing industry and the effect of regional policy', *Oxford Economic Papers.*

Ashcroft B. and Taylor J. (1978), 'The effect of regional policy on the movement of industry in GB', in Maclennan D. and Parr J. (eds), *Regional Policy in Britain,* Martin Robertson.

Ball R. (1975), *The Journey to Work and Labour Market Areas in Cumbria,* MA Dissertation, University of Lancaster.

Begg H.M., Lythe C.M., Sorley R. and MacDonald D.R. (1975), 'Expenditure on regional assistance to industry: 1960/1-1972/3', *Economic Journal.*

318

Berry B.J.L. (1974), 'Hierarchical diffusion: the basis of development filtering and spread in a system of growth centres', in Hansen N.M. (ed.), *Growth Centres in Regional Economic Development,* Free Press.

Blackaby F. (1976), 'The target rate of unemployment', in Worswick G.D.N. (ed.), *The Concept and Measurement of Involuntary Unemployment,* Allen and Unwin.

Blake C. (1973), 'The gains from regional policy', in Wolfe J.N. (ed.), *Cost Benefit and Cost Effectiveness,* Allen and Unwin.

Blake C. (1976), 'Some economics of investment grants and allowances', in Whiting A. (ed.), *The Economics of Industrial Subsidies,* HMSO.

Borts G.H. (1960), 'The equalisation of returns and regional economic growth', *American Economic Review.*

Borts G.H. (1961), *Regional Cycles of Manufacturing Employment in the United States, 1914-53,* National Bureau of Economic Research.

Borts G.H. and Stein J.L. (1962), 'Regional growth and maturity in the United States: a study of regional structural change', *Schweizerische Zeitschrift fur Volkswirtschaft und Statistik.* Reprinted in Needleman L. (ed.), *Regional Analysis,* Penguin 1968.

Borts G.H. and Stein J.L. (1964), *Economic Growth in a Free Market,* Columbia University Press.

Boudeville J.R. (1966), *Problems of Regional Economic Planning,* Edinburgh University Press.

Bowers J.K. (1975), 'British activity rates: a survey of research', *Scottish Journal of Political Economy.*

Bowsher N.N., Daane J.D. and Einzig R. (1957), 'The flow of funds between regions of the United States', *Papers and Proceedings of the Regional Science Association.*

Branson W.H. (1972), *Macroeconomic Theory and Policy,* Harper and Row.

Brechling F.P.R. (1967), 'Trends and cycles in British regional unemployment', *Oxford Economic Papers.*

Brennan M.J. (1967), 'A more general theory of resource migration', in Brennan M.J. (ed.), *Patterns of Market Behaviour,* Brown University Press.

Broadbent T.A. and Morrison, W.I. (1977), 'Controlling urban change: models of the urban economy', in Leontief W. (ed.), *Structure, System and Economic Policy,* Cambridge University Press.

Brown A.J. (1967), 'The Green Paper on the Development Areas', *National Institute Economic Review.*

Brown A.J. (1972), *The Framework of Regional Economics in the United Kingdom,* Cambridge University Press.

Brownrigg M. (1971), 'The regional income multiplier: an attempt to complete the model', *Scottish Journal of Political Economy.*

Buck T.W. (1970), 'Shift and share analysis — a guide to regional policy?', *Regional Studies.*

Buck T.W. and Atkins M.H. (1976a), 'The impact of British regional policies on employment growth', *Oxford Economic Papers.*

Buck T.W. and Atkins M.H. (1976b), 'Capital subsidies and unemployed labour, a regional production function approach', *Regional Studies.*

Cameron G.C. (1974), 'Regional economic policy in the United Kingdom', in Sant M. (ed.), *Regional Policy and Planning for Europe,* Saxon House.

Cheshire P.C. (1973), *Regional Unemployment Differences in Great Britain,* NIESR, Regional Papers II, Cambridge University Press.

Chiang A.C. (1974), *Fundamental Methods of Mathematical Economics,* McGraw-Hill.

Chisholm M. (1976), 'Regional policies in an era of slow population growth and high unemployment', *Regional Studies.*

Clark C., Wilson F. and Bradley J. (1969), 'Industrial location and economic potential in Western Europe', *Regional Studies.*

Creamer D. (1943), 'Shifts of manufacturing industries', *Industrial Location and National Resources,* US National Resources Planning Board, Washington DC.

Dasgupta K. and Pearce D. (1972), *Cost Benefit Analysis: Theory and Practice,* Macmillan.

Diamond D. (1974), 'The long-term aim of regional policy', in Sant M. (ed.), *Regional Policy and Planning for Europe,* Saxon House.

Dixon R.J. (1973), 'Regional specialisation and trade in the UK', *Scottish Journal of Political Economy.*

Dixon R.J. and Thirlwall A.P. (1975), 'A model of regional growth rate differentials along Kaldorian lines', *Oxford Economic Papers.*

Dixon R.J. and Thirlwall A.P. (1976), *Regional Growth and Unemployment in the United Kingdom,* Macmillan.

Eltis W.A. (1973), *Growth and Distribution,* Macmillan.

Estle E. (1967), 'A more conclusive regional test of the Heckscher-Ohlin hypothesis', *Journal of Political Economy.*

Goldfarb R.S. and Yezer A.M. (1976), 'Evaluating alternative theories of intercity and interregional wage differentials', *Journal of Regional Science.*

Gordon I.R. (1970), 'Activity rates, regional and sub-regional differentials', *Regional Studies.*

Gordon I.R. (1977), 'Regional interdependence in the United Kingdom economy', in Leontief W. (ed.), *Structure, System and Economic Policy,* Cambridge University Press.

Greenwood M.J. (1970), 'Lagged response in the decision to migrate', *Journal of Regional Science.*

Greenwood M.J. (1975), 'Research on internal migration in the USA: a survey', *Journal of Economic Literature.*

Greenwood D. and Short J. (1973), *Military Installations and Local Economies, A Case Study,* Aberdeen Studies in Defence Economics, No. 4.

Greig M.A. (1971), 'The regional income and employment multiplier effects of a pulp mill and a paper mill', *Scottish Journal of Political Economy.*

Greig M.A. (1972), *The Economic Impact of the Highlands and Islands Development Board Investment in Fisheries,* Highlands and Islands Development Board.

Greytak D. (1975), 'Regional consumption patterns and the Heckscher-Ohlin trade theorem', *Journal of Regional Science.*

Grigg D.B. (1967), 'Regions, models and classes', in Chorley R.J. and Haggett P. (eds), *Models in Geography,* Methuen.

Hadley G. (1961), *Linear Algebra,* Addison Wesley.

Hallett G., Randall P. and West E.G. (1973), *Regional Policy for Ever?* Institute of Economic Affairs, Readings 11.

Hansen B. (1970), 'Excess demand, unemployment, vacancies and wages', *Quarterly Journal of Economics.*

Hansen N.M. (1968), *French Regional Planning,* Edinburgh University Press.

Hansen N.M. (1972), *Growth Centres in Regional Economic Development,* Collier-Macmillan.

Hansen N.M. (1977), 'Border regions: a critique of spatial theory and a European case study', *Annals of Regional Science.*

Hart R.A. (1975), 'Interregional economic migration: some theoretical considerations (Parts I and II)', *Journal of Regional Science.*

Hartman L.M. and Seckler D. (1967), 'Towards an application of dynamic growth theory to regions', *Journal of Regional Science.*

Harvey D. (1969), *Explanation in Geography,* Edward Arnold.

Haveman R.H. (1970), 'Evaluating public expenditures under conditions of unemployment', in Margolis J. and Haveman R.H. (eds), *Public Expenditure and Policy Analysis,* Markham.

Haveman R.H. (1976), 'Evaluating the impact of public policies on regional welfare', *Regional Studies.*

Haveman R.H. and Krutilla J.V. (1968), *Unemployment, Idle Capacity and the Evaluation of Public Expenditures,* Johns Hopkins Press.

Havemen R.H. and Margolis J. (1970), *Public Expenditure and Policy Analysis,* Markham.

Hewings G.J.D. (1971), 'Regional input-output models in the UK: some problems and prospects for the use of nonsurvey techniques', *Regional Studies.*

Hirschman A.O. (1958), *The Strategy of Economic Development,* Yale University Press.

Holland S. (1976a), *Capital versus the Regions,* Macmillan.

Holland S. (1976b), *The Regional Problem,* Macmillan.

Hoover E.M. (1963), *The Location of Economic Activity,* McGraw-Hill.

Houston D.B. (1967), 'The shift-share analysis of regional growth: a critique', *Southern Economic Journal.*

Howard R.S. (1968), *The Movement of Manufacturing Industry in the United Kingdom, 1945-65,* HMSO.

Hughes J.J. (1970), *Cost Benefit Aspects of Manpower Retraining,* Department of Employment and Productivity, Manpower Paper No. 2, HMSO.

Hughes J.J. (1974), 'The use of vacancy statistics in classifying and measuring structural and frictional unemployment in Great Britain, 1958-72', *Bulletin of Economic Research.*

Hutton J. and Hartley K. (1968), 'A regional payroll tax', *Oxford Economic Papers.*

Ingram J.C. (1959), 'State and regional payments mechanisms', *Quarterly Journal of Economics.* Reprinted in Needleman L. (ed.), *Regional Analysis,* Penguin 1968.

Innis H. (1920), *The Fur Trade in Canada,* Yale University Press.

Isard W. (1956), *Location and Space Economy,* MIT Press.

Isard W. (1960), *Methods of Regional Analysis: An Introduction to Regional Science,* MIT Press.

Isard W. and Langford T.W. (1971), *Regional Input-Output Study: Recollections, Reflections and Diverse Notes on the Philadelphia Experience,* MIT Press.

Isard W., Schooler E.W. and Vietorisz T. (1959), *Industrial Complex Analysis and Regional Development,* MIT Press.

James B.S. (1964), 'The incompatibility of industrial and trading cultures: a critical appraisal of the growth-point concept', *Journal of Industrial Economics.*

Kaldor N. (1966), *The Causes of the Slow Rate of Economic Growth in the UK,* Cambridge University Press.

Kaldor N. (1970), 'The case for regional policies', *Scottish Journal of Political Economy.*

Kennedy C. and Thirlwall A.P. (1977), *The Input-Output Formulation of the Foreign Trade Multiplier,* University of Kent (mimeo).

Kiker B.F. and Traynham E.C. (1976), 'A comment on "Research and Internal Migration in the United States: A Survey"', *Journal of Economic Literature.*

King D.N. (1973), 'Financial and economic aspects of regionalism and federalism', *Royal Commission on the Constitution,* Research Paper 10, HMSO.

Klaasen T.A. (1973), 'Regional comparative advantage in the United States', *Journal of Regional Science.*

Krauss M.B. and Johnson H.G. (1974), *General Equilibrium Analysis,* Allen and Unwin.

Lambooy J.G. (1973), *Regional Policy in the Framework of Europe's Changing Spatial Economy* (mimeo).

Lande P.S. and Gordon P. (1977), 'Regional growth in the United States: a re-examination of the neoclassical model', *Journal of Regional Science.*

Layard R. (1972), *Cost Benefit Analysis,* Penguin.

Lefeber L. (1964), 'Regional allocation of resources in India', in

Friedmann J.P. and Alonso W. (eds), *Regional Development: A Reader,* MIT Press.

Leven C.L. (1964), 'Establishing goals for regional economic development', *Journal of American Institute of Planners.* Reprinted in Friedmann J.P. and Alonso W. (eds), *Regional Development: A Reader,* MIT Press.

Lever W.F. (1972), 'Industrial movement, spatial association and functional linkages', *Regional Studies.*

Lichfield N., Kettle P. and Whitbread M. (1975), *Evaluation in the Planning Process,* Pergamon.

Loasby B.J. (1967), 'Making location policy work', *Lloyds Bank Review.*

Lund P.J. (1976), 'The econometric assessment of the impact of investment incentives', in Whiting A. (ed.), *The Economics of Industrial Subsidies,* HMSO.

McCrone G. (1968), *Regional Policy in Britain,* Allen and Unwin.

McCrone G. (1969), 'Regional policy in the European Communities', in Denton G.R. (ed.), *Economic Integration in Europe,* Weidenfeld and Nicolson.

McDermott P.J. (1977), 'Capital subsidies and unemployed labour: a comment on the production function approach', *Regional Studies.*

MacKay D.I. (1968), 'Industrial structure and regional growth: a methodological problem', *Scottish Journal of Political Economy.*

MacKay D.I. and Hart R.A. (1975), 'Wage inflation and the regional wage structure', in Parkin M. and Nobay A.R. (eds), *Contemporary Issues in Economics,* Manchester University Press.

MacKay R.R. and Segal L. (1977), *Important Trends in Regional Policy and Regional Employment: A Modified Interpretation,* University of Newcastle-upon-Tyne, Discussion Paper 22.

McKinnon R.I. (1963), 'Optimum currency areas', *American Economic Review.*

Melliss C.L. and Richardson P.W. (1976), 'Value of investment incentives for manufacturing industry', in Whiting A. (ed.) *The Economics of Industrial Subsidies,* HMSO.

Miernyk W.H. (1965), *Elements of Input-Output Economics,* Random House.

Miller D. (1972), *Regional Problems: A Multivariate Approach,* MA Dissertation, University of Lancaster.

Moore B. and Rhodes J. (1973a), 'Evaluating the effects of British regional economic policy', *Economic Journal.*

Moore B. and Rhodes J. (1973b), 'The economic and Exchequer implications of regional policy', Memorandum to the Expenditure Committee, Trade and Industry Sub-committee, *HC Paper 42 XVI,* 1972/73.

Moore B. and Rhodes J. (1975a), 'Regional policy and the Scottish economy', *Scottish Journal of Political Economy.*

Moore B. and Rhodes J. (1975b), 'The economic and Exchequer implications of British regional economic policy', in Vaizey J.

(ed.), *Economic Sovereignty and Regional Policy,* Gill and Macmillan.

Moore B. and Rhodes J. (1976a), 'Regional economic policy and the movement of manufacturing firms', *Economica.*

Moore B. and Rhodes J. (1976b), 'A quantitative analysis of the effects of the Regional Employment Premium and other regional policy instruments', in Whiting A. (ed.), *The Economics of Industrial Subsidies,* HMSO.

Moore B. and Rhodes J. (1977), *Industrial and Regional Policy in the Republic of Ireland,* Department of Applied Economics, University of Cambridge.

Morgan E.V. (1973), 'Regional problems and common currencies', *Lloyds Bank Review.*

Moroney J.R. (1972), *The Structure of Production in American Manufacturing,* North Carolina Press.

Moroney J.R. (1975), 'Natural resource endowments and comparative labour costs: a hybrid model of comparative advantage', *Journal of Regional Science.*

Moroney J.R. and Walker J.M. (1966), 'A regional test of the Heckscher-Ohlin theorem', *Journal of Political Economy.*

Morrill R.L. (1968), 'Waves of spatial diffusion', *Journal of Regional Science.*

Morrison W.I. (1971), 'The application of input-output analysis to urban planning', *Centre for Environmental Studies.*

Morrison W.I. (1973), 'The development of an urban interindustry model: (1) the building of input-output accounts, (2) the structure of the Peterborough economy, (3) input-output multipliers', *Environment and Planning.*

Moseley M.J. (1974), *Growth Centres in Spatial Planning,* Pergamon.

Mundell R.A. (1961), 'A theory of optimal currency areas', *American Economic Review.*

Musgrave P.B. and Musgrave R.A. (1973), *Public Finance in Theory and Practice,* McGraw-Hill.

Myrdal G. (1957), *Economic Theory and Underdeveloped Regions,* Duckworth.

Needleman L. and Scott B. (1964), 'Regional problems and the location of industry policy in Britain', *Urban Studies.*

Nevin E., Roe A.R. and Round J.I. (1966), *The Structure of the Welsh Economy,* University of Wales Press.

North D.C. (1955), 'Location theory and regional economic growth', *Journal of Political Economy.*

Oates W.E. (1972), *Fiscal Federalism,* Harcourt Brace.

Okun B. and Richardson R.W. (1961), 'Regional income inequality and internal population migration', *Economic Development and Cultural Change.*

Pacione M. (1976), 'Development policy in southern Italy: Panacea or polemic?', *Tidschrift voor Econ. en Sociale Geografie.*

Pearce D. (1976), *Environmental Economics,* Longman.

Perlman R. (1969), *Labour Theory,* Wiley.

Perroux F. (1950), 'Economic space: theory and applications', *Quarterly Journal of Economics.*

Perroux F. (1970), 'A note on the concept of growth poles', in McKee D.L. (ed.), *Regional Economics: Theory and Practice,* Free Press Macmillan.

Pratt R. (1967), 'Regional production inputs and regional income generation', *Journal of Regional Science.*

Pred A.R. (1965), 'Industrialisation, initial advantage and American metropolitan growth', *Geographical Review.*

Pred A.R. (1966), *The Spatial Dynamics of US Urban-Industrial Growth,* MIT Press.

Presley J.R. and Dennis G.A. (1976), *Currency Areas,* Macmillan.

Prest A.R. (1976), 'The economic rationale of subsidies to industry', in Whiting A. (ed.), *The Economics of Industrial Subsidies,* HMSO.

Prest A.R. and Turvey R, (1965), 'Cost-benefit analysis: a survey', *Economic Journal.*

Rees A. (1973), *The Economics of Work and Pay,* Harper and Row.

Richardson H.W. (1973), *The Economics of Urban Size,* Saxon House and Lexington.

Samuelson P.A. (1948), 'International trade and the equalisation of factor prices', *Economic Journal.*

Scitovsky T. (1958), *Economic Theory and Western European Integration,* Unwin.

Scott A. (1966), 'Policy for declining regions: a theoretical approach', in *Areas of Economic Stress in Canada,* Queen's University.

Scott A. and Breton A. (1975), *The Theory of the Structure of the Public Sector,* University of British Columbia (mimeo).

Shaw G.K. (1974), *Macroeconomic Policy,* Martin Robertson.

Shearer R.A., Young J. and Munro G. (1971), *Trade Liberalization and a Regional Economy: Studies of the Impact of Free Trade on British Columbia,* Toronto University Press.

Short J. (1977), *The Regional Distribution of Public Expenditure in Great Britain, 1969/70-1973/74,* University of Durham (mimeo).

Sjaastad L.A. (1962), 'The costs and returns of human migration', *Journal of Political Economy,* Supplement.

Smith B. (1975), 'Regional specialisation and trade in the UK', *Scottish Journal of Political Economy.*

Smith D.M. (1975), 'Neoclassical growth models and regional growth in the US', *Journal of Regional Science.*

Spence N.A. and Taylor P.J. (1970), 'Quantitative methods in regional taxonomy', in Board C. *et al.* (eds), *Progress in Geography, 2,* Edward Arnold.

Stabler J. (1968), 'Exports and evolution: the process of regional change', *Land Economics.*

Steele D.B. (1969), 'Regional multipliers in Great Britain', *Oxford Economic Papers.*

Stilwell F.J.B. (1968), 'Location of industry and business efficiency', *Business Ratios*.
Stilwell F.J.B. (1972), *Regional Economic Policy*, Macmillan.
Tait A.A. (1975), *The Economics of Devolution*, University of Strathclyde and Fraser of Allander Institute, Speculative Papers 2.
Taylor J. (1967), 'A note on the definition of industrial diversification', *Journal of Economic Studies*.
Taylor J. (1971), 'A regional analysis of hidden unemployment in GB, 1951-66', *Applied Economics*.
Taylor J. (1974), *Unemployment and Wage Inflation*, Longman.
Thirlwall A.P. (1966), 'Regional unemployment as a cyclical phenomenon', *Scottish Journal of Political Economy*.
Thirlwall A.P. (1969a), 'Types of unemployment: with special reference to non-deficient demand unemployment in GB', *Scottish Journal of Political Economy*.
Thirlwall A.P. (1969b), 'Demand disequilibrium in the labour markets and wage rate inflation in the United Kingdom', *Yorkshire Bulletin of Economic and Social Research*.
Thirlwall A.P. (1970), 'Regional Phillips curves', *Oxford Bulletin*.
Thirlwall A.P. (1974), 'Types of unemployment in the regions of Great Britain', *Manchester School*.
Tiebout C.M. (1956), 'Exports and regional economic growth', *Journal of Political Economy*.
Tietz M.B. (1962), 'Regional theory and regional models', *Papers and Proceedings of the Regional Science Association*.
Todd D. (1974), 'An appraisal of the development pole concept in regional analysis', *Environment and Planning*.
Tooze M.J. (1976), 'Regional elasticities of substitution in the United Kingdom in 1968', *Urban Studies*.
Townroe P.M. (1972), 'Some behavioural considerations in the industrial location decision', *Regional Studies*.
Townsend A.R. (1977), 'The relationship of inner city problems to regional policy', *Regional Studies*.
Trevithick J.A. and Mulvey C. (1975), *The Economics of Inflation*, Martin Robertson.
Vanderkamp J. (1971), 'Migration flows, their determinants, and the effects of return migration', *Journal of Political Economy*.
Vanderkamp J. (1972), 'The effect of out-migration on regional employment', *Canadian Journal of Economics*.
Vining R. (1948), 'The region as a concept in business cycle analysis', *Econometrica*.
Walters A.A. (1961), 'The theory and measurement of private and social costs of highway congestion', *Econometrica*.
Watson J. (1971), *Growth and Structural Change in the UK Regions*, MA Dissertation, University of Lancaster.
Weeden R. (1973), *Interregional Migration Models and their Application to Great Britain*, National Institute of Economic and Social Research, Regional Papers II, Cambridge University Press.

Weiss S. and Gooding E. (1968), 'Estimation of differential employment multipliers in a small regional economy', *Land Economics*.

West E.G. (1973), '"Pure" versus "Operational" economics in regional policy', in Hallett G. (ed.), *Regional Policy for Ever?*, Institute of Economic Affairs.

Whitman M.N. (1967), 'International and interregional payments adjustment: a synthetic view', *Princeton Studies in International Finance*.

Whitman M.N. (1972), 'Place prosperity and people prosperity: the delineation of optimum policy areas', in Perlman M. *et al.* (eds), *Spatial, Regional and Population Economics: Essays in Honor of Edgar M. Hoover*.

Williamson J. (1965), 'Regional inequality and the process of national development', *Economic Development and Cultural Change*.

Woodward R.S. (1974a), 'The capital bias of DREE incentives', *Canadian Journal of Economics*.

Woodward R.S. (1974b), 'Effective location subsidies: an evaluation of DREE industrial incentives', *Canadian Journal of Economics*.

Yan C. (1969), *Introduction to Input-Output Economics*, Holt, Rhinehart and Winston.

Government publications

Commission of the European Communities (1973a), *Report on Regional Problems in the Enlarged Community*, COM(73) 550 final, Brussels.

Commission of the European Communities (1973b), 'Proposals for a Community regional policy', *Official Journal of the European Communities*, OJ C86 of 16 October, and OJ C106 of 6 December, Brussels.

Commission of the European Communities (1975a), 'Regulations establishing a Community regional policy', *Official Journal of the European Communities*, OJ L73 of 21 March, and OJ L128 of 19 May, Brussels.

Commission of the European Communities (1975b), *Fifth Report on Competition Policy in the Community*, Brussels.

Commission of the European Communities (1976), 'First report of the Regional Development Fund', *Bulletin of the European Communities*, Supplement 7/76, Brussels.

Commission of the European Communities (1977a), *Guidelines for a Community Regional Policy*, COM (77) 195 final, Brussels.

Commission of the European Communities (1977b), *Second Report of the Regional Development Fund*, COM (77) 260 final, Brussels.

House of Commons (1973a), Expenditure Committee (Trade and Industry Sub-Committee), *Regional Development Incentives*, House of Commons Paper 327, Session 1972/3, HMSO.

House of Commons (1973b), Expenditure Committee (Trade and Industry Sub-Committee), *Regional Development Incentives, Minutes of Evidence, Appendices and Index*, House of Commons Paper 85-I, Session 1973/4, HMSO.

Howard Report (1968), Board of Trade, *The Movement of Manufacturing Industry in the United Kingdom*, HMSO.

Northern Region Strategy Team (1975), *Evaluation of the Impact of Regional Policy on Manufacturing Industry in the Northern Region*, Technical Report 2.

Northern Region Strategy Team (1976a), *Growth and Structural Change in the Economy of the Northern Region Since 1952*, Technical Report Number 4.

Northern Region Strategy Team (1976b), *Public Expenditure in the Northern Region and Other British Regions*, Technical Report Number 12.

Northern Region Strategy Team (1977), *Strategic Plan for the Northern Region*, Reports, Volumes 1-5, HMSO.

North West Strategy Team (1974), *Report*, HMSO.

Office Statistique des Communautes Europeenes (1972), *Regional Statistics*, Brussels.

Regional Development Programme (1977), *Trade and Industry*, 11, 18 and 25 February.

Treaty of Rome (1958), *Treaty Establishing the European Communities and Connected Documents*, Brussels.

White Paper (1940), *Royal Commission on the Distribution of the Industrial Population* (Barlow Report), Cmnd 6153, HMSO.

White Paper (1963a), *Central Scotland: A Programme for Development and Growth*, Cmnd 2188, HMSO.

White Paper (1963b), *The North East: A Programme for Regional Development and Growth*, Cmnd 2206, HMSO.

White Paper (1965), *The National Plan*, Cmnd 2764, HMSO.

White Paper (1969), *The Intermediate Areas* (Hunt Report), Cmnd 3998, HMSO.

Author Index

Subject Index